Examining Cultural Influences on Leadership Styles and Learning From Chinese Approaches to Management:

Emerging Research and Opportunities

Valerie Zhu
Xi'an University of Science and Technology, China

A volume in the Advances in Logistics, Operations, and Management Science (ALOMS) Book Series

www.igi-global.com

Published in the United States of America by
    IGI Global
    Business Science Reference (an imprint of IGI Global)
    701 E. Chocolate Avenue
    Hershey PA 17033
    Tel: 717-533-8845
    Fax: 717-533-8661
    E-mail: cust@igi-global.com
    Web site: http://www.igi-global.com

Library of Congress Cataloging-in-Publication Data

Names: Zhu, Valerie, 1965- author.
Title: Examining cultural influences on leadership styles and learning from
  Chinese approaches to management : emerging research and opportunities /
  by Valerie Zhu.
Description: Hershey, PA : Business Science Reference, [2017]
Identifiers: LCCN 2016057118| ISBN 9781522522775 (hardcover) | ISBN
  9781522522782 (ebook)
Subjects: LCSH: Management--China. | Leadership--China. | Executive
  ability--China.
Classification: LCC HD70.C5 Z5155 2017 | DDC 658.4/0920951--dc23 LC record available at
https://lccn.loc.gov/2016057118

This book is published in the IGI Global book series Advances in Logistics, Operations, and Management Science (ALOMS) (ISSN: 2327-350X; eISSN: 2327-3518)

British Cataloguing in Publication Data
A Cataloguing in Publication record for this book is available from the British Library.

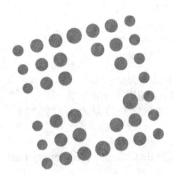

Advances in Logistics, Operations, and Management Science (ALOMS) Book Series

ISSN:2327-350X
EISSN:2327-3518

Editor-in-Chief: John Wang, Montclair State University, USA

MISSION

Operations research and management science continue to influence business processes, administration, and management information systems, particularly in covering the application methods for decision-making processes. New case studies and applications on management science, operations management, social sciences, and other behavioral sciences have been incorporated into business and organizations real-world objectives.

The **Advances in Logistics, Operations, and Management Science** (ALOMS) Book Series provides a collection of reference publications on the current trends, applications, theories, and practices in the management science field. Providing relevant and current research, this series and its individual publications would be useful for academics, researchers, scholars, and practitioners interested in improving decision making models and business functions.

COVERAGE

- Operations Management
- Information Management
- Decision analysis and decision support
- Production management
- Marketing engineering
- Risk Management
- Organizational Behavior
- Computing and information technologies
- Finance
- Networks

IGI Global is currently accepting manuscripts for publication within this series. To submit a proposal for a volume in this series, please contact our Acquisition Editors at Acquisitions@igi-global.com or visit: http://www.igi-global.com/publish/.

Titles in this Series

For a list of additional titles in this series, please visit:
http://www.igi-global.com/book-series/advances-logistics-operations-management-science/37170

Optimal Management Strategies in Small and Medium Enterprises
Milan B. Vemić (Higher School of Academic Studies "DOSITEJ", Serbia)
Business Science Reference ● ©2017 ● 437pp ● H/C (ISBN: 9781522519492) ● US $225.00

Global Intermediation and Logistics Service Providers
Laurence Saglietto (Côte d'Azur University, France) and Cécile Cezanne (University Paris 13 Sorbonne Paris Cité, France)
Business Science Reference ● ©2017 ● 412pp ● H/C (ISBN: 9781522521334) ● US $210.00

Ethics and Sustainability in Global Supply Chain Management
Ulas Akkucuk (Bogazici University, Turkey)
Business Science Reference ● ©2017 ● 350pp ● H/C (ISBN: 9781522520368) ● US $200.00

Supply Chain Management in the Big Data Era
Hing Kai Chan (University of Nottingham Ningbo, China) Nachiappan Subramanian (University of Sussex, UK) and Muhammad Dan-Asabe Abdulrahman (University of Nottingham Ningbo, China)
Business Science Reference ● ©2017 ● 299pp ● H/C (ISBN: 9781522509561) ● US $195.00)

Knowledge Management Initiatives and Strategies in Small and Medium Enterprises
Andrea Bencsik (Széchenyi István University, Hungary & J. Selye University, Slovakia)
Business Science Reference ● ©2017 ● 442pp ● H/C (ISBN: 9781522516422) ● US $200.00

Handbook of Research on Information Management for Effective Logistics...
George Leal Jamil (InescTec, Portugal) António Lucas Soares (University of Porto, Portugal) and Cláudio Roberto Magalhães Pessoa (FUMEC University, Brazil)
Business Science Reference ●©2017 ● 554pp ● H/C (ISBN: 9781522509738) ● US $310.00

Optimum Decision Making in Asset Management
María Carmen Carnero (University of Castilla – La Mancha, Spain) and Vicente González-Prida (University of Seville, Spain)
Business Science Reference ● ©2017 ● 523pp ● H/C (ISBN: 9781522506515) ● US $215.00

For an enitre list of titles in this series, please visit:
http://www.igi-global.com/book-series/advances-logistics-operations-management-science/37170

IGI GLOBAL
DISSEMINATOR OF KNOWLEDGE

www.igi-global.com

701 East Chocolate Avenue, Hershey, PA 17033, USA
Tel: 717-533-8845 x100 ● Fax: 717-533-8661
E-Mail: cust@igi-global.com ● www.igi-global.com

Table of Contents

Preface..vii

Acknowledgment...x

Introduction..xi

Chapter 1
Introduction...1

Chapter 2
Literature Review and Research Hypotheses...8

Chapter 3
Research Methodology 59

Chapter 4
Empirical Testing Results 88

Chapter 5
A Case Study..126

Chapter 6
Conclusions, Implications, and Future Research 156

Appendix 1 164

Appendix 2 169

Appendix 3 177

Appendix 4 182

Appendix 5 185

Related Readings 186

Index 206

Preface

China is the most representative emerging economic entity in BRIC countries. With her astounding economic development in the past thirty years since its reform and opening up policy, more and more scholars and expertise both at home and abroad have paid special attention to conduct researches and relevant projects taking China as the subject. The same is true of Valerie Zhu's research.

I have known her since her undergraduate education in Xian International Studies University (abbreviated as XISU) during which I taught her several courses on cross-cultural communication and translation. After graduation, she has been working as a tourist guide, a project manager in international trade. Later, she went to Aberdeen University, Scotland, the UK to fulfill her master's degree in Management Science & Engineering. Knowing the true meaning of lifelong learning, she continued her PhD program in Management Science & Engineering in Xi'an Jiaotong University (shortened as XJTU), which is one of the leading higher learning universities in China. From her personal experiences both in career and education, I have seen Valerie Zhu as an industrious, hard working and ambitious lady. Actually, she has very well demonstrated the principle of combining theory with practice. It is well known that management is a systematic soft science with strong requirement for practice. Obviously, Valerie's work experiences have, to a great extent, added more tea leaves for her further education in management field. Her affluent background about business operation in China has provided plenty of real time cases in her teaching and learning processes.

From the very ancient times, Chinese people began to investigate the essence of management, but most of them were falling into the scope of state and political management. Though in Chinese history, there have emerged lots of famous business persons like Fan Li in the Spring and Autumn Period, Hu Xue'yan in the Qing Dynasty and various business groups in different areas in China, for example, Jin Shang in Shanxi, Hui Shang in Anhui, Qin Shang in Shaanxi, etc., all these have played an important role in the commercial development in China superficially. However, in Chinese history, business persons had never been seen as a privileged social class as the social strata have been ranked as government officials, farmers, craftsmen and businessmen, which indicated that business persons had been listed as the last in the society. Such inferior position remained till the founding of New China in 1949. Because of such categorization of social strata, business management was not stressed, let alone to say systematic theories of management science. With the reform and opening up, China began to learn the scientific management from the developed countries, namely Europe and the USA. No exaggerating, modern business management theories are almost loan words from foreign countries. In the last thirty years, scholars and experts have noticed that management theories which derived from the soils of the Western world may not apply to Chinese context all the time due to cultural differences. They began to look back into the real Chinese situation and thought about the development of management science deeply rooted in Chinese situation. I could find the similar mindset in Valerie Zhu's research. After communicating and looking through her research topics and academic publications in recently years, I could sense that she has made a close tie between her research and Chinese characteristics. Just like the research she has done with IGI publishing Group *Examining Cultural Influence on Leadership Style and Learning From Chinese Approaches to Management: Emerging Research and Opportunities*. The research topic is of great interest and significance. Leadership theories have been developing fast in the last 50 years with multiple schools of trait theory, behavioral approach, contingency theory, transformational theories, etc. just as above-mentioned, there is not very systematic sole research about Chinese business leaders. Such reality exposes that Valerie's research may to some extent fill in the blank in this field. Not only she has chosen the right topics, but also she has put great efforts in doing it: to determine which surveys she should adopt, she visited Michael Harris Bond in HK for twice to discuss her research; to make a comprehensive literature review, she contacted Schwartz through emails; to secure the quality of questionnaire, she trained those who dispatched the questionnaire on her behalf.... All these have indicated that she has been taking serious attitudes towards this research. In addition, every step she took in the whole process of research was solid and sound, which guaranteed the research quality.

Based on the comprehensive review of her research in this topic and that of her previous research experiences, I have seen very positive opinions about her contribution in this research field and her faithfulness, sincerity to IGI Publishing Group is also revealed from her prudent behavior in academic research.

Mingzhong Zhang
Xi'an University of Science and Technology, China

Acknowledgment

First of all, I should extend my sincere thanks to IGI publishing Group for granting me this valuable opportunity for this research. My special hearted thanks go to Travers, Moore for their excellent collaboration with me in the process of fulfilling this research. The accomplishment of this research is a combined efforts of many people in this field: professor Michael Harris Bond, professor Schwartz, professor Barbara Flynn, Amrik Sohal, Aleda Roth, Daniel Vicky Smith, Jeff Yeung, Chris Voss, etc. They all offered their generous support and assistance in one way or another. Without their support and encouragement, I could not have had the capability to fulfill this research. Also, I would like to thank my mother, my son and my siblings for their understanding and assistance in enabling me to concentrate on my research without the intervention of house chores.

My very unique thanks extent to Professor Jeff Yeung and his research center for their financial support in the process of data collection and processing. Their golden suggestions and very expertise instructions are of great importance in achieving the outcome of this research.

Though this research is temporarily done, being professional personnel in management science field, there is still a long way to explore with time goes by.

Valerie C. Y. Zhu
Xi'an University of Science and Technology, China

Introduction

Culture has been embedded into people's blood. Since his birth, his behaviors will be deeply influenced by the culture in which has been raised and living. Based on substantial amount of literature review and worldwide discussions with professors at home and abroad, the author has collected nearly 800 pieces of questionnaires on values survey and leadership styles on the same population. After processing the raw data, lots of significant results have been found to indicate the correlations between cultures & values systems and leadership styles. Quite a number of magnificent implications have been drawn out from the results. In general, there isn't a one-for-all leadership even for the same person. Leadership style is only a multidimensional tendency of a person which has been closely related to the industry, age, gender, education, tenure, etc. Since questionnaires on values survey and leadership styles, as well as the already well-developed theories on values and leadership styles are all adopted from the western world, this will be a significant pavement for the author and other scholars who are interested in this research topic to do profound comparative studies between China and Western world. Due to the time limits and specific requirements of the word limits for this research, the author has to postpone the further research to the next stage.

Through over two years of survey on the same batch of Guinea pigs on their cultures and values system as well as leadership styles, 778 pieces of valid questionnaires have been collected and processed by appropriate statistical software. Based on the statistical results, the following possible results have been drawn from:

1. Culture and values systems have been ingrained and embedded into people's blood which leaves footprints all the way through his life. Therefore, person's behavior and conducts are the miniatures of the cultures and values systems in which the person is soaked, especially things that they have obtained before 13 years old. Thus, when people come to the post being a leader, their leadership styles will also be significantly influenced by their culture and values system.

2. There is no one-for-all leadership style in the world. Even though the same person's leadership style may alter according to different occasions, when the contexts within which he leads change. It is wrong and at least not exact to say that a person has a specific leadership style all through the periods when he is acting as a leader. It is more reasonable and acceptable to say that a person has a higher tendency in one leadership style over the other leadership styles due to the nature of the industry, the tenure of his career in the firms, as well as the characteristics of the subordinates under which he leads.

3. Additionally, one's leadership styles have been largely affected by numerous other factors which are relevant to the leader. Such as the nature of the industry, the ownership specificity of the enterprise, the education level, gender, age, the competitive environment in which the enterprises belong to, as well as the geographic locations of the enterprises and the tenure. To be specific, in traditional industries such as manufacturing sectors, leaders are more likely to follow autocratic leadership styles; whereas in the high-tech industries, leaders are more likely to adopt democratic and free reign leadership styles; male leaders are more likely to adopt autocratic leadership styles rather than female leaders; leaders with higher education levels are more probably to adopt democratic leadership style and free reign leadership style than those who are at lower education levels.

4. Statistics results have revealed that among the demographic factors, age and education level of the guinea pigs have much greater influence on their leadership styles as against all other demographic factors. This has verified that leader's leadership styles have been deeply affected by his experiences in life and work. With the increase of age, people are intending to have more rational and mature views on lots of things in their life and work and as a result, their leadership styles are more likely to demonstrate in multidimensional scale. They may express different leadership styles according to the specific situation in which they are handling. Education is also a key factor to influence people's leadership style. The higher the education level, the more like the Guinea pigs are intending to conduct in a democratic style or free reign leadership style, as higher education levels have armed themselves on how to empower the subordinates and be delegated by the followers.

5. The geographic location of the enterprise and tenure of the surveyed population will definitely influence the leadership styles. Research results have indicated that business leaders whose enterprises are located along the east-southern coastal lines are more likely to adopt democratic leadership style and free reign leadership style. Moreover, those who have longer tenure in the firms are more probably to adopt democratic and free reign leadership styles. This might be explained as follows: companies which are located in the south-eastern coastal lines have been experiencing more open policy and the location has enabled them to know, understand, and learn more western management styles due to the more and quicker information flow especially during the first half of the period when China has implemented open door policy. The longer the tenure of the leader in the enterprise, the more likely he is to adopt democratic and free reign leadership styles, which is because the longer the time he stays in the enterprises, the more trust and friendliness he has established with his subordinates.

Chapter 1
Introduction

1.1 IDENTIFICATION AND SIGNIFICANCE OF THIS RESEARCH

Culture has been embedded into people's blood. Since his birth, his behaviors will be deeply influenced by the culture in which has been raised and living. Based on substantial amount of literature review and worldwide discussions with professors at home and abroad, the author has distributed 1200 pieces of questionnaire and collected 800 pieces with 778 valid on values survey and leadership styles on the same population. After processing the raw data, lots of significant results have been found to indicate the correlations between cultures & values systems and leadership styles. Quite a number of magnificent implications have been drawn out from the results. In general, there isn't a one-for-all leadership even for the same person. Leadership style is only a multidimensional tendency of a person which has been closely related to the industry, age, gender, education, tenure, etc. Since questionnaires on values survey and leadership styles, as well as the already well-developed theories on values and leadership styles are all adopted from the western world, this will be a significant pavement for the author and other scholars who are interested in this research topic to do profound comparative studies between

DOI: 10.4018/978-1-5225-2277-5.ch001

China and Western world. Due to the time limits and specific requirements of the word limits for this research, the author has to postpone the further research to the next stage.

1.2 STATUS QUO OF LEADERSHIP RESEARCH IN GENERAL

The development of leadership theories and leadership styles has been come across several prominent stages. Such development and the research on the development and evolution of leadership theories and practices are itself a refection and miniature of the social and economic development of the world. As early as at the turn of the 1950s, trait theory was very popular in this research field. Trait theory is trying to identify either a common or universal set of characteristics that distinguishes between:1) Leader – Follower; 2) Effective leader - Ineffective leader. As its main theme suggests the fatal weakness of trait theory is trying to pinpoint universal leadership characteristics. Between 1950s and 1970s, behavioral theory was dominant in the research of leadership styles. The main features of this theory is trying to identify various leadership styles and try to find a general most effective leadership style across all situations. (Bass, 1981; Kerr et al.1974). The drawback of this leadership in general was a simple-minded approach. Since 1980s, in the field of leadership research, there emerged contingency theory which features in 1). Focusing on the dynamic interplay among the leaders, the followers and the situations in which both find themselves (Bass, 1981; Yukl, 1981); 2). Focusing on not only how the leader behaves, but also how the situation and context shape the leaders activities (Bell & Chase, 1995).

The drawbacks of contingency theory are also obvious. To be specific, in this development stage, it ignores the broader managerial roles which leaders must perform; it also ignores the fact that leadership is inherently a process of interpersonal influence.

Then, Mintzberg (1973) suggested in his research that managers might be seen as performing a multitude of roles, which nurtured the appearance of the coming "new phase" - A Managerial Phase. It considers realistic complexities and views leader from an interpersonal influence perspective. The new phase leadership theory embodies the following trends: A focus on leadership as one aspect of management. And it is an elaboration on interpersonal influence process, as well as a concentration on much broader conceptualizations of styles. In the new phase period, there emerged mainly three kinds of leadership theories. That is, Contingency theories; Transactional Leadership;

Transformational Leadership and Reinforcement Strategies, which in a whole have been seen as strategic leadership theory beginning from 1980s. Strategic theories of leadership are concerned with leadership "of" organizations (Hunt, 1991) and are "marked by a concern for the evolution of the organization as a whole, including its changing aims and capabilities" (Selznick, 1984).

The essence of strategic theory is the creation and maintenance of absorptive capacity; adaptive capacity and managerial wisdom. In transactional approach to leadership, it represents the processes of influence and counter-influence among followers in leaderless groups to describe the power leaders have in formal groups, which can be implied as the following: 1) Exchange of Benefits - Leaders give something to followers; 2) mutual rights and understandings - Effective leadership exists when everyone perceives a fair exchange of benefits. As for LMX (Leader-Member Exchange) Theory, which is based on social exchange theory, it emphasize the two relationships between leaders and followers in two aspects: 1) high degree of mutual influence and attraction between the leader and a limited number of subordinates; 2) lesser degree of trust and influence between leader and followers.

No matter how leadership theories develop, to have a better and comprehensive view on leadership theories and research, experts have developed multiple-factor leadership which have been used worldwide to survey the leadership styles at individual level. This is the reason why the author of this research has adopted this survey to conduct her research. In order to match leadership survey, the author has also adopted Schwartz value survey to test the orientation of values system at the individual level.

1.3 GENERAL INTRODUCTION TO THIS RESEARCH AND POTENTIAL RESULTS

Through over two years of survey on the same batch of Guinea pigs on their cultures and values system as well as leadership styles, 778 pieces of valid questionnaires have been collected and processed by appropriate statistical software. Based on the statistical results, the following possible results have been drawn from:

1. Culture and values systems have been ingrained and embedded into people's blood which leaves footprints all the way through his life. Therefore, person's behavior and conducts are the miniatures of the cultures and values systems in which the person is soaked, especially things that they have obtained before 13 years old. Thus, when people

come to the post being a leader, their leadership styles will also be significantly influenced by their culture and values system.

2. There is no one-for-all leadership style in the world, even though the same person's leadership style may alter according to different occasions, when the contexts within which he leads change. It is wrong and at least not exact to say that a person has a specific leadership style all through the periods when he is acting as a leader. It is more reasonable and acceptable to say that a person has a higher tendency in one leadership style over the other leadership styles due to the nature of the industry, the tenure of his career in the firms, as well as the characteristics of the subordinates under which he leads.

3. Additionally, one's leadership styles have been largely affected by numerous other factors which are relevant to the leader. Such as the nature of the industry, the ownership specificity of the enterprise, the education level, gender, age, the competitive environment in which the enterprises belong to, as well as the geographic locations of the enterprises and the tenure. To be specific, in traditional industries such as manufacturing sectors, leaders are more likely to follow autocratic leadership styles; whereas in the high-tech industries, leaders are more likely to adopt democratic and free reign leadership styles; male leaders are more likely to adopt autocratic leadership styles rather than female leaders; leaders with higher education levels are more probably to adopt democratic leadership style and free reign leadership style than those who are at lower education levels.

4. Statistics results have revealed that among the demographic factors, age and education level of the guinea pigs have much greater influence on their leadership styles as against all other demographic factors. This has verified that leader's leadership styles have been deeply affected by his experiences in life and work. With the increase of age, people are intending to have more rational and mature views on lots of things in their life and work and as a result, their leadership styles are more likely to demonstrate in multidimensional scale. They may express different leadership styles according to the specific situation in which they are handling. Education is also a key factor to influence people's leadership style. The higher the education level, the more like the Guinea pigs are intending to conduct in a democratic style or free reign leadership style, as higher education levels have armed themselves on how to empower the subordinates and be delegated by the followers.

5. The geographic location of the enterprise and tenure of the surveyed population will definitely influence the leadership styles. Research re-

sults have indicated that business leaders whose enterprises are located along the east-southern coastal lines are more likely to adopt democratic leadership style and free reign leadership style. Moreover, those who have longer tenure in the firms are more probably to adopt democratic and free reign leadership styles. This might be explained as follows: companies which are located in the east-southern coastal lines have been experiencing more open policy and the location has enabled them to know, understand, and learn more western management styles due to the more and quicker information flow especially during the first half of the period when China has implemented open door policy. The longer the tenure of the leader in the enterprise, the more likely he is to adopt democratic and free reign leadership styles, which is because the long the time he stays in the enterprises, the more trust and friendliness he has established with his subordinates.

The general research framework has been constructed in the following diagram (as can be seen in Figure 1 below).

Figure 1. The procedural research framework of this project

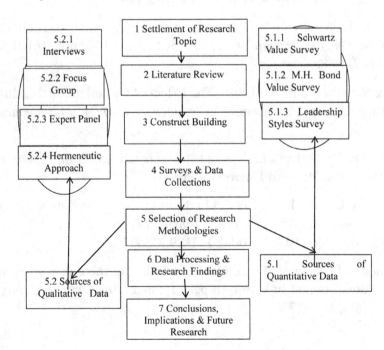

REFERENCES

Abram, D., Ando, K., & Hinkle, S., & ThePsychological Attachment to the Group. (1998). Cross-Cultural Differences in Organizational Identification and Subjective Norms as Predictor of Workers Turnover Intentions. *Personality and Social Psychology Bulletin, 24*(10), 1027–1039. doi:10.1177/01461672982410001

Aldrich, H. E. (1979). *Organizations and environments.* Englewood Cliffs, NJ: Prentice-Hall.

Bass, B. M. (1985). *Leadership and performance beyond expectations.* New York: Free Press.

Bass, B. M. (1990). *Bass & Stogdill's handbook of leadership: Theory, research, and managerial applications* (3rd ed.). New York: Free Press.

Burns, T., & Stalker, G. M. (1961). *The management of innovation.* London: Tavistock Publications, Tavistock Centre.

Dickson, M. (1997). *Universality and variation in organizationally cognitive prototypes of effective leadership* (Unpublished doctoral dissertation). Department of Psychology, University of Maryland.

Gerstner, C. R., & Day, D. V. (1994). Cross-cultural comparison of leadership prototypes. *The Leadership Quarterly, 5*(2), 121–134. doi:10.1016/1048-9843(94)90024-8

Goll I. & Sambharya R. B. (1990). The Effect of Organizational Culture and Leadership on Firm Performance. *Advances in Strategic Management,* (6), 183-200.

Lawrence, P. R., & Lorsch, J. W. (1967). *Organization and environment.* Cambridge, MA: Harvard University Press.

Leung, K., & Bond, M. H. (1989). On the empirical identification of dimensions for cross-cultural comparisons. *Journal of Cross-Cultural Psychology, 20*(2), 133–151. doi:10.1177/0022022189202002

Lumpkin, G. T., & Dess, G. G. (1996). Clarifying the entrepreneurial orientation construct and linking it to performance. *Academy of Management Review, 21*(1), 135–172.

McClelland, D. C., Atkinson, J. W., Clark, R. A., & Lowell, E. L. (Eds.). (1953). *The achievement motive.* New York: Appleton-Century-Crofts. doi:10.1037/11144-000

McFarland, L. J., Senen, S., & Childress, J. R. (1993). *Twenty-first-century leadership.* New York: Leadership Press.

Misumi, J. (1985). *The behavioral science of leadership: An interdisciplinary Japanese research program.* Ann Arbor, MI: University of Michigan Press.

Schein, E. H. (1992). *Organizational culture and leadership: A dynamic view* (2nd ed.). San Francisco: Jossey-Bass.

Staw, B. M., Sandelands, L. E., & Dutton, J. E. (1981). Threat-rigidity effects in organizational behavior: A multilevel analysis. *Administrative Science Quarterly, 26*(4), 501–524. doi:10.2307/2392337

Thompson, K. R., & Luthans, F. (1990). Organizational culture: A behavioral perspective. In B. Schneider (Ed.), *Organizational Climate and Culture* (pp. 319–344). San Francisco: Jossey-Bass.

Trice, H. M., & Beyer, J. M. (1984). *The cultures of work organizations.* Englewood Cliffs, NJ: Prentice-Hall.

Yukl, G. A. (1994). *Leadership in organizations* (3rd ed.). Englewood Cliffs, NJ: Prentice-Hall.

Chapter 2
Literature Review and Research Hypotheses

2.1 FRAMEWORK OF THIS RESEARCH

Leadership research is rather odd and abstract, therefore, a triangulation of research methodologies have been adopted. Literature review provides the theoretical support of this study and the research hypotheses and research constructs have been founded based on large quantities of literature review. To achieve valid and reliable research results, multiple research approaches have been implemented as can be seen from the research framework above in Figure 1. Quantitative approaches combine with qualitative methods are interlocking one with another to demonstrate a panoramic picture of the leadership styles of 778 Guinea pigs being surveyed. In the field of research, quantitative methods are enjoying warm embrace in academia. However, in lots of researches such as leadership style study, qualitative approaches are used to compensate for the too static and "hard" features as in quantitative methods. Therefore, in this study, apart from quantitative approaches like questionnaire survey, the author of this study has also implemented qualitative methods as organizational storytelling, hermeneutic method, interviews, on-site observation, etc.

DOI: 10.4018/978-1-5225-2277-5.ch002

2.2 CHALLENGES IN THIS RESEARCH

The research on the correlations between values orientations and leadership styles is very challenging. Previous researches mainly focus on the separated topics on either values systems or leadership styles. However, there is seldom research which entwines them both together and sees it from comprehensive perspective. The most obvious reason might be that values system or cultural research is rather abstract and qualitative and the same is true of the researches on leadership styles as there is not a one-for-all model of leadership style to follow and it is hard for anyone to say one leadership style is better than the others.

As regarding the cultures and values research, the most famous giants like M. H. Bond, Schwartz, Hofstede and others have in their research eyed on the western context. Although M. H. Bond has developed a Chinese values survey, which is mainly derived from the ideas of Confucius thoughts (BVS), it is not as popular as that developed by Schwartz (SVS). Even when the author of this research has in person had a long talk and profound discussion with M. H. Bond, he finally suggested that the author should adopt SVS (Schwartz values survey as the instrument), which again indicates the importance and significance of this research as this research has been conducted for over two years to have obtained 778 samples from the distributed 1000 questionnaires. The research findings, to some extent may fill the gap of the lack of research on Chinese values and the leadership styles of Chinese business leaders.

To speak from the research methodologies, in the past decade, SEM (Structural Equation Modeling) has become very hot in empirical research field. Even some scholars have summarized hundreds of papers from top tier journals to testify that SEM has been widely used in empirical research and there is a tendency of still roaring up in the research field. The author of this paper has been also intending to follow the trend, but the preliminary results obtained from SEM have shown that the testing results are not very attractive as against the author's expectations. Therefore, the author has to abandon SEM as the research methodology but still have puzzlement in mind. With this big puzzlement, the author has been to HK again to seek answers from one of the greatest giants in culture and leadership style research---M. H. Bond. As he suggested that it doesn't mean that every popular tool is good and appropriate in any research. As the most prominent feature of SEM is to find the correlations between multiple factors, it seems that SEM should be very suitable in this research. Actually, values survey and leadership styles survey to a large extent are very abstract and it is hard to measure the exact correlations between values and leadership styles, even though both of the questionnaires have themselves in 9 and 5 Likert scales respectively. Since the items of the surveys can not be absolutely measured, the correlations between cultural value factors and leadership styles can not be in a linear relation. Being a famous guru in this research, seldom of his (M. H. Bond) papers have adopted SEM as the research methodology, though most of his papers have been released in top-tier journals. The failure in adopting SEM methodology might be resulting in the nature of mediocre of Chinese culture and also might be because the questionnaires adopted in this research are not very suitable to people in Chinese culture.

After the visit and magnificent discussion with M.H. Bond, the puzzlement has been eliminated and the author began to focus on the research by using the popular statistical software ---SPSS. Though the research has not got significant results from SEM model due to its non-linearity nature between values and leadership, there are still lots of meaningful findings in this research. Multiple factor analyses have indicated that Chinese business leaders have a unique but not clear-cut leadership style which revolves among the three leadership styles of autocratic, democratic and free-reign at the axles of Chinese core values. When the 778 samples have been displayed in Matlab graph, it again testifies that the core of the Chinese cultures and values systems is mediocre, or the doctrine of mean as proposed by many scholars both from China and other part of the world who are specialized in Chinese cultures and values as many of the dots are overlapping and most of the dots are concentrated in the middle part of the graph. Multiple factor analyses have demonstrated that there are strong correlations between cultural factors and leadership styles, but more have to be probed and investigated for the future research.

Due to the complexity of this research, multidisciplinary and cross-bordering approaches have been adopted during the process of research. Two set of mature questionnaires have been implemented, one is Schwartz Values Survey and the other is multiple factor leadership style survey. Accompanied with the survey questions, supplementary items have been added in the survey which is worked as either moderate variables or mediate variables. With these supplementary factors, author of this research has the resources to investigate into the influential factors on values orientations and leadership styles, as well as it makes it possible to conduct the correlations between values dimensions and leadership styles.

2.3 CONSTRUCT DEVELOPMENT OF THIS RESEARCH

Based on large quantities of literature review both on values orientation and leadership style, the author has summarized the research construct on the following diagram (as can be seen in Figure 1 below). This construct is developed taking into account that human beings are social creatures and because of this ingrained nature, their behaviors will be the outcomes of independent variables such as date of birth, family background, cultures & sub-cultures, gender, etc. as well as the dependent variables as education level, environment in which they are living, so on and so forth.

2.4 PROCEDURES AND ARRANGEMENT OF THIS RESEARCH

This dissertation has been arranged according to the following logic:

First of all, the research framework has been stipulated based on wide and comprehensive discussions with concerning experts in this research field during their teaching in the school of management of XJTU. When they returned to their home countries after teaching, extensive emails have been exchanged to modify and fine tune the research framework. Even telephone calls have been conducted when necessary to clarify any minor misunderstandings or

Figure 1. Research hypotheses have been postulated based on the above mindset

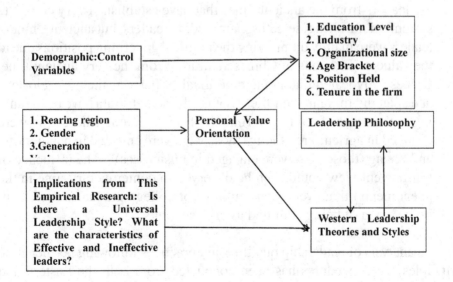

ambiguities on the research. Through many rounds of to and fro discussions either face to face or virtually, the research framework and procedures have been finalized.

Research proposal has been framed and streamlined as in the following steps:

STORIES OF CHINESE LEADERSHIP which have to include the different periods along the development of Chinese economy. To have a panoramic picture of Chinese leadership profile, it is necessary to cover:

Historical Stories of Chinese Leadership (The Past)

Purpose: To identify the historical 'grand stories' of Chinese leadership from the trilogy of Confucianism, Taoism, and Buddhism and to discern similarities and variations in the interpretation of these historical texts from the perspective of traditional Chinese philosophers as well as the discourse on Eastern philosophies in the modern leadership literature. As the leadership stories can only be derived from classical literary works, hermeneutic approach has to be utilized. Leadership profiles have to be drawn from those works based on widely reading and learning, inclusive of getting implications, interpretations and connotations.

Procedures: An expert panel of Chinese philosophers has been asked to identify stories as what the most influential and relevant factors are for Chinese leadership from the perspectives of their views. This is mainly founded on their research results from Chinese philosophies, literature and other sources. Actually, China has an affluent source of producing leaders from the ancient times that have established very complete systems of nurturing, selecting, succeeding leaders, but ancient Chinese leaders were mainly dominating the political governing positions due to the value orientations of Chinese culture. From the very ancient time, Chinese advocated that being a political leader was the most glorious and splendid thing in their life. That is why social strata have been ranking in the order of "Shi (government officials), Nong (those who were engaged in agriculture), Gong (those who were engaged in handicrafts) and Shang (those who were engaged in businesses)". The influence of this ancient view could even be observed in contemporary time in the phenomenon that every year, millions of college graduates rush to sit in the exam of being admitted as civil servants.

Textual analysis of leadership qualities and practices following hermeneutic principles and procedures has been conducted from both the Eastern and the Western perspectives. To establish the Chinese leadership profile, well selected experts have been called for to verify the coding and several rounds of checkup have conducted to finalize the Chinese leadership profile.

Textual analysis of modern interpretations of these Eastern philosophies as presented in the Chinese and Western leadership literature. This involves a literature search in electronic databases for articles as well as books (e.g., Heider's book entitled "Tao of Leadership").

Modern Stories of Chinese Leadership (The Present)

Purpose: To learn the modern stories of Chinese leadership and to discern the extent to which these reflect traditional Chinese philosophies and modern Western leadership theories. Empirical test of theories of cultural convergence, divergence and cross-vergence in Chinese leadership theories in practice have to be implemented.

Procedures

Research Participants: Chinese executives in the EMBA program of XJTU (targeted number of participants = 50 to 60) have been called for in the pilot test. Involvement in the research includes the completion of a survey questionnaire and participation in the qualitative interviews. Actually, to secure the validity and solidity of this research, participants in this part are out-numbered as expected. 1000 sets of questionnaires have been distributed nationwide with EMBA students covering as widely as possible in regions and finally 778 sets of valid surveys have been returned to us with a respondents' rate of 77.8% and the procedures for conducting the questionnaires are in very rigid and international accepted manners.

Step 1: Quantitative Survey Questionnaires

To include validated measures of Chinese leadership style, a thorough check of previous research conducted in China, HongKong, and Taiwan have been done (the Greater China area); work has been done as well to investigate Confucian values measures (e.g., Bond's Chinese Values Survey), cross-culturally validated personal values measure (e.g., Schwartz Value Survey), and the Western leadership styles (e.g., Goleman's emotional intelligence, visionary leadership, transformational leadership, Level 5 leadership).

Questionnaires have been sent to participating executives prior to their interviews and collected at the time of the interview.

Participating executives have been subsequently provided with a "Personal Leadership Profile" report as well as a summary report of study findings.

Quantitative analysis of questionnaires has been focusing on the determining relationships among personal values and leadership styles, demographic differences in values/leadership (e.g., gender, age/generation).

Step 2: Qualitative interviews with Chinese executives who have been asked for telling three stories of leadership based on their work experiences and each story is in a different context.

1.   Their personal story of leadership.
2.   A story about a leader in their work experience who has significantly impacted their leadership philosophy/practice
3.   A story about a leader in their personal/community experience who has significantly impacted their leadership philosophy/practice

Sample probing questions: 1. "Why is it an important story for you?" 2. "In what way is this an interesting story for you?" 3. How has this leader impacted your leadership philosophy and/or practice?

To develop interview protocols, organizational storytelling literature has been reviewed (e.g., David Boje).

Content analysis of leadership stories has been focusing on identifying leadership profile; Common and unique themes within and across contexts have been probed; themes consistent with historical Chinese philosophies have been identified and analyzed; themes consistent with Western leadership theories as against Chinese leadership profile have been investigated.

Step 3: Comparative analysis of qualitative and quantitative leadership data for holistic understanding of antecedents and practice of organizational leadership in the modern Chinese society has been underlined.

Research Report: Based on this research proposal, the research has obtained 778 sets of questionnaires as against the proposed 50 or 60 in order to secure more degree of reliability and generality. The next step follows with the inputting all the raw data into relevant software as SPSS, or LISREL to process the data and present interpretations based on the findings. These findings have been compared with literature review, as most of the leadership literature has been developed in the western world which has obvious contrast to compare with Chinese culture. Personal interviews have been conducted with the participants carefully singled out from the questionnaires list to cover different industries, different geographic areas, different genders and age groups, etc. in order to secure the broad coverage of the research.

2.5 LEADERSHIP LITERATURE REVIEW

2.5.1 Review on Leadership Literature in General

Human beings have always been keenly interested in leaders and leadership. Confucius sought laws of order between leaders and subordinates. Plato described an ideal republic with philosopher-kings providing wise and judicious leadership. Later, Plato and his colleagues established the Paidea, a school for leadership in early Greece. In the sixteenth century, the Italian Niccolo Machiavelli illuminated another side of leadership -- some say the more practical side.

The word "leader" first appeared in the English language in the 1300s; it stems from the root "leden", meaning "to travel" or "show the way." The term "leadership" followed some five centuries later. Indeed, the scientific study of leadership (as opposed to the study of leaders) has arisen primarily in the United States and almost exclusively since the turn of the twentieth century. Ancient Greek philosopher Socrates identified SIX technical functions of a leader which can be iterated as follows: put the right people in the right place at the right time; establish complete, fair and just mechanism for praising and punishment; establish good relationship with his followers; have the personal charms to attract alliances and assistants; have the ability to maintain what they have already got; be industrious and diligent in their work p16 <Strategic Leaders> by John Adel. Different scholars have given different definition on the term "leader", which can be summarized in Table 1.

While certainly not its sole architect, perhaps no other individual has energized leadership research and influenced the emergence of leadership studies as an academic discipline than James Macgregor Burns.

Bernard Bass, a distinguished leadership researcher, dedicated his important book *Leadership beyond Expectations* to Jim Burns. Bass credits Burns' seminal 1978 *Leadership* with the surging interest in both leadership research and leadership studies. "From this piece of work grew empirical studies of attributes and behaviors, literature on charisma, and measurement scales for

Table 1. Definitions about leaders

Scholars	Definition & Implications
Tannenbaum (1961)	Leading is an action which leads a group of people to achieve a common goal
Tannenbaum Wesbhler & Massarik (1961)	Leading is a kind of interpersonal influence which conducts in a specific contingent and through the process of communication, a certain objective is achieved
Bowers & Seashore (1969)	Leading is an action which influences people to achieve a common goal voluntarily
Katz & Kahn (1970)	Leading is an operational procedure for interpersonal relation during which someone provides information in a certain way and others believe that the outcome of their action will be improved if they enact action as per that someone
Davis (1977)	Leading is such that a person can persuade others to pursue an objective with great zeal
Katz & Kahn (1978)	Leading is such that one influence others
Jacobs & Jaques (1990)	Leading is a process in which others put efforts to achieve a set objective
Drath & Palus (1994)	Leading is a process in which a group of people work together
Robbins (1998)	Leading is a kind of capability which influences a group of people to achieve a set goal

Source: Collected and compiled by the author

transformational leadership as well as the enormous growth of leadership studies, research, training programs, and publications.

In 1974, *Stogdill's Handbook of Leadership* listed 4,725 studies of leadership and 189 pages of references. He concluded, however, "The endless accumulation of empirical data has not produced an integrated understanding of leadership."

It might be useful to look back to the 1970s and examine the context and frustration that produced Hunt's lament. Researchers, not theorists, dominated the study of leadership in the twentieth century. These researchers – usually in the field of social, behavioral, or experimental psychology -- were involved in inductive theory building, with gradual but limited success.

Within the tradition of inductive theory building, the analytic dimensions are undefined, and the researcher creates a set of measures that reflect implicit analytic dimensions. After conducting empirical studies, an assessment is made of what measures group together using statistical methods (factor analysis or discriminate analysis). Then the clusters are given names, tested for reliability, refined, and used to do subsequent empirical research.

Factors such as leader intelligence, educational level of followers, dominance, affiliation, achievement orientation, formal and informal leadership, consideration, initiating structure, and every other conceivable variable were tested in self-reports, experimental groups, field studies, and organizations.

But in an important early essay on the topic, Arlun Melcher decries inductive theory construction, because principal attention is given to the reliability of measures and little or no attention to the logical adequacy of the underlying model. Too often, the research yielded models that suggested a set of relationships between variables without offering meaningful explanations of them.

One of the central problems of the inductive approach in constructing a universal leadership theory is the post hoc manner in which it has been developed. That is, "the same studies used to construct it and to provide empirical support for it. This inductive method, in which the theory is being shaped to fit known results makes it impossible for it to conflict with these results" according to Ashour, Graen et al, and McMahon. Much of the leadership research in the present and immediate past demonstrates the limitations of the inductive method.

What then, is good theory? Writing in 1976, Filley, House and Kerr suggested: "A theory should first have internal consistency; that is, its propositions should be free from contradiction. Second, a theory should have external consistency; that is it should be consistent with observations. Third, it must be…stated so that its predictions can be verified. Fourth, a theory should have the characteristic of generality. Finally a practical theory should have the attribute of scientific parsimony.

Using Filley, House and Kerr's framework for good theory, how does Burns' measure up? I would argue that Burns' developed the first comprehensive theory of leadership for modern scholars, utilizing the more abstract, deductive method. He drew upon his vast experience of leaders and leadership, his studies of presidents and movement leaders, and upon an array of disciplines – both his own and those new to him. On the third point of good theory – the verification of predictions -- Burns' has been criticized for his lack of operationalization of key variables and the abstractness of his constructs. But he was looking for universals not particulars – the "grand or generalizable" grail sought by Hunt and others.

Burns' theory brought into focus two vastly important dimensions of leadership – that leadership was relational and that the motivations of leaders and followers were keys to understanding leadership and change.

The Development of Leadership Theories

As regard the research of leadership theories, Bryman (1992) has divided such research into 4 periods according to the time sequence:

1. Prior to 1940, in this period: the dominant theory has been called Trait Theory, which advocated that leaders were born leaders, who have some ingrained characteristics. And as such, researchers were trying to investigate what unique personal traits leaders share;

2. From 1940 to 1960: the dominant leadership theory has been labeled as the Behavior Theory, which proposed that effective leaders definitely expose a certain kinds of behavior. The research of this period has laid focus on the relationship between the effectiveness and efficiency of leadership and leaders' behaviors;

3. From 1960s to 1980s: the dominant theories of this period have been called Contingency Theory, which advocates that effective leadership is such a kind of leadership which is dynamic and always attempts to change as the environment changes.

4. 1980s to date: this period has been called the New Leadership Research Period and such new theories emphasize the importance of vision and the influence that leaders lay upon their subordinates and such influence will be transformed into increased employee performance.

Leadership style refers to the categorization of leaders' behaviors and different scholars have adopted different criteria in categorizing leadership style. To be specific, it can be simplified in Table 2.

Table 2. Conceptions of leadership styles

Leadership Style	Scholars
Autocratic, participative and free reign	Davis & Newstrom (1985) this has been categorized as per the degree of how leaders excel their power
Normative, individual and contingent	Getzel & Guba. This has been categorized as per social systemic theory
Theory X and theory Y	Mcgregor (1957)
Leadership Grid	Blake & Moutom
Bureaucratic, peer and political mode	Bureaucratic concept has been proposed by Max Weber; and peer concept has been proposed by John Millett; political mode has been advocated by J. Vicvo Baldridge
Transactional and transformational	Proposed by Burns & Bass

Source: Collected and compiled by the author

A Relational Approach to Leadership

Burns challenged researchers to abandon the leader-focused model and to take up the study of leadership aimed at "realizing goals mutually held by both leaders and followers." To do so, he suggested involving greater attention to the role of followers as well as the motivations of potential opponents and competition from other actors. Burns speaks of "the reciprocal process of mobilizing by persons with certain motives and values, various economic, political, and other resources, in a context of competition and conflict, in order to realize goals independently or mutually held by both leaders and followers." In short, Burns characterized leadership as a process and not person.

For the most part, leadership research of the first five decades of the 20th century focused on leaders themselves, and has come to be called the era of the "Great Man Theories." These were essentially the study of individual leaders --- "leaderships" rather than "leadership," to paraphrase Burns. Edwin P. Hollander, one of the few researchers at the time who focused on the role of followers in the leadership process, describes this period as the search for traits of good leaders. Hereditary properties such as intelligence, height, and self-confidence were identified as distinguishing characteristics. Whether idealistic or normative, leadership research sought to identify traits or abilities that set leaders apart from non-leaders. But research failed to produce a set of traits that leaders must possess to be effective, Mann (1959) Smith and Krueger (1933) and Stodgill (1948)

As the notion of inherited or inherent leadership was dispelled, the American behaviorist movement scientists measured behaviors of leaders in an attempt to deconstruct leadership. In effect, their operating hypothesis was that the behaviors of effective leaders differed from those of ineffective leaders. Psychologists at Ohio State and the University of Michigan contributed pioneering research in the behavioral understanding of leadership. The Ohio State profiles, after years of study of "consideration" and "initiating structure" and other two-dimensional variables, but failed to either explain or predict leader behavior.

Unknown to Burns, but working in a parallel fashion was an important cadre of social scientists who were generating empirical research findings that would support his reciprocal concept. The Southern Illinois University Leadership Symposia, originating in 1971 produced four important volumes: *Current Developments in the Study of Leadership* (1973); *Contingency Approaches to Leadership* (1974); *Leadership Frontiers* (1975); and *Leadership: the Cutting Edge* 1977). During this period, particular attention was paid to the relationship between leaders and the group, and managerial implications in the workplace. There were twinned variables – "consideration" and "task performance" for example – but the behavior was much more interpenetrating and complex than it appeared.

The key, Burns felt, was in the hypersensitive force field of motivation. "Leaders must assess collective motivation – the hierarchies of motivations in both leaders and followers – as studiously as they analyze the power bases of potential followers and rival leaders." To perceive the working of leadership in social causation as motivational and volitional rather than simply as "economic" or "ideological" or "institutional" is to perceive not a lineal sequence of stimulus-response "sets" or "stages" not even a network of sequential and cross-cutting forces, but a rich and pulsating stream of leadership - followership forces flowing through the whole social process."

Relational -- "a rich and pulsating" process held together by the glue of motivations, both hidden and apparent -- yielded an exquisite internal and external consistency. It was obvious. It was parsimonious. And it was certainly generalizable across sectors of identity, community, and place.

Actually, terms as leader and manager, leadership and management are hard to be defined and normally they are coming out in pairs. Sometimes it is really not an easy job to differentiate one from the other. The demarcation between these pairs of terms is rather blurring free from clear-cut posture. Based on large number of literature reviews, the author has summarized the most transparent and the most frequently mentioned aspects when concerning about manager and leader or management and leadership. Such differentiation can only work as supplementary materials for scholars and researchers who have interest in leadership studies. In real world, they might be used interchangeably (for more details refer to Table 3).

Values-Added Leadership

Burns' theory had a second powerful component, what I like to call a "values-added" dimension. Until Burns' book, the goal of good leadership was seen as "effectiveness." Burns transformed our view of leadership by insisting that great leadership had moral dimensions. "Moral" to Burns did not mean the everyday virtues or daily ethical dimensions, but adherence to the great public values such as liberty, justice, and equality. Moral leadership was the purview of great leadership. He thus made a distinction between two different but compatible leadership behaviors -- transforming and transactional. He defined transactional leadership as "everyday brokerage" and "the process whereby one person takes the initiative in making contact with others for the purpose of an exchange of valued things." This iteration has clearly bridged

Table 3. Differences between management and leadership

Features of Leadership	Features of Management
Guide the direction	Implement tasks
Set up Vision	Accomplish targets
Features of leadership	Features of management
Focus on future	Focus on present
Do the right things	Do things right
Creation & innovation	Maintain & control
Push reform & changes	Maintain stability
Empower & encourage	Terminate constraints
Risk taker	Prudent actions
Rule breaker	Rule follower
Encourage uniqueness	Forge standards
Seek help from art	Lay stress on science
Motivate impetus	Solve problems
Exert personal charisma	Exert power
Establish partnerships with others	Manage others
What happened? Why did it happen?	How did it happen?when did it happen?
To do what and why to do it?	How to do it and when to do it?
Push & promote	Accept & follow
Flexible and open mind	Concise & exact mind
Motivate participation	Hinder blind actions
Encourage morale	Force to implement

Source: Collected and compiled by the author

the gap between leadership and values system, as leaders with good aspects of values dimensions tend to bring about effectiveness and efficiency to the organizations in which he is leading or takes a leadership position in the organizations.

I guess the beauty of fine theory is that eventually it becomes obvious to all. But those of us in the leadership field know our debt to Jim Burns. He pushed us from leaders to leadership, defined leadership as a process between the leaders and the led and put motivation at the core of the leadership process. Leadership scholars emeritus Joseph Rost dedicated his new book <*Leadership for the Twenty-First Century*>, "To James MacGregor Burns, who changed my whole way of thinking about leadership."

The Birth of Leadership Studies in Academia

Leadership research is an emerging field of study in academia. For many years, concepts such as "headship" in anthropology, "roles" in psychology, "power" in political science, and "management" in business were explored in a uni-disciplinary fashion. While sub-fields within disciplines (e.g., educational leadership, political leadership) are still apparent and multidisciplinary research is quite prevalent, the field of leadership studies has become increasingly interdisciplinary since Burns produced *Leadership.*

In a recent analysis of the disciplinary base of leadership faculty by William Howell, business management is the single largest sector. The behavioral and social sciences, together with business management, seem to drive most leadership coursework in America. Interestingly, in Howell's analysis across courses, "moral and ethical leadership is emphasized in 44% of the coursework sample, and 23% focus on "transformational." Five courses studied by Howell curiously focused on "transactional leadership."

To have a clear and panoramic picture of leader, leadership, leadership research, John Gardner in his book <On Leadership > has differentiated two terms "leading manager" and "non-leading manager" as follows:

1. The former is more far-sighted not only concerns about he current crises, not only care about he quarterly financial reports but with more far-reaching ambitions;
2. While considering the departments which they are leading directly, they may not merely consider the benefits of their own departments but take a wide view on the overall benefit of the whole company and facilitate company to have close ties with outside world and keep pace with the world trends;
3. The influence they have bestowed upon the subordinates goes beyond their power domain;
4. They lay special emphasis on intangible assets, such as views, ideas, values system and impetus; they make decisions and understand the interactions between leaders and subordinates by irrational intuitions and unconsciousness;
5. They are politically mature as to tackle the conflicting and contradictory requirements raised by different departments of the organizations;
6. They pursue and embrace innovation and know clearly how to seek contextual solutions to the problems based on different situations.

Leadership research is very challenging as it has to adopt comprehensive, overall view of lots of cross disciplinary and multidisciplinary aspects and leadership is a dead science (David Boje). There is no question that the very word "leadership" stirs up conflicting feelings. But some of its critics who claim that it is not a rigorous discipline or that its theoretical base is not coherent have only to look at the evolution of other disciplines in academia see that leadership is far from unique in these matters.

From the time of Bacon down to the present day, intellectuals have attempted to classify the sciences, to parcel out the world of fact into its natural divisions. Thomas Jefferson parsed the world (and his library) into Memory, Reason, and Imagination.

J.A. Thomson, who writes about the history of science, asserts that science is not defined "by its subject matter, but by its point of view – the particular kind of question it asks." There is no question that leadership research has a unique viewpoint. The same group activity for example, will be looked at differently by a sociologist, a political scientist, or a biologist, for example. A leadership scholar would have a distinct point of view as well, and the questions asked would be quite different.

Critics of leadership studies claim the emerging field lacks coherence and rigor. But Amedeo Giorgi writing in "Toward the Articulation of Psychology as a Coherent Discipline" demonstrates that this is a false aspiration. "Psychology did not have an early or adequate coherence that we lost over time; we were never coherent in the mature sense of the term. While from time to time there has been agreement with respect to a label -- the study of the mind, consciousness, psyche, experience or behavior -- a common in-depth knowledge of each of the terms was never achieved.

In a discipline that embraces behaviorism, psychoanalysis, Gestalt therapy, these sub-fields point to the lack of a comprehensive central perspective that could clarify the meaning of psychology as such, which in turn would provide the basis for unifying apparently disparate sub-fields. He argues "What is the relationship between psycho-physics and psychotherapy?"

In short, the field of leadership studies per se is no more or no less coherent than other disciplines. Indeed, coherence itself may be undesirable, as the disciplines themselves are approaching the boundaries of each other at breakneck speed. Pearsona, for example, warns that, however ingeniously we may map out the territory of knowledge, "every branch of sciences passes, at one or more points, not only into the domain of adjacent, but even of distinct branches." Social psychology, the nether-region between sociology and psychology, has long been an established sub-field.

But even newer enterprises, such as neuro-biology, environmental psychology, and political psychology demonstrate that the twenty-first century will be moving in a rich field of interdisciplinary search for truth. In fact, multiple and interdisciplinary studies is the one fastest growing sectors of academic life, according to the National Center for Educational Statistics. Again, turning to Burns, who sees the future of leadership studies on campuses evolving to play an important synthesizing role: "Leadership research offers the opportunity of true interdisciplinary work. It is the one discipline that can bridge all academic disciplines."

A century from now, observers and scholars will probably see the last half of the twentieth century as an epochal time in the evolution of leadership theory and practice.

In the two decades since *Leadership* was published, the study of leadership has spawned more thousands of publications across numerous disciplines. Professional journals, such as *Leadership Quarterly* and *The Journal of Leadership Studies*, have been established and are devoted exclusively to the study of leadership. The journal *International Leadership Association* brings together scholars, activists, and leaders from all over the world, "everyone with a professional interest in leadership." Leadership studies or research so far has been experiencing diversified and continuous development with different schools.

2.5.2 Brief Summary on Leadership Development and Research

---"Leaders do the right things; while managers do things right."
---"Leadership is to the 20th and 21 century just what God was to the 16th century."

Modern leadership theories initiated in the 1980s which refer to the research on leadership activities of modern leaders, as well as the new views, theories on the leadership performance. These modern leadership theories are inclusive of leadership attribute theory, charismatic leadership theory, leadership replacement theory, transactional leadership theory and transformational leadership theory. In additionally, there are self-leadership theory and super leadership theory, etc.

- **Transactional Leadership Theories:** The basic proposition of transactional leadership theory is that the relationship between the leader and his followers implies a kind of implicit contract. In this contract, leader provides followers with remunerations, promotions, honors and some other forms of reward, while in return, followers obey the rules and regulations of the leader and accomplish the assigned tasks. The whole process is just like a transaction.

The main features of transactional leadership theory can be summarized as follows:

First of all, transactional leadership theory postulates that: 1. Leaders direct and motivate subordinates to be on the way for accomplishing the assigned tasks through clear role description and job description. This means that leaders have the expectation from the subordinates. If such expectations have been satisfied, subordinates will get the concerning rewarding and remuneration. 2. This theory strongly advocates the organizational rewarding and remuneration system to impact the performance of subordinates based on the organizational authority and legitimacy. 3. Thirdly, this theory stresses the work standards, assignment of tasks and profound task orientation which intends to emphasize the accomplishment of tasks and the obedience of subordinates.

- **Transformational Leadership Theory:** As against the transactional leadership theory, transformational leadership theory intends to nurture the sense of idealism and ethical standards of the subordinates through pursuing much higher targets. This theory has been proposed by Burns based on the analyses of personal traits of a large number of political leaders. Later, Bath proposed a more detailed process for changing the subordinates, groups and organizations. In this process, apart from guiding and directing subordinates to finish their assignments, leader's personal charisma is of greatest importance.

The main features of transformational leadership theory can be summed up in the following remarks:

1. This theory has overrun the inducement of transactional leadership theory, it advocates the ways on how to develop the IQ (Intelligence Quotient), EQ (Emotional Quotient) and teamwork spirit so that subordinates are encouraged to accomplish not only their individual tasks but that of the group and organization;
2. It advocates subordinates to focus on long-term goals, to exert their innovative abilities, and stresses on the changes and adjustment of the whole organizational system and establish amicable atmosphere for accomplishing pre-set goals;

3. This theory strongly encourages subordinates to shoulder more duties and responsibilities through long-term orientation and makes the subordinates understand that their personal development will be highly associates with the overall organizational development. Therefore, transformational leadership theory has widened the research scope of leadership theories and development.

Transformational Leadership Theory Contains Four Dimensions

Firstly, charisma dimension advocates the strong motivation on developing subordinates' emotions and the identification and recognition of leader's leadership style. Leaders provide vision and mission for subordinates and ignite subordinates' sense of honor and subordinates have strong belongingness, trust and respect to the leader. This theory stresses on the importance of target and commitment and advocates leader being the model and idol of the subordinates and as a result, subordinates are of strong sense of pride, self-confidence and loyalty; secondly, inspirational motivation dimension refers to the leadership behavior from which leaders provide subordinates with meaningful and challenging jobs, which furthermore includes clarified expected goals, the constraints for accomplishing this goals originated from the overall organizational goals and calls for the team spirit of subordinates through optimistic work attitudes; the third dimension of transformational leadership theory is called intellectual stimulation, which advocates the objections and oppositions against old ideas and outdated traditions; it advocates subordinates to take a new look on all issues with rationality, to utter their view and seek new solutions to the problems and encourage subordinates to accomplish tasks by new approaches. The fourth and the last dimension of transformational leadership theory is individualized consideration, which calls for the consideration and care about every subordinate, to emphasize personalized needs, wants and demands, to offer directions, guidance and suggestions even training to subordinates according to the specific situation of each subordinate.

*   **Charismatic Leadership Theories:** This is the extension and expansion of leadership trait theory. Charisma is the temperament, the feature, the charms of a person which is unique and different from others. It also refers to the ability and capability of a person with which catches the eyes of subordinates. And as a result, leaders formulate their own unique influential power,

strength, attraction and charisma. Charismatic leadership theory was first proposed by Max Web. According to his proposition, the real reason why subordinates can accept their leader is because of a certain kind of personal traits that this leader occupies. Charismatic leaders have unyielding efforts to strive for their lofty visions and this lofty vision has been embraced by their subordinates. Leaders of this type are have the ability to establish the organizational vision and mission and at the same time they know how to associate the vision and mission with the needs, wants, demands of their subordinates. In this way, subordinates are willing to strive for this vision and mission voluntarily. In the implementation of the vision and mission, charismatic leaders normally adopt lots of novel and anti-traditional approaches to accomplish the common vision. Just like John Adel proposes whomever you are treating, inclusive of treating yourself under all circumstances, as a leader, you should always bear in mind the humanity and see humanity as the objective but not merely means (John Adel, *<Strategic Leaders>* P110).

If you stop looking for answers that are always either God or leadership, you will find other underlying factors. (J. Collins 2002, Level 5 Leadership). These remarks have somewhat differentiated the role of leaders and managers, as well as stressed the importance of leadership in the new era, especially in today's information and knowledge oriented century. The word "Lead", derived from Latin origin, meaning to travel, move forward and a leader is a person who is able to partner with followers in the creation and implementations of a common goal or vision. Leadership is a way of focusing and motivating a group to enable them to achieve their aims. It also involves being accountable and responsible for the group as a whole (Demarco et al., 1987). Leadership is the result of the interaction among the superior (leader), the subordinates (followers), and the organization environment (work and the work situation) (Braden, 2000). while leadership development is defined as expanding the collective capacity of organizational members to engage effectively in leadership roles and process (McCauley et al., 1998). The development of leadership theories has been experiencing the following stages: Trait Theory; Behavior Theory; and Contingency Approach (Situational Theories) period. And now comes the period of Current "New Phase" Leadership. In the new phase period of leadership style, there appears the following trends:

1. A focus on leadership as one aspect of management.
2. An elaboration on interpersonal influence process.
3. A concentration on much broader conceptualizations of styles.

In the first trend, practicing managers have long had an interest in issues surrounding delegation and employee participation in decision-making processes (McConkey, 1974; Steinmetz, 1976). A valuable suggestion in this trend is to distinguish the participation and delegation which first proposed by Bass et al. in 1975 and the main contributions in the research of the trend one have been attributed to scholars like Leana (1986,1987) and Vroom and Yetton (1973).

The research in the first trend is mainly focused on the aspects presented in Table 4.

In the new phase period of leadership research, the second trend has been first suggested by Kipnis et al. in 1980 and refined by Hinkin and Schriesheim, who confirmed seven key influence strategies which appear to be operative in a variety of different organizational settings. These seven key influence strategies include rationality, assertiveness, bargaining, coalitions, upward appeals, ingratiation and sanctions. The research preferences of the second trend are mainly expressed in Table 5.

Table 4. Research Focus on the first trend

Decision-Making Form	Definition	Relationship with Job Satisfaction and Commitment
Extreme autocratic	Leader makes decision without any input from the subordinate	Weakly negative with satisfaction; strongly negative with commitment
Autocratic	Leader makes decision after first obtaining information from the subordinate	Zero with satisfaction; weakly positive with commitment
Decision-Making Form	**Definition**	**Relationship with Job Satisfaction and Commitment**
Consultative	Leader makes decision after obtaining the subordinate's advice or recommendation	Zero with satisfaction; weakly negative with commitment
Joint or participate	Leader makes decision jointly with subordinate; both decide as equals	Weakly positive with both
Advisory delegation	Subordinate makes decision after first obtaining recommendation from the leader	Zero with satisfaction; highly positive with commitment
Informational delegation	Subordinate makes decision after first getting needed information from the leader	Moderately positive with satisfaction; zero with commitment
Extreme delegation	Subordinate makes decision without any input form the leader	Moderately negative with satisfaction; zero with commitment

Source: Collected and compiled by the author

Table 5. Research preference on the second trend

Influence tactic	Definition: Attempts to get one's way by the use of …	Relationship with job satisfaction and commitment
Rationality	Logic, data, and rational arguments	Highly positive with both satisfaction and commitment
Assertiveness	Forcefulness in presenting what one wants done	Moderately negative with both satisfaction and commitment
Bargaining	Making trades or offering exchanges	Zero with either satisfaction or commitment
Coalitions	Obtaining support for one's way from peers and subordinates	Zero with either satisfaction or commitment
Upward appeals	Requests which are directed towards higher levels in the organization	Moderately negative with satisfaction; none with commitment
Ingratiation	Flattery and sycophancy	Zero with either satisfaction or commitment
Sanctions	Organizationally based rewards or punishments (or threats/promises or reward and/or punishment)	Very negative with satisfaction; zero with commitment

Source: Collected and compiled by the author

In the third trend of the new phase period of leadership development and research, there emerged several new leadership theories, which are Contingency theories ; Transactional Leadership; Transformational Leadership; and Reinforcement Strategies. From 1980s, Strategic theories of leadership are concerned with leadership "of" organizations (Hunt, 1991) and are "marked by a concern for the evolution of the organization as a whole, including its changing aims and capabilities" (Selznick, 1984). Strategic Leadership activities (Hickman, 1998, House& Aditya, 1997;Hunt, 1991; Ireland& Hitt, 1999;Selznick, 1984; Zaccarro, 1996a). These strategic leadership researchers and scholars have been advocating the roles of leaders to be falling into the activities of the following:

- Making strategic decisions.
- Creating and communication a vision of the future.
- Developing key competencies and capabilities.
- Developing organizational structures, processes and controls.
- Managing multiple constituencies.
- Selecting and developing the next generation of leaders.
- Sustaining an effective organizational culture.
- Infusing ethical value system into an organization's culture.

The researches in the third trend of the new phase period can be summarized in Table 6.

The essence of strategic leadership theory is the creation and maintenance of absorptive capacity, adaptive capacity and managerial wisdom. Even lots of experts have made remarkable comments on leadership and leadership research, for example, "Leadership theory is dead science because it has killed off the leaders." and "Leadership is not about people anymore..", as well as "Theory X, situation, charismatic, transformational and servant leader theories have become clever abstractions. They are not about people struggling with existence while changing society"(David Boje).

2.5.3 Leadership Research and Research Approaches

Unlike natural science research, Leadership Research is very holistic and descriptive, like storytelling. It edges with psychology, anthropology, sociology, etc. That is why David Boje labeled it as "dead science"!!! In leadership research, there is one commonly used approach, which is called Nomothetic Approach. To be specific, it is an approach in leadership research field which insists that leadership phenomenon and leadership content should be applied globally. It is impossible to obtain a one-for-all global leadership style (House, Wright and Aditya, 1997). The other popularly adopted research approach is called Idiographic Approach: this approach admits that leadership phenomenon is a universal issue, but leadership content is embedded into cultures. With the variances of cultures, leadership content is also varying. One leadership style is effective in one culture may not be effective in another

Table 6. Research focus on trend III

Reinforcement behavior	Definition: Leader behavior which provides subordinates with …	Relationship with job satisfaction and organizational commitment
Contingent reward behavior	Rewards when they perform as expected (but not when their performance is unacceptable)	Highly positive with both satisfaction and commitment
Contingent punishment behavior	Punishments when they fail to perform as expected (but not when their performance is acceptable)	Moderately positive with satisfaction; zero with commitment
Non-contingent reward behavior	Rewards whether or not they perform as expected	Zero or weakly positive with satisfaction; zero with commitment
Non-contingent punishment behavior	Punishments whether or not their performance is unacceptable	Highly negative with both satisfaction and commitment

Source: Collected and compiled by the author

culture (Chemes, 993; Hofstede, 1980). Since the birth of leadership theory and leadership theory research, different schools of researchers have in their researches demonstrated different orientations. Table 7 has summarized the most dominant variances in leadership theory and leadership studies.

2.6 LITERATURE REVIEW ON CULTURES AND VALUE SYSTEMS

The term "Culture" is rather abstract and when we consult the definitions of culture in the British Encyclopedia, we may have found over 300 different kinds. When we say "different", actually it is not rigid at all, as we still find these so-called different definitions overlap in one way or another. Just take some of them as examples, as early as in 1962, a cultural research pioneer named Foster has been proposing that "Culture is the way of life of a group of people" (Foster, 1962). In the year 1977, another culture scholar Tylor has iterated culture as "that complete whole which includes knowledge, beliefs, art, law, morals, customs and any capabilities and habits acquired as a member of a society" (Tylor, 1977). Three years later in 1980, maybe one of the culture research giants Hofstede has put the term culture as "the collective programming of the mind which distinguishes the members of one human group from another .... The interactive aggregate of common characteristics that influences a group response to it's environment"(Hofstede, 1980). In 2000, Mitchell has given his definition of culture as "a set of learned core values, beliefs, standards, knowledge, morals, laws, and behaviors shared by individuals and societies that determines how an individual acts, feels, and

Table 7. Focus on Leadership Theories in Western Research

Centralism	Leadership is the way leaders use their power and charisma to influence followers; to direct and guide followers to accomplish goals.	Focus on the ability of leaders
Interaction oriented	Leadership is the process in which leaders and followers interact with each other in order to achieve the goals	Focus on the relationship between leaders and followers.
Structuralism	Leadership is the process of exertion leaders' power in a specific organization structure.	Focus on the organization structure in which leaders posit.
Target oriented	The essence of leadership is to achieve a specific goal.	Focus on the promotion and push function of leaders.

Source: Collected and Compiled by the author of this research project

views oneself and others" (from Mitchell, C. (2000), which has been seen as a much formal definition.

As human beings are social creatures, of course their behaviors will be profoundly influenced by culture or subculture in which they are living. In general, culture plays the following key functions in people's life:

- It enables us to communicate with others through a language that we have learned and that we share in common.
- It makes it possible to anticipate how others in our society are likely to respond to our actions.
- It gives us standards for distinguishing what is right or wrong, beautiful and ugly, reasonable and unreasonable etc.
- It provides with us the knowledge and skills necessary for meeting sustenance needs.
- It enables us to identify with other people.

Geographically speaking, different countries have different cultures and there are three specific aspects of national culture. Namely, It is shared by all or almost all members of some social group; older members try to pass it onto younger members as a heritage; national culture shapes the behavior and structures through one's perception of the world and "national culture explained more of the differences in employees than did professional role, age, gender or race" (Hofstede, 1980). To be specific, national culture has its well-known components as these: Language, Religion, Conflicting Attitudes, Manners and Customs, Education, Humor, Social Organizations and the Arts. In Hofstede's research about national cultures, there are five dimensions of culture: power distance (PDI); Individualism VS Collectivism (IDV); Masculinity VS Femininity (MAS); Uncertainty avoidance index (UAI); Long-term orientation VS Short term orientation (LTO) (Guidham 1999).

2.6.1 Definition of Value

There are two most popular theories that exist for the meaning of value in the value philosophy field. These are the theory of relationship, and the theory of property. According to the theory of relationship, value refers to the fulfillment of objects to the subject's needs, while according to the theory of property, value is considered to be the inherent attribute of an object or subject. This research has adopted the view on the relationship theory of value to feed the purpose for investigating the correlation between values and leadership styles. That is to say, that value is considered to be the fulfillment of an object to the subject's needs. The subject plays a leading and decisive role based on their requirements. From this perspective, people consider object which are positive and able to meet their needs to be valuable, and the positive significance of the objects is that value (Feng, 1997). Kluckhohn (1951) viewed value as a conception, explicit or implicit, distinctive of an individual or characteristic of a group, of the desirable which influences the selection from available modes, means, and ends of action. Rokeach (1968) defined value as follows: "to say that a person 'has a value' is to say that he has an enduring belief that a particular mode of conduct or that a particular end-state of existence is personally and socially preferable to alternative modes of conduct or end-states of existence." Based on the definition of value, a value system is an enduring organization of beliefs concerning preferable modes of conduct or end-states of existence along a continuum of relative importance" (Rokeach, 1973). Schwartz and Bilsky (1987) defined values as conceptions of the desirable that influence the way people select action and evaluate events.

The importance of values system can be summarized by the following statement from (Rokeach, 1973): "Values are determinant of virtually all kinds of behavior that could be called social behavior – of social action, attitude and ideology, evaluations, moral judgments and justifications of self and others, comparisons of self with others, presentations of self to others, and attempts to influence others. "

In a word, for the purpose of this research, values are considered to be lasting beliefs tending to some existing behavior, and a kind of standard which could guide behavior, attitude and judgment. Values govern individuals.

2.6.2 Measuring of Values

Theorists have developed several value measuring systems for empirical studies. The three main value measuring systems which are most commonly used are introduced in this study. Rokeach's value survey (RVS) (Rockeach, 1973) is a popular instrument for the measurement of values. The system consists of two sets of values, with each set containing 18 individual value items. One set is called Terminal values and the other is called Instrumental values. Terminal values refer to desirable end-states of existence. These are the goals that a person would like to achieve during his or her lifetime. Instrumental values refer to morality or capacity. These are preferable modes of behavior, or means of achieving the terminal values. In RVS, there is a brief description of each kind of value. When implementing this survey, the participant will be asked to sequence the two value systems based on their importance. The most important will be ranked first and the sub important one will be ranked second, so on and so forth. In this metrics, the least important one will be ranked the 18th. From the result of this survey, we can determine the sequence of different values, which indicates how important the value is for each person. As all values are viewed as a whole in the survey, RVS demonstrates the systemic and integrity of each value. However, the RVS is not thought to be relevant as it covers collective and societal domains that may not have a direct interest for the marketing research which is why Beatty et.al (1985) suggested that "primarily person-oriented" values are more relevant to consumer behavior in marketing. Hofstede (1994) proposed five dimensions for measuring values. They are Power Distance Index (PDI), Individualism (IDV), Masculinity (MAS), Uncertainty Avoidance Index (UAI) and Long-Term Orientation (LTO). PDI refers to the extent to which the less powerful members of organizations and institutions (like the family) accept and expect that power is distributed unequally. This happens more in Asian countries than in the west. Individualism happens more in western cultures where people tend to be by themselves and be more independent. Masculinity refers to the distribution of roles between the genders, and depending on the culture, the male is often dominant. UAI means how much a society tolerates uncertainty and ambiguity. Long-Term Orientation means one focuses on virtue regardless of truth. Using a questionnaire designed by Chinese scholars, it was found in a study among students in 23 countries around the world, that values associated with Long Term Orientation are thrifty and persevering while Short Term Orientation is associated with respect for tradition, fulfilling social obligations, and protecting one's 'face'. Hofstede's five Cultural Dimensions are very useful when analyzing consumption behavior under different core cultural backgrounds.

The result of Hofstede's research has been widely accepted in international academy as a measure standard of values. However, in accordance with Hofestede, the culture is supposed to be static and continuous. Each dimension of culture is separated into two opposite extremes, and they try to attribute the difference of national management style to differences in national culture only, overlooking the effect of institution. Besides, the sample of Hofstede's research is comprised of the middle management of a large-sized transnational corporation in all corners of the world, but lays particular attention to corporations in western developed countries and regions. The initial purpose of Hofstede's research was to find out the values of middle management in large-sized transnational corporation so as to give recommendations to enterprise management decisions. In view of this, RVS may not be suitable to conduct research under the circumstance of China's changes in the recent 30 years.

Schwartz and Bilsky (1987, 1990) viewed values as a cross-situational concept in terms of three aspects: (1) a value could be either a terminal value or an instrumental value which depends on the situation;(2) a value could be either individual orientation or collective orientation or both in terms of object of application; (3) in reference to the content, the connotation of value can be divided into seven aspects according to the motivational type. Schwartz (1992), expanded the content to 10 aspects based on the result of his cross-cultural empirical research, as is shown in Table 8.

The above 10 dimensions are recognized in all cultures since they are from three different types of universal human needs: biological needs, social co-ordination needs, and needs related to the welfare and survival of groups. In order to describe geography of values all over the world, and map cultural groups, Schwartz (1992, 1994) developed Schwartz Values Survey (SVS), including 57 values representing 10 universal motivational types of values. Schwartz's cultural-difference research is empirical and draws a conclusion based on the analysis of empirical data. With the involvement of the oriental value, SVS is cross-cultural and universal. Therefore SVS is adopted in this dissertation.

Table 8. Schwartz's 10-dimension values theory

Dimension	Explanation	Dimension	Explanation
Self-direction	creativity; freedom; independence; curiosity; choosing your own goals	Benevolence	helpfulness; honesty; forgiveness; loyalty; responsibility; friendship
Power	authority; leadership; dominance	Tradition	accepting one's portion in life; humility; devoutness; respect for tradition; moderation
Achievement	success; capability; ambition; influence; intelligence; self-respect	Conformity	self-discipline; obedience
Hedonism	pleasure; enjoying life	Security	cleanliness; family security; national security; stability of social order; reciprocation of favors; health; sense of belonging
Stimulation	daring activities; varied life; exciting life	Universalism	Broad-mindedness; wisdom; social justice; equality; a world at peace; a world of beauty; unity with nature; protecting the environment; inner harmony

Source: Collected and compiled by the author of this research project

Though the previous pages have introduced three kinds of instruments to measure values systems, each has its own merits and demerits. Rokeach's value survey (RVS) (Rockeach, 1973) demonstrates the systemic and integrity of each value, but it is not thought to be relevant as it covers collective and societal domains that may not have a direct interest for the marketing research which is why Beatty et. al (1985) suggested that "primarily person-oriented" values are more relevant to consumer behavior in marketing. As for the instrument of Hofstede's values survey (1994), in this instrument, Hofstede proposed five dimensions for measuring values. To be specific, they are: Power Distance Index (PDI), Individualism/Collectivism (IDV), Masculinity/Femininity (MAS), Uncertainty Avoidance Index (UAI) and Long-Term Orientation (LTO). Each dimension of culture is separated into two opposite extremes, and they try to attribute the difference of national management style to differences in national culture only, overlooking the effect of institution. Besides, the samples of Hofstede's research is comprised of the middle management of a large-sized transnational corporation in all corners of the world (Guinea pigs for 18,000 of IBM employees all over the world), but lay particular attention to corporations in western developed countries and regions. Therefore, his values survey is at the national level which is inappropriate to test the correlations between the values orientation and consumption behaviors as this should be at individual level. However, Schwartz and Bilsky (1987, 1990) viewed values as a cross-situational concept in terms of the following three aspects: 1. a value could be either a terminal value or an instrumental value which depends on the situation; 2. a value could be either individual orientation or collective orientation or both in terms of object of application; 3. in reference to the content, the connotation of value can be divided into seven aspects according to the motivational type. In this values survey, there are altogether 57 items which can be grouped into ten dimensions and these ten dimensions can again be grouped into four more general dimensions. After the comparison and contrast of these three instruments for measuring values, and under the guidance of the professors who taught the author courses during her PhD. Program (Namely, Carolyn in Fraser University, Canada and M. H. Bond in CUHK, Hong Kong) who are specialized in doing research on cultural issues, the author of this research has accepted their suggestions to adopt Schwartz Values Survey as the instrument to measure the individual values orientations of the Chinese new generation in this research.

It is widely admitted that there are three mainstays while talking about Chinese culture: Confucianism, Buddhism and Taoism. Confucianism advocates the "Doctrine of the mean" and insists that people should be neither conservative nor aggressive in their behaviors. It also strongly supports the idea of "Hierarchy & Order". Meanwhile, Confucianism focuses on "the interest of collectivity over that of individual (Fang 1999). China is the most typical country that enjoys very much the cultural aspects of Long-term Orientation, Collectivism and High Power Distance as compared with other countries. However, with the introduction of Buddhism into China from the third century B.C., it has been developing even more flourishingly than in its original birthplace of India. Buddhist ideas strongly embrace tolerance and obedience and worship for the eternal cycle of birth, suffering, death and rebirth (Fang, 1999). In contrast to the above two mainstays of Chinese culture, there is also "Taoism" established by Lao Tzu, who strongly advocates the idea of "Doing nothing is doing everything[1]" and insists on the balance between "Yin & Yang", as well as the reversion of love & hatred, good & bad, fortune & misfortune (Fang 1999). The relationship between culture and values system is the completely inclusive relation. Values system is the core of culture which has been embedded into people's blood as an ingrained part of their body. The value concept, more than any other, should occupy a central position which is able to unify the apparently diverse interests of all the sciences concerned with human behavior. (Psychologist Rokeach,1973:3, Sociologist Williams, 1968; Anthropologist Kluckhohn, 1951). Values are viewed as the criteria people use to select and justify actions and to evaluate people and events. The charm and also the hardness of this research is that there must have a bridge to gap the distance between value and leadership styles. It is unanimously agreed that human beings are culture creatures, so are leaders and managers; it is also universally true that childhood experiences have been embedded into the blood and will affect their behaviors later on and cultures can evolve with the change of social, economic and technological changes. In the research field of values and cultural issues, one has to take a serious attitude towards the evolution of culture. As for cultural evolution, there are three dimensions to be considered: Convergence (industrialization and technology are the primary driving forces for global merging of work values); Divergence (values system of a society is deeply embedded in its cultural roots); and Cross-vergence (which refers to the business ideology forces leading to convergence and social-cultural forces leading to divergence will synergistically interact with one another).

Figure 2. The three dimensions of culture evolution

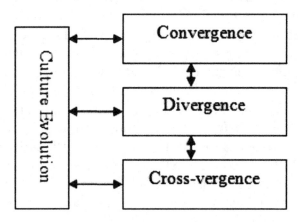

2.6.3 Uniqueness of Chinese Culture and Its Influence on Its Peoples

First of all, this research proposed the general differences of culture as regard the leadership style between the west and the east. As for the Westerners, the following pinpoints have been strongly advocated: the spirit of heroism, which thinks being a hero, is favorable and preferable in an organization; the spirit of individualism has been exerted to its largest extent and making oneself of something has been regarded as the necessary accomplishment and a must to be respected and admired by others. While in the East, leaders do things by using their wisdom and it is non-heroism which plays a key role in the process of leading subordinates. They are robustly propagating the idea of doing nothing is doing everything[2] which has been first proposed by Lao Tzu, the founding-Father of Taoism.

To speak from the perspective of organizational structure, leaders in Chinese firms warmly embrace the tree-shaped structure, which puts the leaders at the bottom of the tree, i.e., the root of the tree, and other subordinates have been presented in the different layers of the tree branches. Such tree-shaped organizational structure is quite varying from that of the pyramid shaped hierarchical organizational structure as dominated the management field for quite some time in the past, which put the leaders at the top of the pyramid and then, middle managers, and other employees.

As regards the emergence and application of various kinds of rules and legitimate regulations throughout the globe, according to traditional Chinese culture, it is a great retreat of the society, the highest level and the most efficient and effective discipline upon human beings should be the morals and ethics, which stipulates the rights and wrongs of people's behaviors and thus substantially reduce the management cost. Therefore, to a large extent, the appearance and adoption of various kinds of rules and regulations have increased the social cost and reduced the efficiency and effectiveness of the social operation, of course inclusive of the management cost.

One of the most important essence of Chinese culture is the idea of "the integration of man and nature" (in Chinese, it is called Tian Ren He Yi[3]). The appearance of the idea could be traced back from the beginning of the agricultural civilization. For the purpose of survival and development, ancient people pursuit the ideal state of being combined with nature (worship nature, pay reverie to nature and expect that nature would do good to their harvest, to give them a harmonious and peaceful life). The integration of Man and Nature has very profound connotations which can be applied to today's business organization and to do so, leaders should make it possible to set organizational goals which could be a combination of the development of the organization and that of the employees. The integration of Man and Nature can be seen as the ultimate objective of the organizational target and vision. If the idea of the integration of Man and Nature can be adopted and applied skillfully in human activity, lots of problems can be avoided and resolved. However, the fact is that the so-called civilized human activities have made the situation from bad to worse. Whenever one problem has been solved, lots of new problems derived from the settlement of the previous problem emerged exponentially which causes human beings even more severe troubles. To some extent, we may say that with the development of modern science and technology, the degree of happiness index has been decreased by and by. Modern civilization has made the society worse than better. The only panacea and cure to solve the human problem is to fully understand the spirit of the integration of Man and Nature and it is of vital importance for Man figure out the ultimate way of how to establish an integral and harmonious relationship with Nature. One attention should be given here: that is, the conformity of the moral lessons and the distribution of happiness. The problem on how to let these two aspects keep abreast with each other and maintain the golden balance whould be a great challenge.

The conception of Confucianist businessmen: in general, Confucianist businessmen (in Chinese, Ru'shang) can be simply defined as those business persons who guide their behaviors and conduct business activities by adopting the creams of Confucianist ideas, i.e. the idea of Benevolence (Ren),Jjustice (Yi), Rituals (Li), Wisdom (Zhi) and Credibility (Xin). Benevolence is the core value of Confucianist ideas, which advocate that only those who are benevolent could love others and the accomplishment of benevolence is reliant on the filial piety, which is the first step to accomplish benevolence. The expression of benevolence follows a certain orders from the most adjacent circle to the most remote circle. To be simplified, such order can be ranked as parents, brothers and sister, relatives, neighbors, friends, acquaintances, nation, country, then the whole world. Such order governs the behavior of people and has become one of the most important norms for Chinese people (can be simply diagramed in the structure of different circles), which resembles the concept of in-groups and out-groups.

The Confucius concept can be categorized roughly into four categories: first of all, the concept of what you do not desire, do not do that to others. While behaving yourself, try to put your feet into other people's shoes-the idea of empathy. Secondly, what you desire will be desired by others as well. These two ideas are based on the assumption that human beings are sharing similar ideas, and thus, they might have the similar reaction towards the behavior of others. This idea is just the same as the modern idea of empathy, which calls for people to stand on other people's position in interacting with others. Thirdly, it is the idea of Togetherness (He, in Chinese) and Sameness (Tong, in Chinese). The former indicates the differences and the latter variances between one and the other. People with the virtue of this embrace and treasure variances, as they uphold the view that although people may have different views about an issue, they still should respect each other and regard the other party's variances as a complimentary part to his own ideas, rather than merely criticize and go against others. This idea has made it possible for people to create a peaceful and harmonious situation, but not conflicts and contradictions. The idea of Sameness and that of Togetherness are the precious cornerstones in Chinese culture which makes it possible for Chinese civilization to sustain and develop for a long time, as the facts demonstrate that all other ancient civilizations have elapsed like Indian civilization, Egyptian civilization, Babylonian civilization which together with China have been unanimously admitted as the Four Most Famous World Civilizations. The capacity and capability of absorption and assimilation of Chinese culture can be undoubtedly regarded as No. one in the world. The evidence could be easily picked up from history: because of the strong capability of assimilation and absorption, in Chinese history, Han Nationality has been ruled by the Mongols, by Manchurians and other minority groups, but in the end, Chinese civilization has assimilated all other cultures. Such can explain why Chinese nation has a very strong and unbending perseverance and persistence. Fourthly, the idea of taking revenge by merely doing something good to those who have done you something bad (in Chinese, it can be called "Yi Zhi Bao Yuan " or "Yi De Bao Yuan"). According to ancient

Chinese culture, even though some people have done something bad to you, the wisest way to take revenge is to do something good instead. But this doesn't mean that you are weak and vulnerable. You are using some tactics to try to gratify your enemy and let him realize that he has done something wrong to you. Of course, you can blame and criticize those who have hurt you; special attention should be paid to the degree of your criticism. In the eye of Confucianist, revolution is a kind of benevolence, as you are fighting for the benefit of the majority by sacrificing the benefit of the minority. Therefore, if the revolution is justified, it should be supported and viewed from a rational perspective, no reason to blame it.

The core value of Chinese philosophy is the idea of Mediocre and the idea of Doing Nothing Is Doing Everything. The former has been proposed by Confucius, the founding father of Confucianism and the latter being proposed by Lao Tzu, the founding father of Taoism. Full and comprehensive understanding and the application of these two ideas can help create a peaceful and harmonious globe for all mankind. The cream of these ideas can be best represented by the Taiji Diagram and Yin Yang Fish (in Chinese, Taiji Tu and Yin Yang Yu). As per the Taoist idea, where there is no Yin, there will be no Yang. Yin is embedded into Yang and vice versa. Actually, the idea of Yin and Yang has originated from the idea of the integration of Man and Nature. These two ideas have well explained the phenomenon that Chinese people are keen on going along with others with long term orientation. This is also the best connotation of the existence of Groupthink and strong clinging to collectivism. In Chinese culture, numerous proverbs and sayings have exposed the cream and tenets of its culture, to name just some: "those birds will get shot who expose their heads first? (Qiang Da Chu Tou Niao in Chinese) ; "people are afraid of being famous just like pigs are afraid of being fat", as a fat pig means that it will be slaughtered for meat (Ren Pa Chu Ming Zhu Pa Zhuang?). Therefore, the safest way is to follow the channels of the majrity's and maintain low key, rather than being standing out on your own way.

"Sheng Ren Yi Bu Ke Yan Wei Ti, Ke Yan Wei Yong"(by Zeng guo'fan, an outstanding official and a business person in the Qing Dynasty) which simply means that sages are those who articulate the least, while those who are talkative are down-to-earth guys. This also expresses in another saying of "Keeping silent is gold". These everyday proverbs have also explained to some extent why Chinese culture has been regarded as mysterious culture.

Looking back to the long hisotry of Chinese culture, it can be generalized into the following episodes:

1.   The period of the unification of tribal groups: in this period, there were number of tribes and among them, the most famous ones are The Yellow Emperor, the Yan Emperor and Chi'you. The three tribes formed a very loose structured union but each underwent their own countries in their own way. The union only functions when they need to fight against other invaders. The most prominent feature of such union is that there is no unification of military force and each tribe has its own military forces which guaranteed the independence and safety of their own country. In Chinese civilization, we call this period the Culture of putting together the military emblem (a piece of leather with some special symbols on it and the war can only be triggered by putting two pieces of the leather sketches together).

2.   The Confucianist culture period: this is a summarization and development of the various schools of cultures during the pre-Qin dynasties, inclusive of Xia, Shang, Zhou, the Spring and Autumn and the Warring Sates Period. This is an amazing period in Chinese history with various schools of ideas like Confucius, Mo'zi, Han'fei'zi, Lao Tzu, etc. This is a period that many schools of thoughts coexisted and developed concurrently. The whole society has provided with a very loose and free platform for various kinds of idea to clash and crash and also it is the period that the complete Chinese cultural system has been accomplished and grown to its full blossom. The unification of feudal system, the currency, the written characters and measurement has been accomplished all in this one period. This period has seen the peak of Chinese civilization and the expressions of Chinese culture in later periods actually are only the modification and adjustment to that of the Confucius period.

3.   The period of Dong'zhong'shu of the Western Han Dynasty: the resonance of Nature and Man (the idea of Tian Ren Gan Ying). This is actually the summarization of the cultural expressions in the Qin and Han Dynasties. Dong zhong'shu, the official and a thinker of the Western Han Dynasty has proposed the slogan of "eliminate all the other schools of thoughts and only maintain the Confucius ideas". But the Confucius ideas here were no long the pure and exact Confucius ideas in its original appearance as that in the Confucius period. Many modifications and adjustment have been made to meet the purpose of the ruling class at his time.

4.   The integration and development of the Buddhist culture in China in the Ming and Qing Dynasties: in this period, the idea of rationalism and reasoning has been strongly advocated. The most outstanding representatives are Zhu'xi and Cheng'yi. The personal freedom has been greatly diminished and personal desires were wiped out to the largest

extent. This period is also called the neo-Buddhist Period. The modification and adjustment of Buddhist doctrines were made to meet with the purpose of the Ruling Class at that period. While tracing back to the different stages of the development of Chinese culture, it is not hard to find that for the same pieces of works like <Da Xue, Zhong Yong, Lun'yu, Mencuis>, the most famous Four Books in Chinese history, different people in different period have different explanations about the ideas of the Books and also given different notes and comments to the Books, which contributes a lot to the sustainable development of traditional Chinese culture, and as such, traditional Chinese culture has been remained and handed down from one generation to another.

5.   After 1840—the Opium War Period: this is in the Qing Dynasty, the Chinese feudal system was declining substantially with lots of turmoil and chaos. New civilization from the Industrial Revolution in Europe and the young nation USA came to China and smashed lots of traditional ideas of Chinese culture. With the clash and crash of the western culture, Chinese civilization has to encounter its fifth integration.

6.   The contemporary period with the Mao Period (1949-1978) and Deng Period (after 1978) as the most typical symbols. This period has witnessed the total Westernization of the Generation X in China especially those who were born in the 1980s and 1990s. Can we still find the pure traditional Chinese culture now? As it is discussed in previous text, the most prominent features of Chinese culture can be summarized as: Collectivism, High Power Distance and Long-term Orientation, but it is also true of the value shift with the generation X.

Taking into account the five dimensions of culture proposed by Hofstede, the vivid description of the contrast between Chinese culture and Western culture can be illustrated as the above. The five cultural dimensions are: power distance index, which is seen as *Power Distance Index (PDI)*. It focuses on the degree of equality, or inequality, between people in the country's society. A High Power Distance ranking indicates that inequalities of power and wealth have been allowed to grow within the society. These societies are more likely to follow a caste system that does not allow significant upward mobility of its citizens. A Low Power Distance ranking indicates the society de-emphasizes the differences between citizen's power and wealth. In these societies equality and opportunity for everyone is stressed. Individualism VS Collectivism *Individualism (IDV)* focuses on the degree the society reinforces individual or collective achievement and interpersonal relationships. A High Individualism ranking indicates that individuality and individual

Figure 3. The contrast between Chinese culture and Western Cultures
Source: The author has adapted from Hofstede Value Survey results

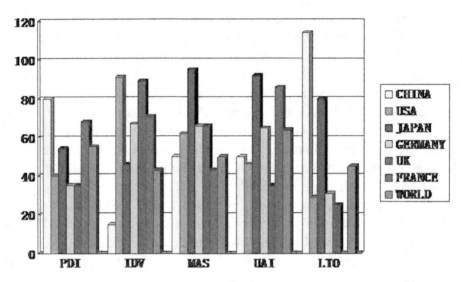

rights are paramount within the society. Individuals in these societies may tend to form a larger number of looser relationships. A Low Individualism ranking typifies societies of a more collectivist nature with close ties between individuals. These cultures reinforce extended families and collectives where everyone takes responsibility for fellow members of their group. Masculinity VS Femininity, i.e. *Masculinity (MAS)* focuses on the degree the society reinforces, or does not reinforce, the traditional masculine work role model of male achievement, control, and power. A High Masculinity ranking indicates the country experiences a high degree of gender differentiation. In these cultures, males dominate a significant portion of the society and power structure, with females being controlled by male domination. A Low Masculinity ranking indicates the country has a low level of differentiation and discrimination between genders. In these cultures, females are treated equally to males in all aspects of the society. The next dimension is Uncertainty Avoidance. i.e. the *UAI* focuses on the level of tolerance for uncertainty and ambiguity within the society - i.e. unstructured situations. A High Uncertainty Avoidance ranking indicates the country has a low tolerance for uncertainty and ambiguity. This creates a rule-oriented society that institutes laws, rules, regulations, and controls in order to reduce the amount of uncertainty. A Low Uncertainty Avoidance ranking indicates the country has less concern about ambiguity and uncertainty and has more tolerance for a variety of opinions. This is reflected in a society that is less rule-oriented, more readily accepts change, and takes more and greater risks and the last cultural dimension is Long Term Orientation index. *LTO* focuses on the degree the society embraces, or does not embrace, long-term devotion to traditional, forward thinking values. High Long-Term Orientation ranking indicates the country prescribes to the values of long-term commitments and respect for tradition. This is thought to support a strong work ethic where long-term rewards are expected as a result of today's hard work. However, business may take longer to develop in this society, particularly for an "outsider". A Low Long-Term Orientation ranking indicates the country does not reinforce the concept of long-term, traditional orientation. In this culture, change can occur more rapidly as long-term traditions and commitments do not become impediments to change. It is of key importance to introduce the national cultural differences between China and Western countries, as national values systems deeply influence personal values orientations, though this research has not adopted Hofstede values survey. The awareness, knowing, understanding and appreciation of cultural differences among countries do have great help in understanding personal and individual values orientations.

2.7 HYPOTHESES OF THIS RESEARCH

Based on the literature review on leadership styles and cultures & values system (both of the questionnaires are on individual level), this research has proposed the following hypotheses:

As this research has adopted two sets of survey questionnaires, in order to avoid the cross-bordering chaos, we also have postulated two separate sets of hypotheses. First of all, we present the hypotheses related with Schwartz value survey as below:

H1: Age brackets play an important role in shaping and reshaping people's values orientations in instrumental value items but less significant in shaping people's terminal value items;

H2: Gender has significant correlations with the values dimensions of power and stimulation;

H3: Permanent residential area of persons has significant correlations with the values dimensions of universalism, self-direction, stimulation, tradition and benevolence;

H4: The education level of persons has strong correlations with the value dimensions of universalism, power, hedonism, self-direction, tradition, benevolence, stimulation and conformity;

H5: The position in the company of the persons has very strong correlations with the value dimensions of universalism, hedonism, self-direction and stimulation;

H6: The work age of persons has significant correlations with the value dimensions of universalism, power, hedonism, self-direction, stimulation, tradition, benevolence and achievement;

H7: The company scale has strong correlations with the values dimension of universalism, benevolence, and conformity;

H8: The nature of company ownership has strong correlations with universalism, hedonism, stimulation, tradition and benevolence;

H9: The nature of business sectors has significant correlations with the values dimensions of power, security, conformity and tradition;

H10: The company location of people has significant correlations with values dimensions of tradition, universalism, conformity and benevolence.

Secondly, based on the literature review of leadership theories and leadership development, as well as the leadership survey, we have postulated the following hypotheses as below:

H11: The age brackets of persons have strong influences upon the persons' leadership style 1 and leadership style 2;

H12: Gender has significant correlations with persons' leadership style 1, style 2 and style 3;

H13: The permanent residential areas of persons have magnificent impact on all the three leadership styles;

H14: The educational level of persons has significant influence upon the persons' all the three leadership styles: autocratic, democratic and free reign;

H15: The persons' position in the business organizations has significant correlations with all the three types of their leadership;

H16: The work age of persons has significant correlations with persons' leadership style 1, style 2 and style 3;

H17: The company scale of persons has strong impact on the formation of persons' leadership styles of all the three types;

H18: The nature of company ownership of the persons has significant correlations with the persons' formation of their leadership styles 1, 2 and 3;

H19: The characteristics of business sector of persons have significant impact upon their leadership styles of all the three types;

H20: The company location of persons has magnificent influence on their leadership styles of all the three types.

Additionally, in this research, we are intending to investigate the following potential propositions, such as, the degree of influence of terminal values on Leadership Styles; the degree of influence of instrumental values on Leadership Styles; the Evolution of managerial work values in China through generations, etc. However, since the ten value dimensions have mixed up the terminal value and instrumental value which makes it hard to meet the purpose of our initial mind. Due to the various kinds of constraints, we will not investigate the further suggested propositions.

REFERENCES

Abram, D., Ando, K., & Hinkle, S., & ThePsychological Attachment to the Group. (1998). Cross-Cultural Differences in Organizational Identification and Subjective Norms as Predictor of Workers Turnover Intentions. *Personality and Social Psychology Bulletin*, *24*(10), 1027–1039. doi:10.1177/01461672982410001

Ajzen, L., & Fishbein, M. (1970). *Understanding attitudes and predicting social behavior*. Englewood Cliffs, NJ: Prentice-Hall.

Allman, J. L., Ohair, D., & Stewart, R. A. (1994). Communication and Aging: A study of the Effects of Cohort-Centrism and Perceived Decoding Ability on Communication Competence and Communication Satisfaction. *Communication Quarterly*, *42*(4), 363–376. doi:10.1080/01463379409369943

Allport, G. W. (1961). *Pattern and Growth in Personality*. New York: Holt, Rinehart & Winston.

Amado, G. (1999). Rivka. Bilateral Transformational Leadership: An Approach for Fostering Ethical Conduct in Public Service Organizations. *Administration & Society*, *31*(2), 247–260. doi:10.1177/00953999922019111

Antal, A. B., Lenhardt, U., & Rosenbrock, R. (2001). Barriers to Organizational Learning. In M. Dierkes, A. B. Antal, J. Child, & I. Nonaka (Eds.), *Handbook of Organizational Learning and Knowledge* (pp. 865–885). Oxford University Press.

Arogyaswarny, B., & Byles, C. M. (1987). Organizational Culture: Internal & External Fits. *Journal of Management*, *13*(4), 647–659. doi:10.1177/014920638701300406

Ashforth, B. E., & Mael, F. (1989). Social Identity Theory and the Organization. *Academy of Management Review*, (14): 20–39.

Badaracco, J. (1992). *Knowledge Link: How Firms Compete Through Strategic Alliance*. Boston: Harvard Business School.

Bandura, A. (1977). Self-Efficacy: Toward a Unifying Theory of Behavioral Change. *Psychological Review*, *84*(2), 191–215. doi:10.1037/0033-295X.84.2.191 PMID:847061

Baransons, J. (1966). Transfer of Technical Knowledge by International Corporations to Developing Economics. *The American Economic Review*, (56): 259.

Barnard, C. (1968). *The Functions of the Executive*. Harvard University Press.

Barnett, J. H., & Karson, M. J. (1987). Personal Values and Business Decision: An Exploratory Investigation. *Journal of Business Ethics*, *6*(17), 371–382. doi:10.1007/BF00382894

Barney, J. (1991). Firm Resources and Sustained Competitive Advantage. *Journal of Management*, *17*(1), 99–120. doi:10.1177/014920639101700108

Barney, J., & Jay, B. (1986). Strategic Factor Markets: Expectation, Luck and Business Strategy. *Management Science*, *32*(10), 1231–1241. doi:10.1287/mnsc.32.10.1231

Bass, B. M. (1981). *Stogdill's Handbook of Leadership* (rev. ed.). New York: Free Press.

Bass, B. M. (1985). *Leadership and Performance Beyond Expectations*. New York Free Press.

Bass, B. M. (1985). *Leadership and performance beyond expectations*. New York: Free Press.

Bass, B. M., & Avlio, B. J. (1990). *Transformational Leadership Questionnaire*. Palo Alto, CA: Consulting Psychologists Press.

Bass, B. M., & Avlio, B. J. (1994). Transformational Leadership and Organizational Culture. *Public Administration Quarterly*, (17): 112–118.

Berman, S. L., Down, J., & Hill, C. W. (2002). Tacit Knowledge as a Source of Competitive Advantage in the NBA. *Academy of Management Journal*, *45*(1), 13–31. doi:10.2307/3069282

Bhatt, G. (2001). Knowledge Management in Organizations: Examining the Interaction between Technologies, Techniques and People. *Journal of Knowledge Management, 5*(1), 68–75. doi:10.1108/13673270110384419

Blanchard, K., & Johnson, S. (1982). *The One Minute Manager*. New York: William Morrow.

Boal, K.B., & Bryson, J.M. (1988). *Charismatic leadership: A phenomenological and structural approach*. Academic Press.

Boje, D.M. (2000). *Storytelling Organizations*. Academic Press.

Bond, M. H. (1988). Finding Universal Dimensions of Individual Variation in Multicultural Studies of Values: The Rokeach and Chinese Value Surveys. *Journal of Personality and Social Psychology, 55*(6), 1009–1015. doi:10.1037/0022-3514.55.6.1009

Boomsma, A. (1982). Non-convergence, Improper Solutions and Starting Values in LISREL Maximum Likelihood Estimation. *Psychometrika*.

Bostrom, R. P. (1989). Successful Application of Communication Techniques to Improve the Systems Development Process. *Information & Management*, 16.

Braden, P. A. (2000). *WVU Parkersburg*. Leadership Theory Lecture.

Braithwaite, V. A., & Law, H. G. (1985). Structure of Human Values: Testing the Adequacy of the Rokeach Value Survey. *Journal of Personality and Social Psychology, 49*(1), 250–263. doi:10.1037/0022-3514.49.1.250

Brown, J. S. (n.d.). *Learning and knowledge are the result of multiple intertwining forces: content, context and community*. Retrieved from www.creatingthe21stcentury.org/Intro4a-How-Larry & JSB.html

Brown, M. H. (1982). That reminds me of a story: Speech action on organizational socialization. University of Texas at Austin.

Bruner, J. (2002). *Making stories*. Harvard.

Bryman, A. (1992). *Charisma and leadership in organizations*. London: Sage.

Burns, J. M. (1978). *Leadership*. New York: Harper & Row.

Cameron, S. W., & Black-Burn, R. T. (1985). Sponsorship and Academic Success. *The Journal of Higher Education*, (52), 369–377.

Canary, D. J., & Spitzberg, B. H. (1987). Appropriateness and Effectiveness Perceptions of Conflict Strategies. *Human Communication Research*, *14*(1), 93–118. doi:10.1111/j.1468-2958.1987.tb00123.x

Cannon-Bowers, J., & Sala, E. (1997). *A Framework for Developing Team Performance Measures in Training*. LEA London.

Carless, S. A. (1998). Gender Difference in Transformational Leadership: An Examination of Superior, Leader, and Subordinate Perspectives. *Sex Role*, (39), 887-902.

Charles, W. L. (2001). *Strategies Management*. Houghton Mifflin Company.

Chatman, J. A., & Jehn, K. A. (1994, June). Assessing the Relationship between Industry Characteristics and Organizational Culture: How Different Can You Be?. *Academy of Management Journal*, *37*(3), 522–532.

Child, J. (1981). Culture, contingency, and capitalism in the cross-national study of organization. In L. L. Cummings (Ed.), Research in organizational behavior (pp. 303–356). Academic Press.

Chinese Culture Connection. (1987). Chinese Values and the Search for Culture-Free Dimensions of Culture. *Journal of Cross-Cultural Psychology*, (18), 143–164.

Comeau-Kirchner, C. (2000). The Sharing Culture. *Management Review*, *89*(1), 8–9.

Conger, J. A., & Kanungo, R. N. (1988). Behavioral Dimensions of Charismatic Leadership. In *Charismatic Leadership*. Jossey Bass.

Damodaran, L., & Olphert, W. (2000). Barriers and Facilitators to the Use of Knowledge Management Systems. *Behaviour & Information Technology*, *19*(6), 405–413. doi:10.1080/014492900750052660

Dart, J. (1999). A story Approach for Monitoring Change in an Agricultural Extension Project. Conference of the Association for Qualitative Research, Melbourne, Australia.

Davenport, T. H. (1998). De Long, David and Michael Beers. Successful Knowledge Management Projects. *Sloan Management Review*, *39*(2), 43–57.

Davenport, T. H., & Prusak, L. (2000). *Working Knowledge: How Organizations Manage What They Know*. Harvard Business School Press.

David, W., & Hutchings, K. (2005). Cultural Embeddedness and Contextual Constraints: Knowledge Sharing in Chinese and Arab Cultures. *Knowledge and Process Management, 12*(2), 89–98. doi:10.1002/kpm.222

Dawson, P. (2003a). Understanding organizational change: the contemporary experience of people at work. Routledge.

De Long, D. W., & Fahey, L. (2000). Diagnosing Cultural Barriers to Knowledge Management. *The Academy of Management Executive, 14*(4), 113–127.

Deluge, R. J., & Souza, J. (1991). The Effects of Transformational and Transactional Leadership Style on the Influencing Behavior or Subordinate Police Officers. *Journal of Occupational Psychology, 64*(1), 49–55. doi:10.1111/j.2044-8325.1991.tb00540.x

Demarco, T. & Lister, T. (1987). *People-ware: Productive Projects and Teams*. Dorset House.

DeVito, J. D. (1999). *Essentials of Human Communication* (Vol. 3). New York: Addison Wesley Longman.

Dewey, J. (1957). *Human Nature and Conduct*. New York: Modern Library.

Dodgson, M. (1993). Organizational Learning: A Review of Some Literatures. *Organization Studies, 14*(3), 375–394.

Donaldson, L. (1993). *Anti-management theories of organization: A critique of paradigm proliferation*. Cambridge, UK: Cambridge University Press.

Dorfman, P. W. (1996). International and cross-cultural leadership research. In B. J. Punnett & O. Shenkar (Eds.), *Handbook for international management research* (pp. 267–349). Oxford, UK: Blackwell.

Downton, J. V. (1973). *Rebel Leadership*. New York: Free Press.

Drucker, P. (1993). *The Post-Capitalism*. New York: Harper & Row Publisher.

Duran, R. L. & Kelly, L. (1988). An Investigation into the Cognitive Domain of Competence: The Relationship between Communicative Competence and Interaction Involvement. *Communication Research Reports*, (5), 91-96.

Dutton, J. E., Dukerich, J. M., & Harquail, C. V. (1994). Organizational Images and Member Identification. *Administrative Science Quarterly, 39*(34), 239–263. doi:10.2307/2393235

Endsley, M. R. (1995). Towards a Theory of Situation Awareness in Dynamic System. *Journal of Human Factors, 1*(37), 32–64. doi:10.1518/001872095779049543

Felix, C. (2000). Cultural Variation of Leadership Prototypes. *Journal of Occupational and Organizational Psychology, 73,* 1–29.

Fiedler, F. E. (1995). Cognitive resources and leadership performance. *Applied Psychology, 44*(1), 5–28. doi:10.1111/j.1464-0597.1995.tb01378.x

Fielder, F. E., & Garcia, J. E. (1987). *New Approaches to Effective Leadership:Cognitive Resources and Organizational Performance.* New York: Wiley.

Finkelstein, S., & Hambrick, D. C. (1996). *Strategic leadership: Top executives and their effects on organizations.* St. Paul, MN: West Publishing Company.

Ford, D. P., & Chan, Y. E. (2003). Knowledge Sharing in Multicultural Setting: A Case Study. *Knowledge Management Research and Practice, 1*(1), 11–27. doi:10.1057/palgrave.kmrp.8499999

Freud, S. (1930). *Civilization and Its Discontents.* London: Hogarth Press.

Freud, S. (1933). *New Introductory Lectures in Psychoanalysis.* New York: Norton.

Friedman H. H. & Langbert M. (2000). Transformational Leadership: Instituting Revolutionary Change in Your Accounting Firm. *The National Public Accountant, 45*(8).

Gold, A. H., Malhotra, A., Egars, S., & Knowledge Management, A. H. (2001). An Organizational Capabilities Perspective. *Journal of Management Information Systems, 18*(1), 185–214.

Gudykunst, W. B. (1991). *Bridging Differences: Effective Inter-group Communication.* Newbury Park, CA: Sage.

Hartog, D. N. D., & House, R. J. (1999). Culture Specific and Cross-culturally Generalizable Implicit Leadership Theories: Are Attitudes of Charismatic/Transformational Leadership Universally Endorsed?. *The Leadership Quarterly, 10*(10), 219–256. doi:10.1016/S1048-9843(99)00018-1

Hickson, D. J., Hinings, C. R., McMillan, J., & Schwitter, J. P. (1974). The culture-free context of organization structure: A tri-national comparison. *Sociology, 8*(8), 59–80. doi:10.1177/003803857400800104

Hofstede, G. (1980). *Culture's consequences: International differences in work-related values*. London: Sage.

Hofstede, G. (1980). *Culture's Consequences: International Differences in Work-Related Values*. Beverly Hills, CA: Sage.

Hofstede, G., & Bond, M. H. (1988). The Confucius connection. From cultural roots to economic growth. *Organizational Dynamics*, (16): 4–21.

House, R. J. (n.d.). Theory of Charismatic Leadership. In J. G. Hunt & L. L. Larson (Eds.), *Leadership: The Cutting Edge*. Carbondale, IL: Southern Illinois University Press.

House, R. J., & Aditya, R. N. (1997). The social scientific study of leadership: Quo vadis? *Journal of Management*, *23*(3), 409–473. doi:10.1177/014920639702300306

House, R. J., Wright, N. S., & Aditya, R. N. (1997). Cross-cultural research on organizational leadership: A critical analysis and a proposed theory. In P. C. Earley & M. Erez (Eds.), *New Perspectives in International Industrial Organizational Psychology* (pp. 535–625). San Francisco: New Lexington.

Hunt, S. D. (1991). *Modern marketing theory: Critical issues in the philosophy of marketing science*. Cincinnati, OH: South-Western.

Jacalyn, S. (1997). *Corporate Culture, Team Culture: Removing the Hidden Barriers to Team Success*. Corporate Management Developers.

Jacobs, T. O., & Jaques, E. (1989). *Executive leadership*. Alexandria, VA: U.S. Army Research Institute.

Keller, G. F., & Kronstedt, C.R. (2005). *Connecting Confucianism, communism and the Chinese culture of commerce*. Academic Press.

Khandwalla, P. N. (1977). *The sign of organizations*. New York: Harcourt Brace Jovanovich.

Kluckhohn, F. R., & Strodtbeck, F. L. (1961). *Variations in value orientations*. New York: HarperCollins.

Kopelman, R. E., Brief, A. P., & Guzzo, R. A. (1990). The role of climate and culture in productivity. In B. Schneider (Ed.), *Organizational climate and culture* (pp. 282–318). San Francisco: Jossey-Bass.

Leung, K., & Bond, M. H. (1989). On the empirical identification of dimensions for cross-cultural comparisons. *Journal of Cross-Cultural Psychology*, *20*(2), 133–151. doi:10.1177/0022022189202002

Lord, R., & Maher, K. J. (1991). *Leadership and information processing: Linking perceptions and performance*. Boston: Unwin-Everyman.

Lumpkin, G. T., & Dess, G. G. (1996). Clarifying the entrepreneurial orientation construct and linking it to performance. *Academy of Management Review*, *21*(1), 135–172.

Maczynski, J. (1997). GLOBE: The Global Leadership and Organizational Behavior Effectiveness research program. *Polish Psychological Bulletin*, *28*(3), 215–254.

Marin, G., Triandis, H. C., Betancourt, H., & Kashima, Y. (1983). Ethnic affirmation versus social desirability: Explaining discrepancies in bilinguals responses to a questionnaire. *Journal of Cross-Cultural Psychology*, *14*(2), 173–186. doi:10.1177/0022002183014002003

McClelland, D. C. (1961). *The achieving society*. Princeton, NJ: Van Nostrand. doi:10.1037/14359-000

McClelland, D. C. (1985). *Human motivation*. Glenview, IL: Scott, Foresman.

McClelland, D. C., & Atkinson, J. W. (1948). The projective expression of needs, I: The effect of different intensities of the hunder drive on perception. *The Journal of Psychology*, *25*(2), 205–222. doi:10.1080/00223980.1948.9 917371

McClelland, D. C., Atkinson, J. W., Clark, R. A., & Lowell, E. L. (Eds.). (1953). *The achievement motive*. New York: Appleton-Century-Crofts. doi:10.1037/11144-000

McConkey, D. (1974). *No-nonsense Delegation*. New York: AMACON.

McFarland, L. J., Senen, S., & Childress, J. R. (1993). *Twenty-first-century leadership*. New York: Leadership Press.

Medley, F., & Larochelle, D. R. (1995). Transformational Leadership and Job Satisfaction. *Nursing Management*, *26*(9), 47–64. doi:10.1097/00006247-199509000-00017 PMID:7659370

Miller, D., & Droge, C. (1986). Psychological and traditional determinants of structure. *Administrative Science Quarterly,* *31*(4), 539-560.

Misumi, J. (1985). *The behavioral science of leadership: An interdisciplinary Japanese research program*. Ann Arbor, MI: University of Michigan Press.

O'Connell, M. S., Lord, R. G., & O'Connell, M. K. (1990, August). *Differences in Japanese and American leadership prototypes: Implications for cross-cultural training*. Paper presented at the Meeting of the Academy of Management, San Francisco, CA.

Putnam, R. D. (1993). *Making democracy work*. Princeton, NJ: Princeton University Press.

Ralston, D. A., Egri, C. P., Stewart, S., Terpstra, R. H., & Kaicheng, Y. (1999, June). Doing Business in the 21st Century with the New Generation of Chinese Managers: A Study of Generational Shifts in Work Values in China. *Journal of International Business Studies*, *30*(2), 415–427. doi:10.1057/palgrave.jibs.8490077

Ralston, D. A., Pounder, J., Lo, C. W. H., Wong, Y.-Y., Egri, C. P., & Stauffer, J. (2006). Stability and Change in Managerial Work Values: A Longitudinal Study of China, Hong Kong, and the U. S. A. *Management and Organization Review*, *2*(1), 67–94. doi:10.1111/j.1740-8784.2006.00031.x

Rokeach, M. (1969). *Introduction to Value Theory*. Englewood Cliffs, NJ: Prentice Hall.

Rokeach, M. (1973). *The nature of human values*. New York: Free Press.

Rokeach, M. (1973). *The Nature of Human Values*. New York: Free Press.

Sathem, V. (1983). Implications of Corporate Culture: A Managers Guide to Action. *Organizational Dynamics*, *12*(10), 5–23. doi:10.1016/0090-2616(83)90030-X

Schein, E. H. (1992). *Organizational culture and leadership: A dynamic view* (2nd ed.). San Francisco: Jossey-Bass.

Schneider, B. (1987). The people make the place. *Personnel Psychology*, *40*(3), 437–454. doi:10.1111/j.1744-6570.1987.tb00609.x

Schneider, B., Goldstein, H. W., & Smith, D. B. (1995). The ASA Framework: An update. *Personnel Psychology*, *48*(4), 747–783. doi:10.1111/j.1744-6570.1995.tb01780.x

Schwartz, S. H. (1990a). Individualism-Collectivism: Critique and Proposed Refinements. *Journal of Cross-Cultural Psychology*, *21*(2), 139–157. doi:10.1177/0022022190212001

Schwartz, S. H. (1990b). Cultural Dimensions of Values: Toward an Understanding of National Differences. In U. Kim & H. Triandis (Eds.), Individualism-Collectivism. London: Sage.

Schwartz, S. H., & Bilsky, W. (1987). Toward a Psychological Structure of Human Values. *Journal of Personality and Social Psychology*, *53*(3), 550–562. doi:10.1037/0022-3514.53.3.550

Schwartz, S. H., & Bilsky, W. (1990). Toward a Theory of the Universal Content and Structure of Values: Extensions and Cross-Cultural Replications. *Journal of Personality and Social Psychology*, *58*(5), 878–891. doi:10.1037/0022-3514.58.5.878

Scott, W. A. (1965). *Values and Organizations*. Chicago: Rand McNally.

Selznick, P. (1984). *Leadership in administration: A sociological interpretation*. Berkeley, CA: University of California Press.

Shaw, J. B. (1990). A cognitive categorization model for the study of intercultural management. *Academy of Management Review*, *15*(4), 626–645.

Shenkar, O., & Von Glinow, M. A. (1994). Uncovering paradox in organizational theory and research: Using the case of China to illustrate national contingency. *Management Science*, *40*(1), 56–71. doi:10.1287/mnsc.40.1.56

Simonton, D. K. (1994). *Greatness: Who makes history and why*. New York: Guilford Press.

Sipe, W. P., & Hanges, P. J. (1997). Reframing the glass ceiling: A catastrophe model of changes in the perception of women as leaders. In R. G. Lord (Chair), *Dynamic systems, leadership perceptions, and gender effects*. Symposium presented at the Twelfth Annual Conference of the Society of Industrial and Organizational Psychology.

Smith, P. B., & Bond, M. H. (1993). *Social psychology across cultures: Analysis and perspectives*. London: Harvester Wheatsheaf.

Smith, P. B., Misumi, J., Tayeb, M. H., Paterson, M., & Bond, M. H. (1989). On the generality of leadership style across cultures. *Journal of Occupational Psychology*, (30): 526–537.

Spitzberg, B., & Cupach, W. (1984). *Interpersonal Communication Competence.* Sage.

Staw, B. M., Sandelands, L. E., & Dutton, J. E. (1981). Threat-rigidity effects in organizational behavior: A multilevel analysis. *Administrative Science Quarterly, 26*(4), 501–524. doi:10.2307/2392337

Thompson, K. R., & Luthans, F. (1990). Organizational culture: A behavioral perspective. In B. Schneider (Ed.), *Organizational Climate and Culture* (pp. 319–344). San Francisco: Jossey-Bass.

Tichy, N. M., & Devanna, M. A. (1994). *The Transformational Leader.* New York: John Wiley.

Triandis, H. C. (1990). Cross-Cultural Studies of Individualism and Collectivism. In J. Merman (Ed.), *Nebraska Symposium on Motivation,* (pp. 41-133). Lincoln, NE: University of Nebraska Press.

Triandis, H. C. (1993). The contingency model in cross-cultural perspective. In M. M. Chemers & R. Ayman (Eds.), *Leadership theory and research: Perspectives and directions* (pp. 167–188). San Diego, CA: Academic Press.

Triandis, H. C. (1995). *Individualism and Collectivism.* Boulder, CO: Westview Press.

Triandis, H. C., McCusker, C., & Hui, C. H. (1990). Multi-method Probes of Individualism and Collectivism. *Journal of Personality and Social Psychology, 59*(5), 1006–1020. doi:10.1037/0022-3514.59.5.1006

Trice, H. M., & Beyer, J. M. (1984). *The cultures of work organizations.* Englewood Cliffs, NJ: Prentice-Hall.

Tushman, M. L., Newman, W. H., & Nadler, D. A. (1988). Executive leadership and organizational evolution: Managing incremental and discontinuous change. In R. H. Kilman & T. J. Covin (Eds.), *Corporate transformation: Revitalizing organizations for a competitive world* (pp. 102–130). San Francisco: Jossey-Bass.

Walsh, J. P., & Ungson, G. R. (1991). Organizational Memory. *Academy of Management Review, 16*(1), 57–91. doi:10.5465/AMR.1991.4278992

Weishut, D. J. (1989). *The Meaningfulness of the Distinction Between Instrumental and Terminal Values* (Unpublished Master's Thesis). The University of Jerusalem, Israel.

William, J. B., & Gerald, L. B. (1996). A Cross-National Study of Managerial Values. *Journal of International Business Studies.*

Yukl, G. (1981). *Leadership in Organizations.* Englewood Cliff, NJ: Prentice-Hall.

Yukl, G. (1994). *Leadership in Organizations.* Englewood Cliffs, NJ: Prentice Hall.

Yukl, G. (1998). *Leadership in Organizations.* Englewood Cliffs, NJ: Prentice Hall.

Yukl, G. (1999). An evaluation of conceptual weaknesses in transformational and charismatic leadership theories. *The Leadership Quarterly*, *10*(10), 285–306. doi:10.1016/S1048-9843(99)00013-2

Yukl, G. A. (1994). *Leadership in organizations* (3rd ed.). Englewood Cliffs, NJ: Prentice-Hall.

Chapter 3
Research Methodology

The research on the correlations between values orientations and leadership styles is very challenging. Previous researches mainly focus on the separated topics on either values systems or leadership styles. However, there is seldom research which entwines them both together and sees it from comprehensive perspective. The most obvious reason might be that values system or cultural research is rather abstract and qualitative and the same is true of the researches on leadership styles as there is not a one-for-all model of leadership style to follow and it is hard for anyone to say one leadership style is better than the others.

As regarding the cultures and values research, the most famous giants like M. H. Bond, Schwartz, Hofstede and others have in their research eyed on the western context. Although M. H. Bond has developed a Chinese values survey, which is mainly derived from the ideas of Confucius thoughts (BVS), it is not as popular as that developed by Schwartz (SVS). Even when the author of this research has in person had a long talk and profound discussion with M. H. Bond, he finally suggested that the author should adopt SVS (Schwartz values survey as the instrument), which again indicates the importance and significance of this research as this research has been conducted for over two years to obtain 778 samples from the distributed 1000 questionnaires. The

DOI: 10.4018/978-1-5225-2277-5.ch003

research findings, to some extent may fill the gap of the lack of research on Chinese values and the leadership styles of Chinese business leaders.

3.1 WHY NOT SEM?

To speak from the research methodologies, in the past decade, SEM (Structural Equation Modeling) has become very hot in empirical research field. Even some scholars have summarized hundreds of papers from top tier journals to testify that SEM has been widely used in empirical research and there is a tendency of still roaring up in the research field. The author of this paper has been also intending to follow the trend, but the preliminary results obtained from SEM have shown that the testing results are not very attractive. Therefore, the author has to abandon SEM as the research methodology but still have puzzlement in mind. With this big puzzlement, the author has been to HK again to seek answers from one of the greatest giants in culture and leadership style research---M. H. Bond. As he suggested that it doesn't mean that every popular tool is good and appropriate in any research. As the most prominent feature of SEM is to find the correlations between multiple factors, it seems that SEM should be very suitable in this research. Actually, values survey and leadership styles survey to a large extent are very abstract and it is hard to use an absolute number to measure, though both of the questionnaires have themselves in 9 and 5 Likert scales respectively. Since the items of the surveys can not be absolutely measured, the correlations between cultural value factors and leadership styles can not be in a linear relation. Being a big giant in this research, none of his (M. H. Bond) papers have adopted SEM in research, though most of his papers have been released in top-tier journals. The failure in adopting SEM might result in the too mediocre culture of Chinese and also might be because the questionnaires adopted in this research are not very suitable to people in Chinese culture.

After this visit and magnificent discussion, my puzzlement has been eliminated and the author began to focus on the research by using another popular statistical tool --- SPSS. Though the research has not got significant results from SEM model, there are still lots of meaningful findings. Multiple factor analyses have indicated that Chinese business leaders have a unique but not clear-cut leadership style which revolves among the three leadership styles of autocratic, democratic and free-reign at the axles of Chinese core values. When the 778 samples have been displayed in Matlab graph, it again testifies that the core of the Chinese cultures and values systems is mediocre, as many of the dots are overlapping and most of the dots are concentrated in the middle part of the graph. Multiple factor analyses have demonstrated that there are strong correlations between cultural factors and leadership styles, but more have to be probed and investigated in the future research.

3.2 QUESTIONNAIRES AND PILOT TESTS

Questionnaires adopted in this research are popularly used and widely accepted globally to guarantee the validity and reliability of the survey results. As questionnaires have been developed by western scholars based on the western cultures, in order to secure its adaptability and validity in Chinese cultural background, rigid procedures have been implemented. First of all, specialized experts have been invited to translate the questionnaires into Chinese and the transcripts have been compared and discrepancies have been pointed out for discussions of several rounds until all the variances have been solved and mutual agreement achieved. Then the transcripts have been again back-translated, compared, discrepancies discussed and consensus reached. Items which are not fully understood in the questionnaire have been discussed with the designers of the questionnaire through emails and face-to-face discussions before final version has been settled. After that, a small population of 35 samples has been summoned to do the pilot test with careful attention of the wordings and understanding in the questionnaire. The participants in the pilot test have been asked to raise questions of any kind relevant to the questionnaires, and then the questions have been collected; categorized and summarized for experts to have further and deeper discussions until there is no misunderstanding and ambiguity in the questionnaires. Then, large size of the questionnaires has been printed for large scale survey.

3.3 SAMPLING AND DATA COLLECTION

To guarantee the high quality survey results, people who have helped to conduct the questionnaires have been trained and pre-tested with the questionnaires for thrice in different times in order to make sure that they themselves have a complete understanding of every survey questions. Questionnaire skills and techniques, as well as interpersonal skills have been trained for them so that they have the full ability to answer all the questions the Guinea pigs might raise in the process of survey. They are also asked to note down all the questions that they can not answer but can be clarified by the experts. To encourage, motivate and extend thanks to the population who has conducted the survey, a small and memorial gift has been provided for all the participants in the survey. All the questionnaires are conducted anonymously without offending the privacy of the participants in order to secure the reality ad reliability of the survey quality and response bias can be minimized.

This survey has been conducted from September 2006 to July 2008 with a total dispatch of 1200 sets all over the country and collected 778 valid sets with a response rate of 65%. To fit the purpose of this research, questionnaires have been only distributed to senior managers and middle management of business organizations. As EMBA program is mostly applied to higher and middle managers in China, therefore, it can not be regarded as convenient sampling in this research.

3.4 Data Encoding, Input and Double Check

To guarantee the quality of data input, because of the heavy workload of 778 pieces questionnaires, twelve postgraduates and PhD candidates have been paid for inputting and double checking the raw data. Before assigning the raw data to different groups, all the data have been marked, encoded and then distributed to different groups. Each two of them has been working as a group, one reads it and the other one input it, and then shift the role for double check as this is a tedious and boring work which needs high attention and concentration, as well as the perfect coordination of eyes and fingers. After all the raw data have been input into the computer, three of the teachers inclusive of the author herself have randomly checked the input with the original sheets as different group has its own code with the original data and the electronic data, so it is easy to check. When input has been finished, invalid data (five items are missing; three or more items neighboring each other in the questionnaires have got the same value; obvious mistakes as proposed by M. H. Bond) have been ticked off. In the end, only 778 sets of questionnaire responses have been seen as valid for processing in statistical software.

3.5 DATA PROCESSING AND TESTING RESULTS

3.5.1 Descriptive Statistical Analysis

In 1986, at the 4th plenary session of the 6th People's Congress, China has been divided into three main districts: the Eastern part, the Central part and the Western part and such geographic division has been promulgated formally in the Seventh Five-Year Plan in China. To be specific, the Eastern part includes

Beijing, Tianjin, Shanghai and provinces of He'bei, Liao'ning, Jiang'su, Fu'jian, Shan'dong, Guang'dong and Hai'nan. The Central part includes Shan'xi Province, Inner Mongolia Autonomous Regions, Ji'lin Province, Heilong'jiang Province, Anhui, Jiang'xi, He'nan, Hu'nan and Guang'xi provinces, while the Western part consists of provinces and regions like Si'chuan, Gui'zhou, Yun'an, Tibet Autonomous Regions, Shaanxi Province, Qing'hai Province, Ning'xia Hui Autonomous Regions and Xin'jiang Ugur Autonomous Regions.

In 1997, at the fifth Plenary Session of the 8th People's Congress, Chong'qing has been set up as the fourth municipal city directly governed by the Central Government apart from the previous three municipal cities as Beijing, Shang'hai and Tianjin, and as a result, it has been counted into the Western part which makes the Western part to have 10 provinces and cities.

Since the per capita level of GDP in Inner Mongolia and Guang'xi Zhuang Autonomous Regions keeps the similar level with that of the Western 10 provinces and regions, in order to make a balanced economic development and decrease the development gaps between the Western and Eastern parts, Inner Mongolia and Guang'xi Zhuang Autonomous Regions have also been put into the Western part in 2000 when the Central Government was stipulating the Grand West Development Policy. In this way, Inner Mongolia and Guang'xi Zhuang Autonomous Regions will also have the honor to enjoy the favorable policies with other 10 provinces in the Western part of China.

Therefore, to date, the Western part of China consists of 12 administrative regions, or rather Si'chuan, Yun'nan, Gui'zhou, Shaanxi, Gan'su,provinces and 5 autonomous regions as Ning'xia Hui Autonomous Regions, Xin'jiang Urgur Autonomous Regions, Inner Mongolia Autonomous Regions, Guang'xi Zhuang Autonomous Regions and Xi'zang Tibetan Autonomous Regions. As for the Middle part of China, it is made up of 8 princes and regions, inclusive of Shan'xi, Ji'lin, Heilongjiang, An'hui, Jiang'xi, He'nan, Hu'bei, Hu'nan provinces, whereas the Easterns part of 11 provinces and municipalities remain unchanged.

From the profile of the research participants, it is clearly expressed that 570 samples (which takes up 73.5% of the total population) are males and only 205 samples are females (which takes up 26.5% of the total participants). This is in conformity with the real world situation as men dominate the middle and senior management not only in China, but also true in other parts of the world, even inclusive of the most advanced countries that there are more male leaders than female leaders. As it is a vast and general topic, this research only focuses on the correlations between values orientation and leadership styles, but

Table 1. Profile of the respondents in this research

Characteristics of Firms		No. (Share in Total)
Gender	Male	570(73.5%)
	Female	205(26.5%)
	Unmarked	0(0.0%)
Age	Less 30	204(26.3%)
	31-35	199(25.7%)
	36-40	151(19.5%)
	41-45	163(21.0%)
	46-50	40(5.2%)
	Over 51	18(2.3%)
	Unmarked	0(0.0%)
Permanent Residential Areas	East	134(17.3%)
	Middle	124(16.0%)
	West	440(56.8%)
	Others	76(9.8%)
	Unmarked	1 (0.1%)
Education	<5 years	99(12.8%)
	5-8 years	41(5.3%)
	9-12 years	53(6.8%)
	13-16 years	392(50.6%)
	Master& PhD	150(19.4%)
	Unmarked	40(5.2%)
Position	Grassroots	83(10.7%)
	Primary leaders	74(9.5%)
	Middle management	354(45.7%)
	Senior management	228(29.4%)
	Unmarked	36(4.6%)
Tenure	< 6 years	144(18.6%)
	6-10 years	209(27.0%)
	11-15 years	133(17.2%)
	16-20 years	144(18.6%)
	21-25 years	97(12.5%)
	Over 25	48(6.2%)
	Unmarked	0(0.0%)

continued on next page

Table 1. Continued

Characteristics of Firms		No. (Share in Total)
Nature of Ownership	State-owned & collective enterprises	290(37.4%)
	Characteristics of firms	No. (share in total)
	Private	58(7.5%)
	Joint-venture	40(5.2%)
	Wholly-owned subsidiaries	160(20.6%)
	Others	189(24.4%)
	Unmarked	38(4.9%)
Number of Formally Enrolled Employee	1-100	190(24.5%)
	101-1000	241(31.1%)
	Over 1000	343(44.1%)
	Unmarked	2(0.3%)
Industries	Agriculture, mining, forestry, fishery	149(19.2%)
	Construction	41(5.3%)
	Manufacturing	212(27.4%)
	Transportation, communications, energy	110(14.2%)
	Wholesaler and retailer	29(3.7%)
	Financing, insurance he real estate	73(9.4%)
	Tertiary industry (hotels & restaurants)	47(6.1%)
	Public administration	66(8.5%)
	Health-care and beauty industry	2(0.3%)
	others	1(0.1%)
	Unmarked	45(5.8%)
Company Locations	East of China	100(12.9%)
	North of China	57(7.4%)
	Middle of China	28(3.6%)
	South of China	133(17.2%)
	Northwest of China	399(51.5%)
	Southwest of China	11(1.4%)
	Northeast of China	2(0.3%)
	Unmarked	45(5.8%)

not on sexism or Women's Liberation Movement, or other feminist movements. Therefore, we will not tangle on this obvious difference.

As regards age groups, in this research, we have categorized the participants into 6 age groups with a five-year interval between each neighboring groups. Therefore, we get 204 populations which are under 30 years old, which takes up 26.3% of the total population, and 199 samples who are between 31-35 years old. These two categories take up 52% of the total Guinea pigs, which have indicated that Chinese business leaders are tending to be very young as against the normal phenomenon before the year 1978 - the beginning of Reform and Opening Up in China when business leaders were normally 40 or over years old. We also get 151 samples who are between 36 and 40 years old and 163 samples who are between 41 to 45 years old and 40 participants who are between 46 to 50 years old, only 18 (2.3% of the total population) who are over 51 years old. We need to further investigate the potential reasons why 97.7% of the participants in this study are less than 50 years old. Is it because that Chinese values system has been shifted and young people are granted more opportunity to posit in high ranking positions? Or are there any restrictions or regulations that those who are participating EMBA studies must be below 50 years old?

In regard to permanent residential areas, among the 778 samples, there are 134 Guinea pigs come from the Eastern part of China; 124 samples from the Middle part of China and 440 samples are from the Western part of China (which takes up 56.8% of the total population) and 76 from other areas of China. Though this survey has been conducted nationwide, it seems that more participants in this study are living permanently in the western part of China. This obvious bias might affect the research results a bit because of the obvious reasons that people in the Eastern part of China might have quite different values orientations and leadership styles than that that come from the Middle and the Western parts of China. The author of this research is fully aware of this bias, but due to the limited research funds and the unappealing education system of China, it is unavoidable. This research dilemma which should be avoided but can not avoid may call attention for the concerning parties to ponder the real purpose of higher education. Such embarrassment may be avoided in the future when the government realizes that they should provide sufficient funds for PhD. candidates to do their research; it may also call attention of the business personnel who should learn from foreign business persons to grant research funds for the higher learning organizations especially in management field which calls for the combination of theories and practice. After all, academic research should be closely linked with the real business practices in the marriage of the two.

From the demographic analysis, we have categorized the education levels of all the participants into five groups: those who have got less than 5 years of schooling, meaning less than a primary school graduate and this portion comes to 12.8% (99 samples); those who have received 5-8 years of schooling, meaning who have graduated from junior middle school which take up 5.3% of the total population (in 41 samples) and those who have got 9-12 years of schooling, they are probably senior middle school graduates and we have 53 guinea pigs which takes up 6.8% of the total population. Those who have received 13-16 years of education takes up the largest portion, reaching 392 samples (50.6% of the total population), which means that over half of the participants in this study have got bachelor's degree and they are university students. This finding coincides with the government policy since the reform and opening up, government has advocated leaders have to be young, knowledgeable, specialized in a specific field. We have also got 150 samples who are masters or PhD earners, which takes up 19.4% of the total population. Such finding has revealed that more and more Chinese people are seeking for higher degrees but not clinging to only a bachelor's degree. There are still 40 participants who have missed this point and keep the survey blank. We are not sure it is because they forgot to fill in the blank or they have a very low education level and do not want to "lose face" even though the survey has been conducted anonymously.

When we test the position of those participants in this study, we have found that middle and senior managers take up 75.1% of the total population with middle managers in 354 samples (45.7% of the total population) and 228 samples (29.4% of the total population) for senior managers. Grassroots, primary leaders and unmarked samples come to 83 (10.7%), 74 (9.5%) and 36 (4.6%) respectively. As we lack sufficient information to propose why senior and middle managers take up 75.1% of the total population in this research, but one thing is clear that EMBA education in China mainly opens to middle and senior managers due to market positioning of EMBA program. Also, it might be true is that EMBA education is expensive investment and it is only affordable by the middle and senior managers in China no matter they pay themselves or they have been paid by their organizations. Still, we have found that though EMBA education is so-called elite education, quite a lot of people are eager to participate in the program with one reason or another.

As regards the tenure of the participants in this study, those who are working in the organizations between 6-10 years takes up 27% (209 samples) and those who are working in the organizations less than 6 years, between 11-15 years and 16-20 years, as well as between 21-25 years are distributed evenly with 144 samples, 133 samples, 144 samples and 97 samples respectively.

These four tenure groups take up 56.9% of the total population (in total number of 518 samples). There are also 48 samples who have been working in the organizations for over 25 years (6.2% of the total population) which have reflected very high loyalty. The reasons for such high loyalty to the organizations have to be investigated with the support of more information.

Regarding the nature of ownership of the organizations, there are five categories which the 778 samples have been grouped into. Among the samples, state-owned enterprises (SOEs) take up the largest portion of 290 samples (37.4%) and wholly-owned subsidiaries (WOSs), as well as marked others take up 20.6% (160 samples) and 24.4% (189 samples) respectively. Private firms, joint-ventures and unmarked firms take up only 17.6% of the total population with 58 samples, 40 samples and 38 samples respectively. This means that EMBA participants are mainly from SOEs, Wholly-owned subsidiaries and those marked "others". It also indicates that there might be very promising business organizations and the nature of these organizations is unidentified which mean the lack of policy or regulation. It is presumable that these business organizations might be the newly born babies with the reform and opening up which are beyond the identification of government policy.

Among the 778 surveyed participants, it has been demonstrated that 44.1% of the participants are working in organizations with employees over 1000 heads; there are 241 participants who are working in organizations with 101—1000 employees and still 190 participants who are working in the organizations with employees between 1—100 heads. The other two samples do not mark the scale of their business organizations. This is obvious that China has large number of firms with over 1000 employees, bearing in mind most of the participants (56.8%) are from the western part of China, which implies that there are even more larger business organizations in the middle part and eastern part of China, as there are big gap in economic development in the eastern and western part of China.

In the surveyed participants, we have also observed the nature of their industries. According to the survey, there are altogether ten groups as regards the nature of the industries: agriculture, mining, forestry and fishery have been seen as in the same group which takes up 19.2% of the total population with 149 samples. Manufacturing sector comes to be the No. 1 with 212 samples and 27.4% of the total population, and then followed by transportation, telecommunications and energy sector which occupies 110 samples with 14.2% in the total population. Financing, insurance, real estate as a whole takes up 73 samples (9.4% of the total population), public administration, 66 samples (8.5% of the total) and 47 samples (6.1%) for tertiary industry and 41 samples (5.3%) for construction. Health-care, beauty industry, as well as other unidentified sectors only take up 2 (0.3%) and 1 (0.1%) respectively. This statistic has revealed that China has a very imbalanced structure its industries with manufacturing and agriculture as the two mainstays which still fall into the traditional economic structure. There is much room for China to develop her tertiary industry, as well as health-care and beauty industry.

Regarding the locations of business organization, the study has revealed that 399 organizations have been located in the Northwestern part of China, which takes up 51.5% of the total population. There are 133 (17.2% of the total) organizations located in the South of China and 100 organizations (12.9% of the total population) which are located in the Eastern part of China. Altogether 81.6% of the participants have their business organizations located in the Northwestern part of China, the South of China and the East of China. Organizations located in the north of China takes up 7.4% of the total population with 57 samples, 45 participants have not marketed the locations of their business organization for no reasons and 28 samples have their organizations located in the Middle of China and 11 in Southwestern of China, only two have the organizations located in Northeastern part of China.

3.5.2 Construct Measures

We followed the procedures suggested by Churchill (1979) in scale development. First, the domain of each construct was clearly defined in terms of what would be included or excluded. Second, the literature was searched to locate any relevant scales. Measures were adopted or adapted from the existing literature where appropriate. If none were available or appropriate, new measures were developed.

Construct Validity

Construct validity is mainly tested by CFA (certified Factor Analysis). The higher the loading of the items in the survey, the better the construct validity. The testing results have demonstrated that loading of all the items are significant and the whole research model has been tested by Chi-Square and the overall testing results have shown that there is a good construct validity (Chi-Square = 4079.56, df = 901, RMSEA) = 0.072, NNFI = 0.94, CFI = 0.95, SRMR = 0.071, GFI = 0.79). For more details, please refer to Table 8.

In this study, the scales for measuring values orientation falls into ten dimensions based on the Schwartz values survey as the primary stage and then the ten value dimensions can again be categorized into four grand values dimensions as the secondary stage. To be specific, the primary ten value

Table 2. CFA values of value dimensions

Construct	Item	Std. loading	*t*-value
Universalism	Universalism1	0.35	-
	Universalism2	0.56	8.7
	Universalism3	0.64	9.08
	Universalism4	0.59	8.85
	Universalism5	0.65	9.12
	Universalism6	0.66	9.15
	Universalism7	0.62	9.02
	Universalism8	0.65	9.12
Power	Power1	0.61	-
	Power2	0.55	12.41
	Power3	0.71	15.05
	Power4	0.59	13.22
Hedonism	Hedonism 1	0.56	-
	Hedonism 2	0.62	11.42
Self-direction	Self-direction1	0.46	-
	Self-direction2	0.66	11.89
	Self-direction3	0.6	11.32
	Self-direction4	0.65	11.79
	Self-direction5	0.58	11.18
Security	Security1	0.52	-
	Security2	0.54	11.75
	Security3	0.58	12.34
	Security4	0.45	10.37
	Security5	0.66	13.3
Stimulation	Stimulation1	0.54	-
	Stimulation2	0.69	13.71
	Stimulation3	0.73	14.12
Conformity	Conformity1	0.67	-
	Conformity2	0.62	15.81
	Conformity3	0.55	14.17
	Conformity4	0.54	14.07
Tradition	Tradition1	0.58	-
	Tradition2	0.5	11.37

continued on next page

Table 2. Continued

Construct	Item	Std. loading	*t*-value
	Tradition3	0.68	14.22
	Tradition4	0.34	8.17
	Tradition5	0.54	12.05
Benevolence	Benevolence1	0.7	-
	Benevolence2	0.63	17.12
	Benevolence3	0.72	19.96
	Benevolence4	0.65	17.74
	Benevolence5	0.7	19.38
Achievement	Achievement1	0.7	-
	Achievement2	0.69	5.88
	Achievement3	0.58	6.87
	Achievement4	0.59	6.65

Chi-Square = 4079.56, df = 901, RMSEA) = 0.072, NNFI = 0.94, CFI = 0.95, SRMR = 0.071, GFI = 0.79

dimensions are: power, universalism, achievement, hedonism, stimulation, self-direction, universalism, benevolence, tradition, conformity and security. However, these primary ten value dimensions again can be grouped into four grant value dimensions as openness-to-change, conservation, self-enhancement and self-transcendence (four more details please refer to Appendix 2 Schwartz Value Survey). For the scales of measuring leadership styles, we have adopted the widely used western questionnaire of Leadership style survey, in which there are 30 statements of each describes a specific situation in business world. Then, the participants grade those thirty statements along the 5 point Likert scale, representing "always so for 5" to "often so for 4"., down through "sometimes so for 3" and "seldom so for 2".and "never so for 1".. Then, each participant has 30 grades and these grades have been added up according to the instructions of the questionnaire (for more details please refer to Appendix 3 Leadership style survey).

3.5.3 Reliability Analysis

Reliability refers to the degree of possibilities for observing the same object and in the same observing approaches. The higher the reliability of the observed objects, the higher the degree of repeatability, and the lower the degree of variance between the data the the average value of the data. There are three kinds of factors to indicate reliability: Stability, Equivalence and Internal Consistency. Among them, repeatability refers to the fact that items can be used to measure the same construct or variable repeatedly and has high stability. Internal consistency is an important measurement for testing the correlation-ability of a certain item in measuring the other indicators of the same variable, which refers to the degree of variance in testing different items. The most popularly adopted index for measuring the internal consistency is the value of Cronbach α, which is also called the co-efficiency of internal consistency. The value of Cronbach α can be calculated through the following formula:

$$\alpha = \frac{k \times \overline{\text{cov}} \, / \, \overline{\text{var}}}{1 + (k-1)\overline{\text{cov}} \, / \, \overline{\text{var}}} \tag{1}$$

k is the number of indices, $\overline{\text{cov}}$ is the standard deviation and $\overline{\text{var}}$ is the average standard deviation. Cronbach α is currently the most popularly adopted indicator to evaluate the reliability of variables. The value of Cronbach α falls into the domain of 0 and 1. The higher the value of Cronbach α, the more the reliability. Generally speaking, all the items to measure the same index should have the value of Cronbach α larger than 0.7. The values of Cronbach α in this research can be demonstrated as in the table below: (For Cronbach αvalues, please see Table 2). From the table of values of Cronbach α, it indicates that variable adopted in this research have good reliability. Reliability is operationalized using the internal consistency method that is estimated using Cronbach's alpha (Hull & Nie, 1981). Typically, reliability coefficients of 0.70 or higher are considered adequate. Therefore, an alpha value of 0.70 is considered as the critical value.

To evaluate the internal consistency of the scales for reliability, we use the internal consistency method that is estimated using Cronbach's alpha and item-to-total analysis. Typically, reliability coefficients of 0.70 or higher and the item loading on the factors of 0.60 or higher are considered adequate (Hull & Nie, 1981). For each of the four factors, we calculated Cronbach reliability coefficient (alpha), and the item-to-total correlations for every item. The results are presented in Table 3. the analyses have shown that all the Cronbach's alpha values are larger than 0.6, which indicates that research items are of better internal consistency and with high reliability. Even though, one of the then values dimensions--- Hedonism only have two items to measure, it also enjoys good reliability.

Table 3. Cronbach alpha of value dimensions

Construct	Item	Mean	S.D.
Universalism Cronbach's alpha = 0.7887	Universalism1	6.55	1.76
	Universalism2	6.57	1.65
	Universalism3	5.96	1.65
	Universalism4	6.78	1.44
	Universalism5	5.89	1.69
	Universalism6	6.69	1.46
	Universalism7	6.93	1.34
	Universalism8	6.50	1.48
Power Cronbach's alpha = 0.6902	Power1	5.60	1.80
	Power2	6.47	1.52
	Power3	5.87	1.70
	Power4	5.88	1.62
Hedonism Correlation = 0.334**	Hedonism 1	6.82	1.49
	Hedonism 2	6.41	1.56
Self-direction Cronbach's alpha = 0.7021	Self-direction1	7.00	1.53
	Self-direction2	6.46	1.51
	Self-direction3	6.61	1.62
	Self-direction4	6.71	1.44
	Self-direction5	5.76	1.69
Security Cronbach's alpha = 0.6782	Security1	6.89	1.57
	Security2	7.07	1.61
	Security3	6.79	1.43
	Security4	7.75	1.24
	Security5	6.32	1.43
Stimulation Cronbach's alpha = 0.6640	Stimulation1	6.44	1.52
	Stimulation2	5.55	1.79
	Stimulation3	5.94	1.64
Conformity Cronbach's alpha = 0.6539	Conformity1	6.75	1.33
	Conformity2	6.50	1.48
	Conformity3	7.37	1.20
	Conformity4	6.07	1.55

continued on next page

Table 3. Continued

Construct	Item	Mean	S.D.
Tradition Cronbach's alpha = 0.6571	Tradition1	5.78	1.60
	Tradition2	5.44	1.80
	Tradition3	6.44	1.42
	Tradition4	4.34	2.29
	Tradition5	5.06	2.00
Benevolence Cronbach's alpha = 0.7900	Benevolence1	6.91	1.31
	Benevolence2	6.95	1.32
	Benevolence3	6.41	1.31
	Benevolence4	7.11	1.28
	Benevolence5	6.69	1.33
Achievement Cronbach's alpha = 0.7019	Achievement1	6.33	1.62
	Achievement2	6.24	1.50
	Achievement3	6.98	1.28
	Achievement4	6.82	1.53

**Correlation is significant at 0.05 level

Apart from calculating the value of Cronbach α, we also calculated CR (Composite Reliability), CR can be obtained from the following formula:

$$CR = \frac{\left(\sum loading\right)^2}{\sum\left(1 - loading^2\right) + \left(\sum loading\right)^2} \tag{2}$$

In which, factor loading of each item falls into the domain of 0 and 1. just like Cronbach α, for CR, the larger the value of CR (composite reliability), the higher the degree of reliability. According to Bagozzi and Yi(1988), if the value of CR is larger than 0.7, it means that the measured items have good reliability.

As can be seen from Table 3, Cronbach's alpha values of the factors are well above the critical value and ranged from 0.65 to 0.78. These results suggest that the theoretical constructs exhibit good psychometric properties.

3.6 VALIDITY ANALYSIS

Validity has been used to measure if the testing results are in conformity with that of the researchers expected. Therefore, it refers to the variance between the testing results and the ideal value. In analyzing the validity of items, we normally have to take into account the four aspects of validity from difference perspectives. That is, Content Validity, Structural Validity, Convergent Validity and Discriminant Validity.

3.6.1 Content Validity

Since the survey questionnaires of both values system and leadership styles have been tested for a long time and they are mature questionnaires designed by expertise in the research field many years ago. The questionnaires have been widely used globally. Though the adopted surveys have been developed in the context of western cultures, they have well translated Chinese versions done by research experts in values and leadership research field and have been used in the realm of Pan-China culture circles, such as HK, Singapore, Taiwan and other areas. Very rigid procedures have been designed in this research and pilot tests have been conducted prior to the large samples being distributed. Therefore, questionnaires adopted in this research should have high content validity.

Content validity refers to, to what extent that the variable has provided sufficient information to reflect the nature and essence of the object under observation (Churchill,1979). The judgment on content validity can not merely from the superficial figure but a kind of subjective judgment. In order to guarantee the content validity, we have adopted sufficient and workable measures: in the questionnaires adopted in the research, we have provided the instructions to answer the survey questions; clearly manifested the Guinea pigs on how to fill up the surveys and promised them that the questionnaires will be treated confidentially and if they require, the results in addition, we have modified or fine tuned some of the items in the questionnaires with the purpose of adapting better in Chinese situation, as the questionnaires we have adopted in this research are from foreign contexts. Pilot tests have been made for several rounds to guarantee that each participants fully understand every single item of the questionnaires and at the same time, the quality of questionnaires have been secured. The above mentioned measures adopted in conducting surveys have guaranteed the content validity of this research. The content validity of an instrument is the extent to which it provides adequate coverage for the construct domain or essence of the domain being measured

(Churchill, 1979). The determination of content validity is not numerical, but subjective and judgmental (Emory, 1980). Prior to data collection, the content validity of the instrument was established by grounding it in existing literature including over 400 articles. Pre-testing the measurement instrument before the collection of data further validated it. Professors who have helped to conduct the survey in this study and the carefully selected potential EMBA students have been involved in the pretest process to guarantee that they are fully understand not only the superficial meaning but also the implied meaning of each item in the questionnaires. Concerning experts were asked to review the questionnaire for structure, readability, ambiguity, and completeness (Dillman, 1978). The final survey instrument incorporated minor changes to remove a few ambiguities that were discovered during this validation process. These tests indicated that the resulting measurement instrument represented the content of the supply chain management factors.

3.6.2 Convergent Validity

In this research, we have adopted two approaches to measure the convergent validity of variables. First of all, we have calculated the factor loading of each item and all the factors loading of the observed items are over 0.5, which indicates that factors are of good convergent validity. In general, if the factor loading is over 0.7 (in other words, the ANOVA values can explain over half of the items), it means that the research construct is of good appropriate quality (Fornell and Larcker,1981). Some scholars think it a rigid requirement for accepting factor loadings to be over 0.7, later the academic field has stipulated factor loading 0.5 is the maximum tolerant value. The following formula can be used to calculate the AVE (Average Variance Extracted) (Fornell and Larcker,1981):

$$A VE = \frac{\left(\sum loading^2\right)}{\sum\left(1 - loading^2\right) + \left(\sum loading^2\right)} \tag{3}$$

Loading refers to the factor loading of each item, the value of factor loading falls into the domain of 0 and 1. The larger the AVE value, the better the fitness of items. In this research, we have calculated the AVE values of each item and can be seen in the table below(For values of convergent validity, please see the Table 4). If the AVE value is more than 0.7 or near 0.7, it means that factors have good convergent validity. Convergent validity is

Table 4. Convergent validity of value dimensions

Construct	Item	mean	S.D.	Loading
Universalism	s17	6.546	1.656	0.52
	s24	5.930	1.650	0.59
	s26	6.754	1.446	0.55
	s30	6.662	1.459	0.62
	s35	6.908	1.338	0.61
	s38	6.486	1.483	0.63
Power	s3	5.562	1.794	0.59
	s12	6.445	1.522	0.52
	s27	5.846	1.687	0.70
	s46	5.841	1.604	0.55
Hedonism	s4	6.795	1.492	0.55
	s50	6.379	1.563	0.59
Self-direction	s16	6.437	1.509	0.63
	s31	6.595	1.621	0.57
	s41	6.692	1.444	0.62
	s53	5.733	1.688	0.55
Security	s8	6.868	1.567	0.48
	s13	7.072	1.603	0.53
	s15	6.779	1.426	0.58
	s56	6.287	1.426	0.63
Stimulation	s9	6.418	1.521	0.53
	s25	5.521	1.782	0.66
	s37	5.911	1.635	0.70
Conformity	s11	6.732	1.327	0.68
	s20	6.484	1.476	0.59
	s40	7.355	1.201	0.54
Tradition	s18	5.750	1.596	0.55
	s32	5.413	1.794	0.47
	s36	6.414	1.419	0.65
	s44	4.308	2.271	0.30
	s51	5.012	1.992	0.51

continued on next page

Table 4. Continued

Construct	Item	mean	S.D.	Loading
Benevolence	s33	6.900	1.319	0.66
	s45	6.925	1.320	0.59
	s49	6.388	1.310	0.69
	s52	7.093	1.282	0.62
	s54	6.662	1.333	0.68
Achievement	s34	6.299	1.618	0.64
	s39	6.212	1.493	0.66
	s43	6.951	1.283	0.54
	s55	6.799	1.530	0.56

demonstrated by the statistical significance of the loading at a given alpha (e.g., $P = 0.05$). A loading of 0.7 indicates that about one-half of the item's variance (the squared loading) can be attributed to the construct; thus, 0.7 is the suggested minimum level for item loading on established scales.

3.6.3 Discriminant Validity

Discriminant validity can be measured by the following two approaches: first, choose two variables at random, compare the ANOVA values when the fixed correlation co-efficiency is 1 and when the correlation co-efficiency is stipulated at random. The values obtained from this variance indicate the divergent validity. The larger the values, the larger the divergence. Second, compare the square root of AVE and the correlation co-efficiency between this variable and another one. If the square root of AVE is larger than correlation co-efficiency, it means that there exists better divergent validity (Fornell and Larcker,1981). In addition to convergent validity, discriminant validity is another important test to ensure adequacy of the measurement model. Discriminant validity measures the extent to which individual items intended to measure one latent construct do not at the same time measure a different latent construct (DeVellis, 1991).

In this study, discriminant validity is established using CFA and the control variables are age, gender, permanent residential area, education level, position in the organization, tenure with the company, company scale, the ownership nature of the company, the nature of industry and company location; while independent variables are 10 dimensions of values orientation based on Schwartz's 57 value survey items, which specifically can be expressed as universalism (UNIVER. in short), power, hedonism, self-direction, security, stimulation, conformity, tradition, benevolence and achievement. To facilitate the arrangement of these terms in this dissertation, short forms are adopted as UNIVER., POWER, HEDO., S-DIR. SECU., STI., CONF., TRADI., BENEV., ACHIEV. respectively and the dependent variables in this research are the three kinds of leadership styles---- to be specific, autocratic leadership style, democratic leadership style and free reign leadership style.

Discriminant validity measures the extent to which individual items intending to measure one latent construct do not at the same time measure a different latent construct (DeVellis, 1991). In this study, discriminant validity is established using CFA. Models were constructed for all possible pairs of latent constructs. These models were run on each selected pair, (1) allowing for correlation between the two constructs, and (2) fixing the correlation between the constructs at 1.0. A significant difference in Chi-square values for the fixed and free solutions indicates the distinctiveness of the two constructs (Bagozzi et al., 1991).

We assessed the discriminate validity of each construct using the procedure recommended by Bagozzi, Yi, and Phillips (1991). This entails analyzing all possible pairs of constructs in a series of two-factor confirmatory factor analysis (CFA) models (Wu et al., 2006). We built a constrained CFA model for each possible pair of latent constructs, in which the correlations between the paired constructs were fixed to 1.0. This was compared with the original unconstrained model, in which the correlations were freely estimated. A significant difference in the chi-square statistics between the fixed and unconstrained models indicates high discriminate validity (Bagozzi et al., 1991). In this study, the critical value ($c2(1) > 3.84$) was exceeded in all 45 pairs, which indicated significant differences at the 0.05 level (Table 5). Therefore, the construct exhibit discriminate validity.

3.6.4 Structural Validity

Structural validity refers to the observed variable has, to what extent, measured the structure of the variable observed, but not other variables(Churchill,1979). The measuring of structural validity not only has to consider the degree of dependence of the observed variables (convergent validity), but also has to secure that this index has not measured other variables (divergent validity) (Campbelland Fiske,1959). Convergent validity refers to the fact that indices have demonstrated the observed construct or variables, free from existing factor cross loading. Divergent validity refers to the fact that there are significant variances between one variable and another, there does not exist

Table 5. Discriminant validity of value dimensions

	Universalism	Power	Hedonism	Self-Direction	Security	Stimulation	Conformity	Tradition	Benevolence
Universalism									
Power	59.5								
Hedonism	78.39	16.53							
Self-Direction	67.26	40.04	55						
Security	52.27	26.56	46.81	59.59					
Stimulation	59.42	21.53	57.09	45.91	58.61				
Conformity	58.92	23.35	63.97	62.94	15.18	50.25			
Tradition	47.04	19.32	55.17	62.1	36.81	25.72	15.06		
Benevolence	55.97	32.28	56.18	51.04	39.45	50.13	27.02	27.63	
Achievement	44.37	10.01	43.05	20.49	31.28	12.26	16.62	16.84	15.12

All chi-square differences are different at 0.05 level

such construct which measures two or more variables at the same time. In empirical study, these two validities are widely used.

In summary, due to the complexity of the research, methodologies adopted in this study have to be of the nature of triangulation: qualitative approaches include hermeneutic methods, literature review, storytelling and narrative, interviews; and for quantitative approaches have to consist of questionnaire surveys with reasonable and acceptable Likert scales. Though SEM as a popular tool in current research, it is not suitable in this study. The most predominant approach adopted in this research is SPSS 11.5, which not at all affect the effectiveness and efficiency of the research results in this study.

REFERENCES

Ajzen, L., & Fishbein, M. (1970). *Understanding attitudes and predicting social behavior*. Englewood Cliffs, NJ: Prentice-Hall.

Allan, J. (2000). *Power of the tale*. John Wiley & Sons Publishing House.

Allman, J. L., Ohair, D., & Stewart, R. A. (1994). Stewart, R. Communication and Aging: A study of the Effects of Cohort-Centrism and Perceived Decoding Ability on Communication Competence and Communication Satisfaction. *Communication Quarterly, 42*(4), 363–376. doi:10.1080/01463379409369943

Allport, G. W. (1961). *Pattern and Growth in Personality*. New York: Holt, Rinehart & Winston.

Amado, G. (1999). Rivka. Bilateral Transformational Leadership: An Approach for Fostering Ethical Conduct in Public Service Organizations. *Administration & Society, 31*(2), 247–260. doi:10.1177/00953999922019111

Anderson, J. C., & Gerbing, D. W. (1988). Structural Equation Modeling in Practice: A review and Recommended Two-Step Approach. *Psychological Bulletin*, 103.

Antal, A. B., Lenhardt, U., & Rosenbrock, R. (2001). Barriers to Organizational Learning. In M. Dierkes, A. B. Antal, J. Child, & I. Nonaka (Eds.), *Handbook of Organizational Learning and Knowledge* (pp. 865–885). Oxford University Press.

Babbie, E. (2004). *The Practice of Social Research* (10th ed.). Belmont, CA: Wadsworth Publishing.

Bass, B. M. (1997). Does the transactional-transformational leadership paradigm transcend organizational and national boundaries? *The American Psychologist, 52*(2), 130–139. doi:10.1037/0003-066X.52.2.130

Bass, B. M., & Avlio, B. J. (1990). *Transformational Leadership Questionnaire*. Palo Alto, CA: Consulting Psychologists Press.

Boal, K.B., & Bryson, J.M. (1988). *Charismatic leadership: A phenomenological and structural approach*. Academic Press.

Boje, D. M. (1991). the storytelling organization: A study of story performance in an office-supply firm. *Administrative Science Quarterly, 36*(1), 106–126. doi:10.2307/2393432

Boje, D. M. (1995). Stories of the storytelling organization: A post-modern analysis of Disney as Tamara-Land. *Academy of Management Journal, 38*(4), 997–1035. doi:10.2307/256618

Boje, D. M., Luhman, J. T., & Baack, D. E. (1999). Hegemonic stories and encounters between storytelling organizations. *Journal of Management Inquiry, 8*(8), 340–360. doi:10.1177/105649269984002

Boomsma, A. (1982). Non-convergence, Improper Solutions and Starting Values in LISREL Maximum Likelihood Estimation. *Psychometrika*, 50.

Boyce, M. (1995a). Collective centering and collective sense-making in the stories and storytelling of one organization. *Organization Studies*, *16*(1), 107–137. doi:10.1177/017084069501600106

Boyce, M. (1995b). Organizational Story and Storytelling. *Critical Review*.

Brislin, R. W. (1986). The wording and translation of research instruments. In W. J. Lohner & J. W. Berry (Eds.), *Field methods in cross-cultural research* (pp. 137–164). Beverly Hills, CA: Sage Publications.

Brown, M. H. (1982). That reminds me of a story: Speech action on organizational socialization. University of Texas at Austin.

Brownlee, K. A. (1975). A note on the effects of non-response on surveys. *Journal of the American Statistical Association*, *52*(227), 29–32.

Bruner, J. (2002). *Making stories*. Harvard.

Buchanan, D., & Badham, R. (1999). *Power, politics and organizational change: winning the turf game*. London: Sage Publication.

Cannon-Bowers, J., & Sala, E. (1997). *A Framework for Developing Team Performance Measures in Training*. LEA London.

Carter. (2001, November 20). A tale of the unexpected: The journey of a white paper. *Knowledge Management*.

Czarniawska, B. (1997a). *Narrating the Organization: Dramas of Institutional Identity*. Chicago: University of Chicago Press.

David, W., & Hutchings, K. (2005). Cultural Embeddedness and Contextual Constraints: Knowledge Sharing in Chinese and Arab Cultures. *Knowledge and Process Management*, *12*(2), 89–98. doi:10.1002/kpm.222

Dawson, P. (2000). Technology, work restructuring and the orchestration of a rational narrative in the pursuit of Management objectives: The political processes of plant-level change. *Technology Analysis and Strategic Management*, *12*(1), 2000. doi:10.1080/095373200107229

Dawson, P. (2003b). Reshaping change: a processual approach. Routledge. doi:10.4324/9780203451830

Dawson, P. (2003-2004). *Organizational change stories and management research: Facts or fiction*. Academic Press.

Denning, S. (2000). *The Springboard: How Storytelling Ignites Action in Knowledge-era Organizations*. Butterworth-Heinemann.

Denning, S. (2001). The Springboard: How Storytelling Ignites Action in Knowledge-era Organizations. *Journal of Organizational Change Management, 14*(6), 609-614.

Denning, S. (2002). Using stories to spark organizational change. *Journal of Storytelling and Business Excellence*. Retrieved from http://www.storytellingcenter.com/articles.htm

Denning, S. (2002). *Organizational storytelling -- the narrative angle: the seven most valuable forms of organizational storytelling*. Academic Press.

Denning, S. (2002). The narrative lens: storytelling in the 21st century organizations. *Knowledge Directions, 3*(2), 92-101.

Fornell, C., & Larcker, D. F. (1981). Evaluating Structural Equation Models with Unobservable Variables and Measurement Error. *JMR, Journal of Marketing Research, 18*(1), 39–51. doi:10.2307/3151312

Forray, J.M. (2002, November). Temporal spans in talk: doing consistency to consult fiar organization. *Administrative Science Quarterly*.

Fröhlich, P., & Karandikar, H. (2002, March 18). Driving organisational change: Using story to transform work processes at ABB. *Knowledge Management*.

Gabriel, Y. (2000a). *Storytelling in organizations: an introduction*. Academic Press.

Gabriel, Y. (2000b). *Storytelling in organizations: Facts, fictions and fantasies*. Academic Press.

Gagliardi, P. (1986). The creation and change of organizational cultures: A conceptual framework. *Organization Studies, 7*(2), 117–134. doi:10.1177/017084068600700203

Gephart, R. P. Jr. (1991). Succession, sense making, and organizational change: A story of a deviant college president. *Journal of Organizational Change Management, 4*(4), 35–44. doi:10.1108/EUM0000000001196

Grundstein-Amado, R. (1999). Bilateral Transformational Leadership: An Approach for Fostering Ethical Conduct in Public Service Organizations. *Administration & Society, 31*(2), 247–260. doi:10.1177/00953999922019111

Hanges, P. J., Braverman, E. P., & Rentsch, J. R. (1991). Changes in raters impressions of subordinates: A catastrophe model. *The Journal of Applied Psychology, 76*(6), 878–888. doi:10.1037/0021-9010.76.6.878

Hannabuss, S. (2000). Narrative knowledge: eliciting organizational knowledge from storytelling. *Aslib Proceedings: New Information Perspectives, 52*(10), 402-413.

Hargies, O. (2003-2004). *Crisis Management and Organizational Communication.* Academic Press.

Homer, P. M., & Kahle, L. R. (1988). A Structural Equation of the Value-Attitude-Behavior Hierarchy. *Journal of Personality and Social Psychology, 54*(4), 638–646. doi:10.1037/0022-3514.54.4.638

House, R. J., Hanges, P., Ruiz-Quintanilla, S. A., & Dickson, M. W. (1997). *The development and validation of scales to measure societal and organizational culture.* Under review.

James, L. R., Demaree, R. G., & Wolf, G. (1984). Estimating within-group interrater reliability with and without response bias. *The Journal of Applied Psychology, 69*(1), 85–98. doi:10.1037/0021-9010.69.1.85

Jobber, D., Mirza, H., & Wee, K. H. (1991). Incentives and response rates to cross-national business surveys: A logit model analysis. *Journal of International Business Studies, 22*(4), 711–719. doi:10.1057/palgrave.jibs.8490852

Judge, T. A., & Bono, J. E. (2000). Five-Factor Model of Personality and Transformational Leadership. *The Journal of Applied Psychology, 85*(5), 751–765. doi:10.1037/0021-9010.85.5.751 PMID:11055147

Kahan, S. W. (2001). *Are you sitting comfortably? Using the power of storytelling to build communities* (Vol. 10). Knowledge Management.

Leana, C. R. (1987). Power Relinquishment vs. Power Sharing: Theoretical Clarification and Empirical Comparison of Delegation and Participation. *The Journal of Applied Psychology, 72*(2), 754–774. doi:10.1037/0021-9010.72.2.228

Leung, K., & Bond, M. H. (1989). On the empirical identification of dimensions for cross-cultural comparisons. *Journal of Cross-Cultural Psychology, 20*(2), 133–151. doi:10.1177/0022022189202002

Leung, K., & Bond, M. H. (1989). On the Empirical Identification of Dimensions for Cross-Cultural Comparison. *Journal of Cross-Cultural Psychology*, *20*(2), 133–151. doi:10.1177/0022022189202002

Li, J., & Tsui, A. (2002). A citation analysis of management and organization research in the Chinese context: 19841999. *Asia Pacific Journal of Management*, *19*(1), 87–107. doi:10.1023/A:1014891624018

Lumpkin, G. T., & Dess, G. G. (1996). Clarifying the entrepreneurial orientation construct and linking it to performance. *Academy of Management Review*, *21*(1), 135–172.

Lyness, K. S., & Kropf, M. B. (2007). Cultural values and potential non-response bias: A multilevel examination of cross-national differences in mail survey response rates. *Organizational Research Methods*, *10*(2), 210–225. doi:10.1177/1094428106291060

Maczynski, J. (1997). GLOBE: The Global Leadership and Organizational Behavior Effectiveness research program. *Polish Psychological Bulletin*, *28*(3), 215–254.

Marin, G., Triandis, H. C., Betancourt, H., & Kashima, Y. (1983). Ethnic affirmation versus social desirability: Explaining discrepancies in bilinguals responses to a questionnaire. *Journal of Cross-Cultural Psychology*, *14*(2), 173–186. doi:10.1177/0022002183014002003

Matsuda, Y. (1990). Survey systems and sampling designs of Chinese household surveys. *The Developing Economics*, (36), 329-352.

McAdams, D. P. (1997). *The stories we live by: personal myth and the making of the self.* Guilford Press.

McClelland, D. C. (1961). *The achieving society.* Princeton, NJ: Van Nostrand. doi:10.1037/14359-000

McClelland, D. C., & Atkinson, J. W. (1948). The projective expression of needs, I: The effect of different intensities of the hunder drive on perception. *The Journal of Psychology*, *25*(2), 205–222. doi:10.1080/00223980.1948.9917371

McFarland, L. J., Senen, S., & Childress, J. R. (1993). *Twenty-first-century leadership.* New York: Leadership Press.

Miller, D., & Droge, C. (1986). Psychological and traditional determinants of structure. *Administrative Science Quarterly, 31*(4), 539-560.

Misumi, J. (1985). *The behavioral science of leadership: An interdisciplinary Japanese research program*. Ann Arbor, MI: University of Michigan Press.

Morrison, R. S., & Jones, L. (1997). The Relation Between Leadership Style and Empowerment on Job Satisfaction of Nurses. *Occupational Health and Industrial Medicine, 37*(2), 62–63.

O'Connell, M. S., Lord, R. G., & O'Connell, M. K. (1990, August). *Differences in Japanese and American leadership prototypes: Implications for cross-cultural training*. Paper presented at the meeting of the Academy of Management, San Francisco, CA.

Peverill, S. (1988). Why the 1936 Literary Digest Poll failed?. *Public Opinion Quarterly*, (52), 125–133.

Ren, S., & Wood, R. (2015). Business leadership development in China. *Asia Pacific Business Review*. doi:10.1080/13602381.2015.1113658

Rokeach, M. (1973). *The nature of human values*. New York: Free Press.

Schein, E. H. (1992). *Organizational culture and leadership: A dynamic view* (2nd ed.). San Francisco: Jossey-Bass.

Schein, E. H. (1996). Three Cultures of Management: The Key to Organizational Learning. *Sloan Management Review, 38*(1), 9–21.

Schneider, B. (1987). The people make the place. *Personnel Psychology, 40*(3), 437–454. doi:10.1111/j.1744-6570.1987.tb00609.x

Schneider, B., Goldstein, H. W., & Smith, D. B. (1995). The ASA Framework: An update. *Personnel Psychology, 48*(4), 747–783. doi:10.1111/j.1744-6570.1995.tb01780.x

Sekaran, U. (1983). Methodological and theoretical issues and advancements in cross-cultural research. *Journal of International Business Studies, 14*(3), 61–73. doi:10.1057/palgrave.jibs.8490519

Shaw, J. B. (1990). A cognitive categorization model for the study of intercultural management. *Academy of Management Review, 15*(4), 626–645.

Sipe, W. P., & Hanges, P. J. (1997). Reframing the glass ceiling: A catastrophe model of changes in the perception of women as leaders. In R. G. Lord (Chair), *Dynamic systems, leadership perceptions, and gender effects*. Symposium presented at the Twelfth Annual Conference of the Society of Industrial and Organizational Psychology.

Smith, P. B., Misumi, J., Tayeb, M. H., Paterson, M., & Bond, M. H. (1989). On the generality of leadership style across cultures. *Journal of Occupational Psychology*, (30): 526–537.

Thompson, K. R., & Luthans, F. (1990). Organizational culture: A behavioral perspective. In B. Schneider (Ed.), *Organizational Climate and Culture* (pp. 319–344). San Francisco: Jossey-Bass.

Triandis, H. C. (1993). The contingency model in cross-cultural perspective. In M. M. Chemers & R. Ayman (Eds.), *Leadership theory and research: Perspectives and directions* (pp. 167–188). San Diego, CA: Academic Press.

Triandis, H. C. (1995). *Individualism and Collectivism*. Boulder, CO: Westview Press.

Walumbwa, F. O., Avolio, B. J., & Wang, P. (2005). Transformational Leadership and Work-Related Attitudes: The Moderating Effects of Collective and Self-Efficacy Across Cultures. *Journal of Leadership & Organizational Studies*, *11*(11), 2–16. doi:10.1177/107179190501100301

Yukl, G. A. (1994). *Leadership in organizations* (3rd ed.). Englewood Cliffs, NJ: Prentice-Hall.

Chapter 4
Empirical Testing Results

4.1 INFLUENCE OF VALUES SYSTEM AND DEMOGRAPHIC FACTORS ON LEADERSHIP STYLES

The factors which influence leadership styles to speak from the perspective of values system include gender, age, tenure, position, residential region, education level, nature of the enterprise, scale of the enterprise, as well as enterprise location.

The influential factors on leadership style include gender, age, tenure, position, residential region, education, nature of the enterprise, enterprise scale and enterprise location.

Among the influential factors on leadership styles, there are three kinds of variables to be considered during the investigation of the research: independent variables, mediate variables and moderate variables. Age, gender, rearing place and family background can be seen as the independent variables, as these factors are ingrained and can not be changed by people; while education level, nature of business sector, company location, position, tenure in the company, company size, business scope, etc. can work as mediate variables and moderate variables. No matter what sorts of variables, being part of human life, these factors lay influence on leadership styles at different degrees.

DOI: 10.4018/978-1-5225-2277-5.ch004

4.2 RELIABILITY TEST AND VALIDITY TEST

According to Churchill's (1979) paradigm for construct measurement, after defining the domain of values systems and the leadership styles measurement constructs and developing a measurement instrument, we need to test the reliability and validity of the constructs. The values orientation can be used to measure an individual's personal behaviors and can be worked as the benchmark for leadership profile; while the leadership style of an individual is the real behaviors one has expressed on the post of being a leader in different contexts. In our study, we want to test if there are cultural influences (values orientation) on the leadership styles. if it meets the requirements of reliability and validity (Chen and Paulraj, 2004). Reliability reflects the consistency or repeatability of measurement, which is a necessary but not sufficiency condition for validity. Validity is concerned with the extent to which a specific set of items reflects a content domain (DeVellis, 1991).

4.2.1 Reliability Test

To evaluate the internal consistency of the scales for reliability, we use the internal consistency method that is estimated using Cronbach's alpha and item-to-total analysis. Typically, reliability coefficients of 0.70 or higher and the item loading on the factors of 0.60 or higher are considered adequate (Hull and Nie, 1981).

For each of the items in this research, we calculated Cronbach reliability coefficient (alpha), and the item-to-total correlations for every item. As can be seen from Table 4 of Chapter 3, all Cronbach's alpha values of the factors are well above the critical value and ranged from 0.65 to 0.78, meanwhile the item loading on the factors are all acceptable. These results confirm the proposed research models meet the requirements of the internal consistency of the scales for reliability.

4.2.2 Validity Test

Evaluating validity helps to ensure that the items used to operationalize the construct actually measure what they are supposed to measure (Churchill, 1979). Validity includes unidimensinoality which estimates whether items reflect one but not more than one construct (Gerbing and Anderson, 1988), and construct validity which is the extent to which the items in a scale measure the abstract or theoretical construct (Carmines and Zeller, 1979). Testing of construct validity concentrates not only on finding out whether or not an item loads significantly on the factor it is measuring – convergent, but also on ensuring that it measures no other factors – discriminant (Campbell and Fiske, 1959). The following section will assess the three types of validity respectively.

4.2.3 Unidimensionality Test

Unidimensionality refers to the phenomenon that any index can indicate the only single variable but not multiple variables. Unidimensionality test must go along with the following two requirements: first, any one of the indicator has significant factor loading on the variable under testing; secondly, any one of the variable has no cross factor loading. That is to say, for any one of the indicator, it can not have significant factor loading on Factor A and at the same time, have significant factor loading on Factor B. According to this requirement, this research has adopted EFA (Exploratory Factor Analysis) to test the unidimensionality of each index. In the process of (EFA) Exploratory Factor Analysis, every variable has been analyzed and those that have factor loading less than 0.4 have been ticked off. Then, variable contained in this research have been gathered to conduct exploratory factor analysis, in the process of EFA, items with cross factor loading have been eliminated. in our research, there is not any single variable which has factor loading less than 0.4, and there is not items which have cross factor loading. This demonstrates that items we have used in this research have good unidimensionality.

There are two implicit conditions for establishing unidimensionality. First, an empirical item must be significantly associated with the empirical representation of a construct. Second, it must be associated with one and only one construct. Only when a measure satisfies both of these conditions, it can be considered unidimensional (Chen and Paulraj, 2004).

In this study, unidimensionality was established using confirmatory factor analysis (CFA). As recommended by researchers, multiple fit criteria were utilized to assess the tenability of the measurement models (Hu et al., 1992). The measures of model fit used in this study include the ratio of the chi-square statistic to the degrees of freedom (χ^2/d.f.), comparative fit index (CFI), normed fit index (NFI), non-normed fit index (NNFI), root mean square error of approximation (RMSEA). These fit indices considered are those most commonly recommended for this type of analysis (Bagozzi and Yi, 1988).

4.2.4 Convergent Validity

Convergent validity measures the similarity or the convergence between the individual items measuring the same construct. One way to test convergent validity is to use CFA. In CFA, convergent validity can be assessed by testing whether each individual item's standardized coefficient from the measurement model is significant, namely greater than twice its standard error (Gerbing and Anderson, 1988). In addition, according to Bollen (1989), the larger *t*-values or the standardized coefficients are, the stronger the evidence that the individual items represent the underlying factors. The results of CFA reveal that the standardized coefficients for all items greatly exceed twice their standard errors, and that the standardized coefficients for all variables are large (>0.6) and significant (all the t-values are larger than 2). Therefore, all items are significantly related to their underlying theoretical constructs.

4.2.5 Discriminant Validity

Discriminant validity measures the extent to which individual items intending to measure one latent construct do not at the same time measure a different latent construct (DeVellis, 1991).

In this study, discriminant validity is established using CFA. Models were constructed for all possible pairs of latent constructs. In this study, control variables are age, gender, permanent residential area, education level, position in the organization, tenure with the company, company scale, the ownership nature of the company, the nature of industry and company location; while independent variables are 10 dimensions of values orientation based on Schwartz's 57 value survey items, which specifically can be expressed as universalism (UNIVER. in short), power, hedonism, self-direction, security, stimulation, conformity, tradition, benevolence and achievement. To facilitate the arrangement of these terms in this dissertation, short forms are adopted as UNIVER., POWER, HEDO., S-DIR. SECU., STI., CONF., TRADI., BENEV., ACHIEV. respectively and the dependent variables in this research are the three kinds of leadership styles---- to be specific, autocratic leadership style, democratic leadership style and free reign leadership style.

4.2.6 Mediating and Moderating Effect in this Research

Mediating Effect

- **Mediate Variables:** also called mediators, which are the factors that play the role of mediator when independent variables have effect on dependent variables (Baron & Kenny,1986). The functioning mechanism of mediators can be illustrated in the figure below (2). When there is a void of mediator B, the effect of A on C is c; while there exists mediators, the effect of A to C is c', the effect of variable A on C through mediator B is ab, which demonstates that the effect of independent variable A on mediator B is a and the effect of mediator B on dependent variable C is the multiplication of a and b, which can be indicated as: c = c' + ab

In testing the mediating effect, it is necessary to investigate the relationship between A, B and C. suppose that there is high correlation between independent variable and dependent variable, when there exists a mediator between them, the correlation between the independent variable and dependent variable will decrease, which means that there is significant mediating effect. In other words, mediator can explain the relationship between independent variable and dependent variable effectively. According to Baron and Kenny(1986), if the following four conditions can be met, it means that there exists significant mediating effect: first of all, independent variable has significant effect on dependent variable; secondly, independent variable has significant effect on mediator; thirdly, mediator has significant effect on dependent variables; and lastly, when mediator has been introduced into the model, the effect of independent variable on dependent variable will decrease.

Figure 1. The effect of mediators

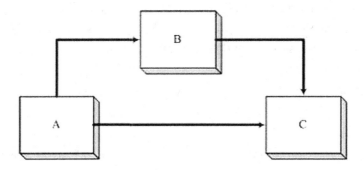

According to Wen Zhong'lin, Hou Jietai, Zhang Lei and others (2004), mediating effect is a kind of indirect effect. No matter there is latent variable or not, SEM or regression can be used to analyze and test the mediating effect, which the mediating effect can be compared

Moderate Effect

According to Baron, Kenny(1986)and Wen Zhong'lin(2004), if the relationship between variable A and C is the function of variable B, then B is called moderator. In other words, the relationship between variable C and A has been influenced by variable C. Such relationship can be demonstrated in the figure below (see Figure 2):

There are lots of approaches to test the moderating effect: some researchers have adopted the ANOVA analyses to test moderating effect, that is, to scrutinize the interaction between independent variable and other variables under different contexts (Baron & Kenny,1986). However, the most frequently used approach to test the moderating effect is called MRA (Moderated Regression Analysis) and normally, regression equations have been used to test the moderating effect of variables.

4.3 TESTING RESULTS FROM SVS (SCHWARTZ VALUES SURVEY)

First of all, we will investigate how the demographic factors influence the values systems of the participants in this study. In the research, we will probe the influences on an individual's values systems from the following

Figure 2. Illustration of moderating effect

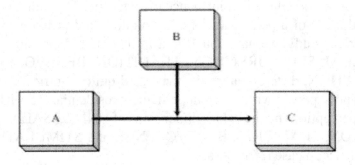

demographic factors. To be specific, gender, age, tenure, position, residential areas, education level, nature of the organizations, scale of the organization, as well as location of the organizations. We have adopted the single factor ANOVA analysis and the mean values have been compared, and then the sampled population have been queued according to the mean values.

4.3.1 The ANOVA Analysis of Age on Values Orientation

From the Table 1, it is obvious that values orientation in the values dimensions of POWER and SELF-DIRECITON, there are significant variances among different age groups, which means that different age groups have different perceptions on the value dimensions of POWER and SELF-DIRECITON (as can be seen in Table 1)

4.3.2 The ANOVA Analysis of Genders on Values System

Different sexes have different perceptions on different values dimensions. Males and females due to their ingrained differences, they demonstrate different orientations towards values dimensions. This can be testified empirically from our research as can be implied in Table 2. The testing results have embodied that in the values dimensions of POWER and STIMULATION, both male and female have transparent differences. (For more details, please refer to the Table 2 of this study).

4.3.3 The Impact of Permanent Residential Areas on Values Orientation

It can be seen as common knowledge, the place where people live permanently or at least for a long time during their whole life cycle especially before 15 years old will leave very profound footprints on the people in life habit, values orientation and even accents and such influences may embed deep in their blood which will influence the later life. Therefore, permanent residential areas of a person works as a unique brand or trademark. From this empirical study, we have found that in the value dimensions of UNIVERSALISM, SELF-DIRECTION, TRADITION, BENEVOLENCE and STIMULATION, different areas demonstrated quite significant variances. In other words, people with different permanent residential areas have rather different perceptions on the values dimensions of UNIVERSALISM, SELF-DIRECTION, TRADITION, BENEVOLENCE and STIMULATION. (for more evidence, please refer to Table 3).

Empirical Testing Results

Table 1. ANOVA analysis of ages on values

		Sum of Squares	df	Mean Square	F	Sig.
UNIVER	Between Groups	3.588	5	0.718	0.725	0.605
	Within Groups	761.075	769	0.990		
	Total	764.662	774			
POWER	Between Groups	15.419	5	3.084	2.169	0.056*
	Within Groups	1093.500	769	1.422		
	Total	1108.919	774			
HEDO	Between Groups	7.525	5	1.505	.968	0.436
	Within Groups	1195.070	769	1.554		
	Total	1202.595	774			
S_DIR	Between Groups	12.219	5	2.444	2.213	0.051*
	Within Groups	849.226	769	1.104		
	Total	861.445	774			
SECURI	Between Groups	2.600	5	0.520	0.556	0.734
	Within Groups	719.617	769	0.936		
	Total	722.217	774			
STIMUL	Between Groups	14.508	5	2.902	1.780	0.114
	Within Groups	1253.358	769	1.630		
	Total	1267.866	774			
CONFOR	Between Groups	2.809	5	0.562	0.589	0.709
	Within Groups	733.849	769	0.954		
	Total	736.658	774			
TRADI	Between Groups	10.161	5	2.032	1.415	0.216
	Within Groups	1104.068	769	1.436		
	Total	1114.229	774			
BENEV	Between Groups	4.384	5	0.877	0.937	0.456
	Within Groups	719.876	769	0.936		
	Total	724.260	774			
ACHIEVE	Between Groups	2.516	5	0.503	0.429	0.828
	Within Groups	901.338	769	1.172		
	Total	903.854	774			

Table 2. The ANOVA analysis of genders on values

		Sum of Squares	df	Mean Square	F	Sig.
UNIVER	Between Groups	0.021	1	0.021	0.021	0.883
	Within Groups	764.641	773	0.989		
	Total	764.662	774			
POWER	Between Groups	4.315	1	4.315	3.020	0.083*
	Within Groups	1104.604	773	1.429		
	Total	1108.919	774			
HEDO	Between Groups	2.958	1	2.958	1.906	0.168
	Within Groups	1199.637	773	1.552		
	Total	1202.595	774			
S_DIR	Between Groups	1.267	1	1.267	1.139	0.286
	Within Groups	860.178	773	1.113		
	Total	861.445	774			
SECURI	Between Groups	1.985	1	1.985	2.131	0.145
	Within Groups	720.232	773	0.932		
	Total	722.217	774			
STIMUL	Between Groups	4.568	1	4.568	2.795	0.095*
	Within Groups	1263.298	773	1.634		
	Total	1267.866	774			
CONFOR	Between Groups	0.115	1	0.115	0.121	0.728
	Within Groups	736.542	773	0.953		
	Total	736.658	774			
TRADI	Between Groups	1.957	1	1.957	1.360	0.244
	Within Groups	1112.272	773	1.439		
	Total	1114.229	774			
BENEV	Between Groups	0.000	1	0.000	0.000	0.992
	Within Groups	724.260	773	0.937		
	Total	724.260	774			
ACHIEVE	Between Groups	0.198	1	0.198	0.169	0.681
	Within Groups	903.656	773	1.169		
	Total	903.854	774			

Empirical Testing Results

Table 3. ANOVA analysis of permanent residential areas on value orientations

		Sum of Squares	df	Mean Square	F	Sig.
UNIVER	Between Groups	7.117	3	2.372	2.412	0.066*
	Within Groups	757.389	770	0.984		
	Total	764.507	773			
POWER	Between Groups	5.456	3	1.819	1.269	0.284
	Within Groups	1103.461	770	1.433		
	Total	1108.917	773			
HEDO	Between Groups	8.934	3	2.978	1.923	0.124
	Within Groups	1192.424	770	1.549		
	Total	1201.358	773			
S_DIR	Between Groups	11.598	3	3.866	3.503	0.015*
	Within Groups	849.763	770	1.104		
	Total	861.360	773			
SECURI	Between Groups	0.519	3	0.173	0.185	0.907
	Within Groups	720.624	770	.936		
	Total	721.143	773			
STIMUL	Between Groups	13.163	3	4.388	2.694	0.045*
	Within Groups	1254.225	770	1.629		
	Total	1267.388	773			
CONFOR	Between Groups	2.501	3	0.834	0.874	0.454
	Within Groups	734.151	770	0.953		
	Total	736.652	773			
TRADI	Between Groups	29.942	3	9.981	7.088	0.000*
	Within Groups	1084.251	770	1.408		
	Total	1114.193	773			
BENEV	Between Groups	7.290	3	2.430	2.610	0.050*
	Within Groups	716.822	770	0.931		
	Total	724.112	773			
ACHIEVE	Between Groups	4.054	3	1.351	1.156	0.326
	Within Groups	899.792	770	1.169		
	Total	903.845	773			

4.3.4 The Influence of Education Levels on Values Orientations

Education plays a key role in the whole life cycle of human beings. People are born with lots of features that are die-hard which can not be changed and eliminated, but education can work as a powerful tool in changing people's life. Therefore, we always say knowledge changes people's fortune but knowledge are mainly obtained through education. No boasting that education gives people second life. Due to different education background, people are definitely behaving very differently. Our empirical study has extremely strongly proved this statement. Among the ten value dimensions, people's education levels have very significant influence on eight value dimensions (as shown in Table 4). These eight values dimensions are: UNIVERSALISM, POWER, HEDONISM, SELF-DIRECTION, STIMULATION, CONFORMITY, TRADITION and BENEVOLENCE.

4.3.5 The Influence of Position on Values Orientations

Different positions of a person in an organization confer different decision powers and excel different attitudes towards their subordinates. These different power or position-driven behaviors can be traced back to their values orientations. Our empirical study has demonstrated that different position levels have significant variance in the perception of the following values dimensions: UNIVERSALISM, HEDONISM, SELF-DIRECTION AND STIMULATION (as can be shown in Table 5).

4.3.6 The Influence of Tenure on Values Orientations

People are environmental driven creatures; specific working environment will have profound influences on people in their attitudes, work habits, reflections to the external environment as well as their perceptions on security, achievement and other ideological factors. In this study, from the 778 Guinea pigs, we have found that different groups with different tenures in the working organizations have quite different values orientations in the following eight values dimensions: namely UNIVERSALISM, POWER, HEDONISM, SELF-DIRECTION, STIMULATION, TRADITION, BENEVOLENCE AND ACHIEVEMENT (as can be referred to Table 6).

Table 4. ANOVA analysis of education on values orientations

		Sum of Squares	df	Mean Square	F	Sig.
UNIVER	Between Groups	13.344	5	2.669	2.732	0.019*
	Within Groups	751.318	769	0.977		
	Total	764.662	774			
POWER	Between Groups	27.624	5	5.525	3.929	0.002*
	Within Groups	1081.296	769	1.406		
	Total	1108.919	774			
HEDO	Between Groups	36.069	5	7.214	4.756	0.000*
	Within Groups	1166.526	769	1.517		
	Total	1202.595	774			
S_DIR	Between Groups	21.643	5	4.329	3.964	0.001*
	Within Groups	839.802	769	1.092		
	Total	861.445	774			
SECURI	Between Groups	6.639	5	1.328	1.427	0.212
	Within Groups	715.578	769	0.931		
	Total	722.217	774			
STIMUL	Between Groups	39.801	5	7.960	4.985	0.000*
	Within Groups	1228.065	769	1.597		
	Total	1267.866	774			
CONFOR	Between Groups	17.366	5	3.473	3.713	0.003*
	Within Groups	719.291	769	.935		
	Total	736.658	774			
TRADI	Between Groups	30.091	5	6.018	4.269	0.001*
	Within Groups	1084.138	769	1.410		
	Total	1114.229	774			
BENEV	Between Groups	12.205	5	2.441	2.636	0.023*
	Within Groups	712.055	769	0.926		
	Total	724.260	774			
ACHIEVE	Between Groups	7.266	5	1.453	1.246	0.286
	Within Groups	896.588	769	1.166		
	Total	903.854	774			

Table 5. ANOVA analysis of positions on values orientations

		Sum of Squares	df	Mean Square	F	Sig.
UNIVER	Between Groups	7.455	3	2.485	2.495	0.059*
	Within Groups	732.076	735	.996		
	Total	739.531	738			
POWER	Between Groups	2.300	3	0.767	0.533	0.659
	Within Groups	1056.461	735	1.437		
	Total	1058.761	738			
HEDO	Between Groups	10.671	3	3.557	2.396	0.067*
	Within Groups	1091.086	735	1.484		
	Total	1101.756	738			
S_DIR	Between Groups	7.482	3	2.494	2.236	0.083*
	Within Groups	819.682	735	1.115		
	Total	827.165	738			
SECURI	Between Groups	5.684	3	1.895	1.984	0.115
	Within Groups	701.904	735	0.955		
	Total	707.588	738			
STIMUL	Between Groups	11.255	3	3.752	2.367	0.070*
	Within Groups	1164.890	735	1.585		
	Total	1176.145	738			
CONFOR	Between Groups	3.634	3	1.211	1.262	0.286
	Within Groups	705.598	735	0.960		
	Total	709.232	738			
TRADI	Between Groups	8.571	3	2.857	2.086	0.101
	Within Groups	1006.712	735	1.370		
	Total	1015.283	738			
BENEV	Between Groups	5.733	3	1.911	2.031	.108
	Within Groups	691.626	735	.941		
	Total	697.359	738			
ACHIEVE	Between Groups	6.485	3	2.162	1.856	0.136
	Within Groups	855.942	735	1.165		
	Total	862.427	738			

Empirical Testing Results

Table 6. ANOVA analysis of tenure on values orientations

		Sum of Squares	df	Mean Square	F	Sig.
UNIVER	Between Groups	14.325	5	2.865	2.936	0.012*
	Within Groups	750.337	769	0.976		
	Total	764.662	774			
POWER	Between Groups	15.486	5	3.097	2.178	0.055*
	Within Groups	1093.433	769	1.422		
	Total	1108.919	774			
HEDO	Between Groups	29.654	5	5.931	3.888	0.002*
	Within Groups	1172.941	769	1.525		
	Total	1202.595	774			
S_DIR	Between Groups	27.264	5	5.453	5.027	0.000*
	Within Groups	834.181	769	1.085		
	Total	861.445	774			
SECURI	Between Groups	3.588	5	0.718	0.768	0.573
	Within Groups	718.629	769	0.934		
	Total	722.217	774			
STIMUL	Between Groups	38.783	5	7.757	4.853	0.000*
	Within Groups	1229.083	769	1.598		
	Total	1267.866	774			
CONFOR	Between Groups	3.558	5	0.712	0.746	0.589
	Within Groups	733.100	769	0.953		
	Total	736.658	774			
TRADI	Between Groups	27.808	5	5.562	3.937	0.002*
	Within Groups	1086.421	769	1.413		
	Total	1114.229	774			
BENEV	Between Groups	13.152	5	2.630	2.844	0.015*
	Within Groups	711.109	769	0.925		
	Total	724.260	774			
ACHIEVE	Between Groups	12.206	5	2.441	2.105	0.063*
	Within Groups	891.647	769	1.159		
	Total	903.854	774			

4.3.7 The Influence of Organization Scale on Values Orientations

People who are working in organizations with different scales (total employees, total annual turnover, etc.) may create different feelings in self-esteem, self-actualization, etc. but how does company scale influences the values orientations of the staff? Our empirical study has shown that among the ten values dimensions, nine of them do not have significant influence on the perceptions of the staff. Only one value dimension UNIVERSALISM brings strong perceptions to peoples who are working in different scales of the organizations (as can be seen in Table 7).

4.3.8 The Influence of Company Nature on the Values Orientations

According to the questionnaires of SVS and leadership styles, participants have to choose from 12 categories of company natures such as SOE, collectively owned enterprises, joint ventures, private firms, etc. on the postulation that different natures of organizations will influence their employees differently in values orientations. Our empirical study has revealed that among different categories of company natures, they have demonstrated quite differently in the fowling five values dimensions: UNIVERSALISM, HEDONISM, STIMULATION, TRADITION AND BENEVOLENCE, while the company nature does not have significant influence on the perception of the other five values dimensions (for more details, please refer to Table 8).

4.3.9 The Influence of Industries on Values Orientation

Different industries have different features just as heavy manufacturing firms as steelmaking will be quite different from that of hi-tech firms like software developing firms. Due to the big differences of different industries, people who are working in such big contrasted firms will behave differently. In this empirical study, it is obviously found that different industries have demonstrated different perceptions in the following four value dimensions: POWER, SECURITY, CONFORMITY, TRADITION (as can be seen in Table 9).

Empirical Testing Results

Table 7. ANOVA analysis of company scales on values orientations

		Sum of Squares	df	Mean Square	F	Sig.
UNIVER	Between Groups	6.223	2	3.112	3.162	0.043*
	Within Groups	757.617	770	0.984		
	Total	763.840	772			
POWER	Between Groups	0.225	2	0.112	0.078	0.925
	Within Groups	1107.513	770	1.438		
	Total	1107.738	772			
HEDO	Between Groups	6.721	2	3.361	2.168	0.115
	Within Groups	1193.849	770	1.550		
	Total	1200.571	772			
S_DIR	Between Groups	4.569	2	2.284	2.054	0.129
	Within Groups	856.288	770	1.112		
	Total	860.857	772			
SECURI	Between Groups	1.011	2	0.506	0.541	0.583
	Within Groups	720.076	770	0.935		
	Total	721.087	772			
STIMUL	Between Groups	4.532	2	2.266	1.383	0.252
	Within Groups	1261.898	770	1.639		
	Total	1266.430	772			
CONFOR	Between Groups	2.221	2	1.111	1.166	0.312
	Within Groups	733.651	770	0.953		
	Total	735.872	772			
TRADI	Between Groups	1.681	2	0.841	0.584	0.558
	Within Groups	1107.608	770	1.438		
	Total	1109.289	772			
BENEV	Between Groups	1.227	2	0.614	0.655	0.520
	Within Groups	721.890	770	0.938		
	Total	723.118	772			
ACHIEVE	Between Groups	2.312	2	1.156	0.990	0.372
	Within Groups	898.849	770	1.167		
	Total	901.161	772			

Table 8. T he influence of nature of company ownership on values orientations

		Sum of Squares	df	Mean Square	F	Sig.
UNIVER	Between Groups	10.817	4	2.704	2.722	0.029*
	Within Groups	727.275	732	0.994		
	Total	738.092	736			
POWER	Between Groups	8.595	4	2.149	1.512	0.197
	Within Groups	1040.339	732	1.421		
	Total	1048.934	736			
HEDO	Between Groups	20.623	4	5.156	3.540	0.007*
	Within Groups	1066.156	732	1.456		
	Total	1086.779	736			
S_DIR	Between Groups	5.465	4	1.366	1.221	0.300
	Within Groups	819.097	732	1.119		
	Total	824.563	736			
SECURI	Between Groups	6.529	4	1.632	1.706	0.147
	Within Groups	700.272	732	0.957		
	Total	706.801	736			
STIMUL	Between Groups	26.171	4	6.543	4.167	0.002*
	Within Groups	1149.289	732	1.570		
	Total	1175.460	736			
CONFOR	Between Groups	7.194	4	1.798	1.887	0.111
	Within Groups	697.756	732	0.953		
	Total	704.950	736			
TRADI	Between Groups	21.044	4	5.261	3.872	0.004*
	Within Groups	994.500	732	1.359		
	Total	1015.544	736			
BENEV	Between Groups	9.226	4	2.306	2.470	0.043*
	Within Groups	683.454	732	0.934		
	Total	692.680	736			
ACHIEVE	Between Groups	6.382	4	1.596	1.370	0.243
	Within Groups	852.624	732	1.165		
	Total	859.006	736			

Empirical Testing Results

Table 9. Influence of industries on values orientations

		Sum of Squares	df	Mean Square	F	Sig.
UNIVER	Between Groups	8.632	9	0.959	0.964	0.469
	Within Groups	716.301	720	0.995		
	Total	724.934	729			
POWER	Between Groups	22.900	9	2.544	1.796	0.066*
	Within Groups	1019.982	720	1.417		
	Total	1042.883	729			
HEDO	Between Groups	11.397	9	1.266	0.846	0.574
	Within Groups	1077.652	720	1.497		
	Total	1089.049	729			
S_DIR	Between Groups	10.546	9	1.172	1.049	0.399
	Within Groups	804.245	720	1.117		
	Total	814.792	729			
SECURI	Between Groups	16.212	9	1.801	1.902	0.049*
	Within Groups	682.049	720	0.947		
	Total	698.261	729			
STIMUL	Between Groups	21.967	9	2.441	1.541	0.130
	Within Groups	1140.605	720	1.584		
	Total	1162.572	729			
CONFOR	Between Groups	14.448	9	1.605	1.690	0.088*
	Within Groups	684.028	720	0.950		
	Total	698.476	729			
TRADI	Between Groups	30.719	9	3.413	2.531	0.007*
	Within Groups	970.861	720	1.348		
	Total	1001.580	729			
BENEV	Between Groups	7.198	9	0.800	0.845	0.575
	Within Groups	681.710	720	0.947		
	Total	688.908	729			
ACHIEVE	Between Groups	10.530	9	1.170	1.014	0.427
	Within Groups	830.808	720	1.154		
	Total	841.337	729			

4.3.10 The Influence of Company Location on Values Orientations

Company location play a crucial role in business practices and sometimes company location works as a label even a fame to determine business success, however, as regards the values orientations; company locations are not as determinant as it works in marketing or sales. Our empirical study has clearly demonstrated that only one values dimension TRADITION is sensible to company locations and all other nine value dimensions are null sensible to company locations (for more can be perceived from Table 10).

In order to have a more straight-forward and simplistic picture of the influence of demographic factors on values orientations, the following diagram works well for this purpose (please refer to Figure 3):

4.4 TESTING RESULTS FROM LEADERSHIP STYLE SURVEY

The research on the correlations between values orientations and leadership styles is very challenging. Previous researches mainly focus on the separated topics on either values systems or leadership styles. However, there is seldom research which entwines them both together and sees it from comprehensive perspective. The most obvious reason might be that values system or cultural research is rather abstract and qualitative and the same is true of the researches on leadership styles as there is not a one-for-all model of leadership style to follow and it is hard for anyone to say one leadership style is better than the others.

As regarding the cultures and values research, the most famous giants like M. H. Bond, Schwartz, Hofstede and others have in their research eyed on the western context. Although M. H. Bond has developed a Chinese values survey, which is mainly derived from the ideas of Confucius thoughts (BVS), it is not as popular as that developed by Schwartz (SVS). Even when the author of this research has in person had a long talk and profound discussion with M. H. Bond, he finally suggested that the author should adopt SVS (Schwartz values survey as the instrument), which again indicates the importance and significance of this research as this research has been conducted for over two years to obtain 778 samples from the distributed 1000 questionnaires. The research findings, to some extent may fill the gap of the lack of research on Chinese values and the leadership styles of Chinese business leaders.

Empirical Testing Results

Table 10. Influence of company locations on values orientations

		Sum of Squares	df	Mean Square	F	Sig.
UNIVER	Between Groups	2.432	6	0.405	0.401	0.878
	Within Groups	730.677	723	1.011		
	Total	733.110	729			
POWER	Between Groups	9.910	6	1.652	1.153	0.330
	Within Groups	1035.356	723	1.432		
	Total	1045.266	729			
HEDO	Between Groups	6.006	6	1.001	0.665	0.678
	Within Groups	1088.198	723	1.505		
	Total	1094.204	729			
S_DIR	Between Groups	2.587	6	0.431	0.380	0.892
	Within Groups	820.207	723	1.134		
	Total	822.794	729			
SECURI	Between Groups	9.001	6	1.500	1.586	0.148
	Within Groups	683.994	723	0.946		
	Total	692.995	729			
STIMUL	Between Groups	5.248	6	0.875	.549	0.771
	Within Groups	1150.910	723	1.592		
	Total	1156.158	729			
CONFOR	Between Groups	6.838	6	1.140	1.181	0.314
	Within Groups	697.734	723	0.965		
	Total	704.573	729			
TRADI	Between Groups	29.296	6	4.883	3.615	0.002*
	Within Groups	976.607	723	1.351		
	Total	1005.903	729			
BENEV	Between Groups	7.948	6	1.325	1.394	0.214
	Within Groups	686.965	723	0.950		
	Total	694.913	729			
ACHIEVE	Between Groups	4.691	6	0.782	.664	0.679
	Within Groups	851.557	723	1.178		
	Total	856.249	729			

Figure 3. Correlations between demographic factors and values orientations

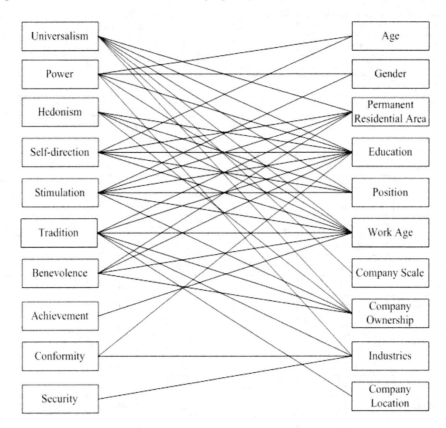

To speak from the research methodologies, in the past decade, SEM (Structural Equation Modeling) has become very hot in empirical research field. Even some scholars have summarized hundreds of papers from top tier journals to testify that SEM has been widely used in empirical research and there is a tendency of still roaring up in the research field. The author of this paper has been also intending to follow the trend, but the preliminary results obtained from SEM have shown that the testing results are not very attractive. Therefore, the author has to abandon SEM as the research methodology but still have puzzlement in mind. With this big puzzlement, the author has been to HK again to seek answers from one of the greatest giants in culture and leadership style research---M. H. Bond. As he suggested that it doesn't mean that every popular tool is good and appropriate in any research. As the most prominent feature of SEM is to find the correlations between multiple factors, it seems that SEM should be very suitable in this research. Actually, values survey and leadership styles survey to a large extent are very abstract and it is hard to use an absolute number to measure, though both of the questionnaires have themselves in 9 and 5 Likert scales respectively. Since the items of the surveys can not be absolutely measured, the correlations between cultural value factors and leadership styles can not be in a linear relation. Being a big giant in this research, none of his (M. H. Bond) papers have adopted SEM in research, though most of his papers have been released in top-tier journals. The failure in adopting SEM might result in the too mediocre culture of Chinese and also might be because the questionnaires adopted in this research are not very suitable to people in Chinese culture.

After this visit and magnificent discussion, my puzzlement has been eliminated and the author began to focus on the research by using another popular statistical tool --- SPSS. Though the research has not got significant results from SEM model, there are still lots of meaningful findings. Multiple factor analyses have indicated that Chinese business leaders have a unique but not clear-cut leadership style which revolves among the three leadership styles of autocratic, democratic and free-reign at the axles of Chinese core values. When the 778 samples have been displayed in Matlab graph, it again testifies that the core of the Chinese cultures and values systems is mediocre, as many of the dots are overlapping and most of the dots are concentrated in the middle part of the graph. Multiple factor analyses have demonstrated that there are strong correlations between cultural factors and leadership styles, but more have to be probed and investigated in the future research.

4.4.1 Optimal Clustering of Leadership Styles

778 samples is a large bundle and in order to facilitate processing the raw data, we have adopted a popularly used approach ----- the optimal clustering method to group the 778 samples according to the requirement of the optimal clustering theory. The grouping of the samples has followed the following steps:

Step 1: Pre-processing of raw data, 7 items (135, 220, 656, 711, 712 and 718) have been eliminated due to the items missing (Merisavo, M., Kajalo, S., Karjaluoto, H., Virtanen, V., Salmenkivi, S., Raulas, M., Leppäniemi, M. (2007), "An empirical study of the drivers of consumer acceptance of mobile advertising", Journal of Interactive Advertising, 13 p., available at: www.jiad.org/vol7/no2/merisavo/index.htm, Vol. 7 No.2)

Step 2: Cluster the pending groups by adopting the approach of Hierarchical cluster and calculate the the coefficient of each cluster. Theoretically, it is impossible to cluster 778 survey questionnaires into more than 9 groups; therefore, we only clustered the raw data into nine clusters.

Step 3: Calculate the degree of changes between the nearby two groups and the degree of changes between the adjunct two groups can be demonstrated by the coefficient of clusters, then we get the value for the degree of changes (the variance between the two adjunct clusters divided by the value of the second cluster in each pair, for example between clusters 1 and 2, we use 151.23 minus 136.03 and divided by 136.03, then we 11.2%), so on and so forth. The calculated results have been demonstrated in the tables below:

After the first stage of optimal clustering of leadership styles, we get (see Table 11):

From the above table, we have got the largest degree of changes between two groups is 16.9%, which means that the optimal clustering of the 778 samples should be 3 clusters and in this research of leadership styles, we have named them into style 1, style 2 and style 3. The relevant theory and top tier journal papers have also supported our findings that 778 samples can be grouped into three clusters after the optimal clustering analysis (for more details, please refer to JHY Yeung, W Selen, CC Sum, B Huo. 2006. Linking financial performance to strategic orientation and operational priorities: An empirical study of third-party logistics providers, Journal of Physical Distribution & Logistics Management. Vol. 36, issue 3, 210-230.)According to the clustering result, it is found that three kinds of leadership styles are the most appropriate.

After optimal clustering of samples, there appears such dispersion of samples (see Table 12).

After clustering, three kinds of leadership styles are shown in Table 13.

The ANOVA analysis on three different leadership styles can be demonstrated as shown in Table 14.

The testing results have indicated that the above clustering of leadership styles have significant variances. Therefore, such clustering is meaningful and valid.

Table 11.

No. of cluster	1	2	3	4	5	6	7	8	9
coefficient of cluster	151.23	136.03	116.33	102.01	93.49	88.6	86.7	80.5	77.76
change of		11.2%	16.9%	14.0%	9.1%	5.5%	2.2%	7.7%	3.5%

Table 12. Number of samples in each Cluster

Table 14.

Cluster	No.
1	290.000
2	329.000*
3	159.000

Sample Case	F-Value	Sig
1	55.1	0.00***
2	573.2	0.00***
3	123.1	0.00***

Table 13.

Sample Case	Autocratic	Democratic	Free Reign
1	30.68	33.69	29.07
2	31.53	39.34	33.82
3	37.19	41.74	38.86

ANOVA analysis on different sample clusters can be shown in Table 15. These results have shown that there are significant variances among different sample clusters, which again have testified the validity and magnificence of the optimal clustering of leadership styles.

Table 15.

		Sum of Squares	df	Mean Square	F	Sig.
S1	Between Groups	4517.362	2	2258.681	146.529	.000***
	Within Groups	11792.117	765	15.415		
	Total	16309.479	767			
S2	Between Groups	7983.385	2	3991.692	424.948	.000***
	Within Groups	7185.928	765	9.393		
	Total	15169.313	767			
S3	Between Groups	9816.276	2	4908.138	485.626	.000***
	Within Groups	7731.719	765	10.107		
	Total	17547.995	767			

ANOVA analyses on values orientations under optimal clustering of leadership styles (see Table 16).

This figure has revealed that most of the samples have been overlapped and vast majority of the samples are tending to concentrated in the middle part of the graph, which have side-supported the findings from the leadership survey based on optimal clustering and SPSS testing results. Maybe the sound explanation for such extreme convergence and concentration is that the value of mediocre has played a dominant role in Chinese leaders which have cognitively made them not to disclose their leadership styles transparently and openly. On the other hand, it also shows that Chinese business leaders have the odor of keeping themselves in the middle way which is supposed to be the safest position and also because of such middle way attitude; they have the flexibility to shift their leadership styles from one to another according to the changing contexts.

4.4.2 Analyses of Demographic Factors on the Leadership Styles

1. The Influence of Age on Leadership Styles

Leadership styles may alter with age, though there are lots of factors which can influence a person's leadership style. The ANOVA analyses have shown that there are significant variances in leadership styles 1 & 2 among different age groups but there is no obvious variance among different age group on leadership style 3, as can be shown in the Table 17.

Table 16.

	C1	C2	C3	F-Value	Sig
Universalism	6.4368	6.6464	6.6745	4.206	0.015
Power	5.9767	5.8731	6.1107	2.075	0.126
Hedonism	6.5586	6.6170	6.6745	0.447	0.640
Self-direction	6.2759	6.4369	6.4732	2.186	0.113
Security	6.6724	6.8047	6.8708	2.090	0.124
Stimulation	5.8908	6.0314	6.0291	1.082	0.339
Conformity	6.7690	6.8642	7.1007	5.323	0.005
Tradition	5.3600	5.3757	5.5866	2.002	0.136
Benevolence	6.6966	6.8717	6.9329	3.879	0.021
Achievement	6.5052	6.5927	6.7685	2.931	0.054

Figure 4. The distribution of 778 Leadership participants in Matlab graph.

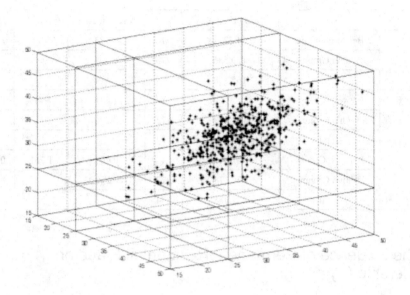

Table 17. The influence of age on leadership styles

		Sum of Squares	**df**	**Mean Square**	**F**	**Sig.**
STYLE1	Between Groups	4.417	5	0.883	4.223	0.001*
	Within Groups	160.842	769	0.209		
	Total	165.258	774			
STYLE2	Between Groups	2.253	5	0.451	2.299	0.043*
	Within Groups	150.746	769	0.196		
	Total	152.999	774			
STYLE3	Between Groups	1.965	5	0.393	1.721	0.127
	Within Groups	175.616	769	0.228		
	Total	177.581	774			

2. The Influence of Sexes on Leadership Styles

Leadership styles may alter with sexes, though there might be lots of factors which can influence a person's leadership style. In this research, our empirical research results (The ANOVA analyses) have shown that there are significant variances in leadership styles 1 & 2 among different sex groups, but there is no obvious variance among different age group on leadership style 3, as can be shown in the Table 18.

Table 18. The influence of gender on leadership styles

		Sum of Squares	df	Mean Square	F	Sig.
STYLE1	Between Groups	4.723	1	4.723	22.741	0.000*
	Within Groups	160.536	773	0.208		
	Total	165.258	774			
STYLE2	Between Groups	1.471	1	1.471	7.504	0.006*
	Within Groups	151.528	773	0.196		
	Total	152.999	774			
STYLE3	Between Groups	0.404	1	0.404	1.761	0.185
	Within Groups	177.178	773	0.229		
	Total	177.581	774			

3. The Influence of Permanent Residential Place on Leadership Styles

The permanent residential place may have influence on leadership styles due to the influential factors relating to geographic locations, though there are lots of factors which can influence a person's leadership style. The ANOVA analyses have shown that there are significant variances in leadership styles 1 & 2 among different age groups but there is no obvious variance among different age group on leadership style 3, as can be shown in the Table 19.

Table 19. The influence of permanent residential place on leadership styles

		Sum of Squares	df	Mean Square	F	Sig.
STYLE1	Between Groups	3.263	3	1.088	5.171	0.002*
	Within Groups	161.924	770	0.210		
	Total	165.187	773			
STYLE2	Between Groups	3.030	3	1.010	5.187	0.001*
	Within Groups	149.916	770	0.195		
	Total	152.945	773			
STYLE3	Between Groups	0.396	3	0.132	0.574	0.633
	Within Groups	177.027	770	0.230		
	Total	177.423	773			

4. The Influence of Education Levels on Leadership Styles

People with different education background behave differently even under the same contexts. People with higher education levels might have more power of knowledge in shifting from one leadership style to another according to the different circumstances. Through the empirical study of 778 samples, the ANOVA analyses have shown that there are significant variances in all the three leadership styles 1, 2 & 3 among different educational groups, as can be shown in the Table 20.

5. The Influence of Business Positions on Leadership Styles

People with different positions in the organization may have different leadership styles. In addition, different positions of the people in the business organization may have different perceptions towards different leadership styles. Our empirical study of 778 business leaders have shown that there are significant variances in all the three leadership styles 1, 2 & 3 among different positional groups in different business organizations, as can be shown in the Table 21.

6. The Influence of Tenures on Leadership Styles

People with different working experiences in business organizations may behave differently due to the degree of familiarity about the organization in which they are working. Do people among different tenure groups share the same or similar perception towards leadership styles? Through the empirical

Table 20. The influence of education levels on leadership styles

		Sum of Squares	df	Mean Square	F	Sig.
STYLE1	Between Groups	3.513	5	0.703	3.340	0.005*
	Within Groups	161.746	769	0.210		
	Total	165.258	774			
STYLE2	Between Groups	6.043	5	1.209	6.324	0.000*
	Within Groups	146.956	769	0.191		
	Total	152.999	774			
STYLE3	Between Groups	2.381	5	0.476	2.090	0.065*
	Within Groups	175.200	769	0.228		
	Total	177.581	774			

Table 21. The influence of business positions on leadership styles

		Sum of Squares	df	Mean Square	F	Sig.
STYLE1	Between Groups	9.919	3	3.306	16.926	0.000*
	Within Groups	143.569	735	0.195		
	Total	153.487	738			
STYLE2	Between Groups	1.679	3	0.560	2.992	0.030*
	Within Groups	137.469	735	0.187		
	Total	139.148	738			
STYLE3	Between Groups	4.167	3	1.389	6.292	0.000*
	Within Groups	162.248	735	0.221		
	Total	166.415	738			

study of 778 samples, the ANOVA analyses have shown that there are significant variances in all the three leadership styles 1, 2 & 3 among different tenure groups, as can be shown in the Table 22.

7. The Influence of Corporate Scales on Leadership Styles

People who are working in different corporate scales may have different feelings which enhance or weaken their personal perceptions in job security, career stability, self-esteem, self-actualization, etc. How about their perceptions towards leadership styles? Through the empirical study of 778 samples, the ANOVA analyses have shown that there are significant variances only

Table 22. The influence of tenure on leadership styles

		Sum of Squares	df	Mean Square	F	Sig.
STYLE1	Between Groups	4.735	5	0.947	4.537	0.000*
	Within Groups	160.523	769	0.209		
	Total	165.258	774			
STYLE2	Between Groups	2.394	5	0.479	2.445	0.033*
	Within Groups	150.605	769	0.196		
	Total	152.999	774			
STYLE3	Between Groups	3.603	5	0.721	3.185	0.007*
	Within Groups	173.978	769	0.226		
	Total	177.581	774			

on leadership style 2, but there are no significant variances in leadership style 1 and style 3 among different corporate scale groups, as can be shown in the Table 23.

8. The Influence of Nature of Company Ownership on Leadership Styles

People who are working with different corporate natures may behave differently and enjoy quite different perceptions in career development, self-pride, self-realization and even job security. How about their perceptions towards leadership styles among different groups of corporate nature? Through the real life business examples of 778 samples, the ANOVA analyses have shown that there are significant variances in the leadership styles 1 & 3 among different educational groups, but there are no transparent differences in leadership style 2, as can be shown in the Table 24.

9. The Influence of Industries on Leadership Styles

People who are working in different industries may have different feelings which might enhance or weaken their personal perceptions in job security, career stability, self-esteem, self-actualization, etc. What about their perceptions towards leadership styles? Through the empirical study of 778 samples, the ANOVA analyses have shown that there are significant variances in the first two kinds of leadership styles 1 & 2, but there are no significant variances in leadership style 3 among different industry groups, as can be shown in the Table 25.

Table 23. The influence of company scales on leadership styles

		Sum of Squares	df	Mean Square	F	Sig.
STYLE1	Between Groups	0.305	2	0.152	0.711	0.491
	Within Groups	164.951	770	0.214		
	Total	165.256	772			
STYLE2	Between Groups	0.932	2	0.466	2.366	0.095*
	Within Groups	151.693	770	0.197		
	Total	152.625	772			
STYLE3	Between Groups	0.102	2	0.051	0.222	0.801
	Within Groups	177.301	770	0.230		
	Total	177.404	772			

Table 24. The influence of nature of company ownership on leadership styles

		Sum of Squares	df	Mean Square	F	Sig.
STYLE1	Between Groups	2.097	4	0.524	2.552	0.038*
	Within Groups	150.344	732	0.205		
	Total	152.441	736			
STYLE2	Between Groups	0.264	4	0.066	0.348	0.846
	Within Groups	138.931	732	0.190		
	Total	139.195	736			
STYLE3	Between Groups	1.502	4	0.376	1.665	0.156*
	Within Groups	165.080	732	0.226		
	Total	166.582	736			

Table 25. Influence of industries on leadership styles

		Sum of Squares	df	Mean Square	F	Sig.
STYLE1	Between Groups	4.622	9	0.514	2.563	0.007*
	Within Groups	144.253	720	0.200		
	Total	148.875	729			
STYLE2	Between Groups	4.303	9	0.478	2.602	0.006*
	Within Groups	132.298	720	0.184		
	Total	136.600	729			
STYLE3	Between Groups	2.265	9	0.252	1.117	0.348
	Within Groups	162.168	720	0.225		
	Total	164.433	729			

10. The Influence of Corporate Locations on Leadership Styles

Corporate locations may provide quite different feelings for its employees. Taking into account the nature of the industry, the nature of the corporate and the nature of the market, corporate location can be very important factor for business success and sometimes even works as a key influential factor to attract talents as it enhance or weaken their personal perceptions in career opportunity, self-esteem, self-actualization, etc. How about their perceptions towards leadership styles? Through the empirical study of 778 samples, the ANOVA analyses have shown that there are significant variances only in the first kind of leadership styles 1, but there are no significant variances in leadership styles 2 and 3 among different corporate location groups, as can be shown in the Table 26.

As expressed in the above tables of this chapter, demographic factors influence leadership styles in one way or another. Some factors may have more significant correlations with a certain leadership style, while others may have less significant correlations with this leadership style. This again has demonstrated that the research is a complex with multiple considerations and the relations between leadership styles and demographic factors are in non-linear conditions. The following figure (Figure 5) illustrates the correlations between leadership styles and demographic factors in a much straight forward manner.

4.5 THE CORRELATIONS BETWEEN VALUES SYSTEM AND LEADERSHIP STYLES

Based on the specific analyses on values systems and leadership styles respectively, taking ten factors as the moderate and mediate variables (age, sex, permanent residential place, education level, position, tenure, corporate scale, corporate nature, industry nature, as well as corporate location), we have been doing further studies on the correlations between values system and leadership styles as a whole in a more comprehensive approach. Then we have got the following research results, as shown in Table 27.

The results have indicated that among then ten values dimensions, there are six value dimensions which have significant positive correlation with the first type of leadership style (that is, POWER, HEDONISM, STIMULATION,

Table 26. The influence of company locations on leadership styles

		Sum of Squares	df	Mean Square	F	Sig.
STYLE1	Between Groups	8.107	6	1.351	6.818	0.000*
	Within Groups	143.279	723	0.198		
	Total	151.386	729			
STYLE2	Between Groups	1.664	6	0.277	1.465	0.187
	Within Groups	136.869	723	0.189		
	Total	138.533	729			
STYLE3	Between Groups	1.022	6	0.170	0.750	0.610
	Within Groups	164.202	723	0.227		
	Total	165.224	729			

Figure 5. The correlations between demographic factors and leadership styles

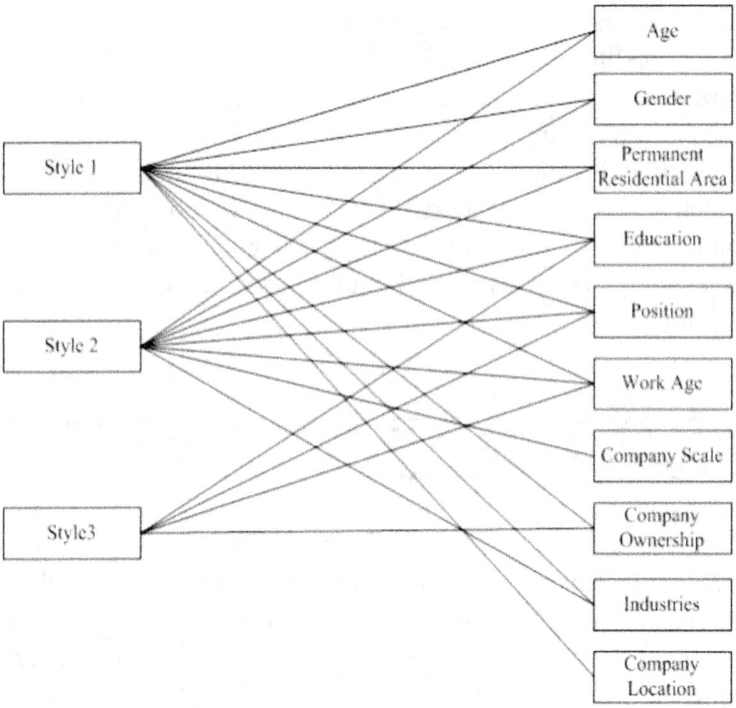

Table 27. The coefficient between values dimensions and leadership styles

	UNIVER	POWER	HEDO	S_DIR	SECURI	STIMUL	CONFOR	TRADI	BENEV	ACHIEVE
STYLE1	-0.017	0.156***	0.062+	0.039	0.009	0.066+	0.071*	0.114**	0.034	0.108**
STYLE2	0.090*	0.045	0.028	0.133***	0.107**	0.083*	0.157***	0.045	0.140***	0.140***
STYLE3	0.052	0.044	-0.016	0.077*	0.015	0.034	0.116**	0.072*	0.083*	0.105**

Note:***$\alpha = 0.001$,**$\alpha = 0.01$,**$\alpha = 0.05$,+$\alpha = 0.10$

CONFORFORMITY, TRADITION & ACHIEVEMENT correlate to leadership style 1: autocratic style); While value dimensions UNIVERSALISM, SELF-DIRECTION, SECURITY, STIMULATION, CONFORMITY, BENEVOLENCE AND ACHIEVEMENT have significant and positive correlations with the leadership style 2 (democratic style) and value dimensions SELF-DIRECTION, CONFORMITY, TRADITION, BENEVOLENCE and ACHIEVEMENT have significant and positive correlations with the third type of leadership style ---the free reign style. To have a straight forward

Figure 6. The interactions between leadership styles and values orientations

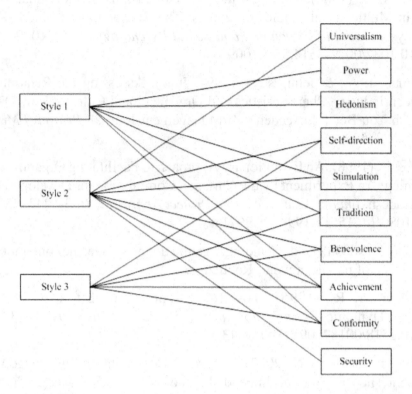

picture of the correlations between leadership styles and values orientations, we have designed the following chart for visual investigation (please refer to Figure 6 for more details):

REFERENCES

Adler, N. J., Campbell, N., & Lauren, A. (1989). In search of appropriate methodology: From outside the Peoples Republic of China looking in. *Journal of International Business Studies*, *20*(1), 61–74. doi:10.1057/palgrave. jibs.8490351

Barnett, J. H., & Karson, M. J. (1987). Personal Values and Business Decision: An Exploratory Investigation. *Journal of Business Ethics*, *17*(5), 371–382. doi:10.1007/BF00382894

Bond, M. H. (1988). Finding Universal Dimensions of Individual Variation in Multicultural Studies of Values: The Rokeach and Chinese Value Surveys. *Journal of Personality and Social Psychology*, *55*(6), 1009–1015. doi:10.1037/0022-3514.55.6.1009

Chatman, J. A., & Jehn, K. A. (1994, June). Assessing the Relationship between Industry Characteristics and Organizational Culture: How Different Can You Be? [J]. Academy of Management Journal. *Briarcliff Manor*, *37*(3), 522–532.

Davies, R. (1998). An Evolutionary Approach to Facilitating Organizational Learning: An Experiment by the Christian Commission for Development in Bangladesh. *Impact Assessment and Project Appraisal*, *16*(3), 243–250. do i:10.1080/14615517.1998.10590213

Dawson, P. (2003a). Understanding organizational change: the contemporary experience of people at work. Routledge.

Endsley, M. R. (1995). Towards a Theory of Situation Awareness in Dynamic System. *Journal of Human Factors*, *1*(37), 32–64. doi:10.1518/001872095779049543

Glisby, M., & Holden, N. (2003). Contextual Constraints in Knowledge Management Theory: Cultural Embeddedness of Nonakas Knowledge Creating Company. *Knowledge and Process Management*, *10*(1), 29–36. doi:10.1002/kpm.158

Hope, V., & Henry, J. (1995). Corporate Cultural Change---Is It Relevant for Organizations of the 1990s?. *Human Resource Management Journal*, *5*(4), 61–73. doi:10.1111/j.1748-8583.1995.tb00383.x

Hult, G. T. M., & Hurley, R. F. (2000). Leadership and Relationship Commitment: A Focus on the Supplier-Buyer-User Linkage. *Industrial Marketing Management*, (29), 111-119.

Jacovs, T. O., & Jaques, E. (1990). Military Executive Leadership. In K. E. Clark & M. B. Clark (Eds.), *Measures of Leadership* (pp. 281–295). West Orange, NJ: Leadership Library of America.

Keller, G. F., & Kronstedt, C.R. (2005). *Connecting Confucianism, communism and the Chinese culture of commerce*. Academic Press.

Kerr, S., Schriesheim, C. A., Murphy, C. J., & Stogdill, R. M. (1974). Toward a Contingency Theory of Leadership Based upon the Consideration and Initiating Structure Literature. *Organizational Behavior and Human Performance, 12*(1), 62–82. doi:10.1016/0030-5073(74)90037-3

Kipnis, D., Schmidt, S.R., & Wilkinson, I. (1980). Intra-organisational Influence Tactics: Explorations in Getting One's Way. *Journal of Applied Psychology, 65*, 440-52.

Kogut, B., & Zander, U. (1993). Knowledge of the Firm and the Evolutionary Theory of the Multinational Corporation. *Journal of International Business Studies, 24*(4), 625–646. doi:10.1057/palgrave.jibs.8490248

Kotter, J. (1996). *Leading Change.* Harvard Business School Press.

Kotter, J. (1997). *Realizing Change.* Harvard Business School Press.

Leana, C. R. (1986). Predictors and Consequences of Delegation. *Academy of Management Journal, 29*(4), 228–233. doi:10.2307/255943

Lewis, P. V. (1975). *Organizational Communications: The Essence of Effective Management.* Grid.

McCauley, C. D., & Brutus, S. (1998). *Management development through job experiences: An annotated bibliography.* Greensboro, NC: Center for Creative Leadership.

McFarland, L. J., Senen, S., & Childress, J. R. (1993). *Twenty-first-century leadership.* New York: Leadership Press.

Miller, D. (1991). *Handbook of Research Design and Social Measurement.* Newbury Park, CA: Sage Publication.

Miller, D., & Droge, C. (1986). Psychological and traditional determinants of structure. *Administrative Science Quarterly, 31*(4), 539-560.

Misumi, J. (1985). *The behavioral science of leadership: An interdisciplinary Japanese research program.* Ann Arbor, MI: University of Michigan Press.

Mohan, T. (2000). Leadership Styles in Information Technology Projects. *International Journal of Project Management,* (8): 235–241.

O'Connell, M. S., Lord, R. G., & O'Connell, M. K. (1990, August). *Differences in Japanese and American leadership prototypes: Implications for cross-cultural training.* Paper presented at the meeting of the Academy of Management, San Francisco, CA.

Pierce, J. L., Kostova, T., & Dirks, K. T. (2001). Toward a Theory of Psychological Ownership in Organizations. *Academy of Management Review*, *26*(2), 298–311.

Podsakoff, P. M., Mackenzie, S. B., Moorman, R. H., & Fetter, R. (1990). Transformational Leader Behaviors and Their Effects on Trust, Satisfaction and Organizational Citizenship Behavior. *The Leadership Quarterly*, (1), 107–142. doi:10.1016/1048-9843(90)90009-7

Putnam, R. D. (1993). *Making democracy work*. Princeton, NJ: Princeton University Press.

Reed, R., & DeFillippi, R. J. (1990). Casual Ambiguity, Barriers to Imitation and Sustainable Competitive Advantage. *Academy of Management Review*, (15), 88–102.

Rokeach, M. (1973). *The nature of human values*. New York: Free Press.

Roy, A., Walters, P. G. P., & Luk, S. T. K. (2001). Chinese puzzles and paradoxes: Conducting business research in China. *Journal of Business Research*, *52*(2), 203–210. doi:10.1016/S0148-2963(99)00071-5

Schein, E. H. (1992). *Organizational culture and leadership: A dynamic view* (2nd ed.). San Francisco: Jossey-Bass.

Schneider, B. (1987). The people make the place. *Personnel Psychology*, *40*(3), 437–454. doi:10.1111/j.1744-6570.1987.tb00609.x

Schneider, B., Goldstein, H. W., & Smith, D. B. (1995). The ASA Framework: An update. *Personnel Psychology*, *48*(4), 747–783. doi:10.1111/j.1744-6570.1995.tb01780.x

Schwartz, S. H. (1990c). *Thoughts in Response to Cross-Cultural Applications and Critiques*. Paper Presented at the 10th International Association of Cross-Cultural Psychology Congress, Nara, Japan.

Shaw, J. B. (1990). A cognitive categorization model for the study of intercultural management. *Academy of Management Review*, *15*(4), 626–645.

Staw, B. M., Sandelands, L. E., & Dutton, J. E. (1981). Threat-rigidity effects in organizational behavior: A multilevel analysis. *Administrative Science Quarterly*, *26*(4), 501–524. doi:10.2307/2392337

Stening, B. W., & Everett, J. E. (1984). Response styles in a cross-cultural managerial study. *The Journal of Social Psychology*, *122*(2), 151–156. doi: 10.1080/00224545.1984.9713475

Thompson, K. R., & Luthans, F. (1990). Organizational culture: A behavioral perspective. In B. Schneider (Ed.), *Organizational Climate and Culture* (pp. 319–344). San Francisco: Jossey-Bass.

Triandis, H. C. (1993). The contingency model in cross-cultural perspective. In M. M. Chemers & R. Ayman (Eds.), *Leadership theory and research: Perspectives and directions* (pp. 167–188). San Diego, CA: Academic Press.

Veiga, J., Lubatkin, M., Calori, R., & Very, P. (2000). Measuring Organizational Culture Clashes: A Two-Nation Post-Hoc Analysis of a Cultural Compatibility Index. *Human Relations*, *53*(4), 539–557. doi:10.1177/0018726700534004

Vroom, V. H., & Yetton, P. W. (1973). *Leadership and Decision Making*. Pittsburgh, PA: University of Pittsburg Press.

Yukl, G. A. (1994). *Leadership in organizations* (3rd ed.). Englewood Cliffs, NJ: Prentice-Hall.

Zack, H. (1999). Managing Codified Knowledge. *Sloan Management Review*, *4*(40), 45–58.

Chapter 5
A Case Study

5.1 WHY CASE STUDY HAS BEEN ADOPTED IN THIS LEADERSHIP RESEARCH?

Theories that come from real world phenomena and can again be applied in real world practices have been regarded as valid and reliable theories. As a very effective approach, case study has been widely used in scientific research. Any theory and hypotheses have to be testified by facts. These facts may come from scientific experiments, and they can also be from case studies. Case studies provide vivid, real lifelike examples, especially in lots of social science research projects, like leadership research. Leadership research as a holistic and abstract topic needs qualitative data to support, apart from quantitative data as depicted in large spaces in the previous chapters. Due to its richness in details, vivid implementation in practice, case study can work as an efficient and effective tool to strengthen and enhance the theoretical suppositions. In order to consolidate the hypotheses proposed in this research, this chapter provides a case study in which the leadership styles of the CEO of a firm has been excavated and investigated from a deeper and wider perspective.

DOI: 10.4018/978-1-5225-2277-5.ch005

5.2 ORGANIZATIONAL STORYTELLING APPROACH

The purpose of fishing net is to catch fish. When fish is caught, the net is forgotten; the purpose of a rabbit snare is to catch rabbit. When rabbit is caught, the snare is forgotten…

The purpose of a story is to entertain the audience, share the personal experiences, exchange information, transmit knowledge, shape and reshape the organizational change programs… A good story will never die. ----

Even a scientist admits, "Knowledge can not be captured via a formula or an equation"

Stories are the best ways to handle complexity, ambiguity, uncertainty and rapid changes within organizations (Allan, J. et.al. 2000).

Traditionally, organizational communications have had a tendency to be somewhat dry and lacking in inspiration. Storytelling uses ranges of techniques to engage, involve and inspire people, using language that is more authentic (opposed to textbook "buzzword" speak) and a narrative form that people find interesting and fun. (http://www.creatingthe21stcentury.org)

Stories make experience meaningful, stories connect us with one another; stories make the character come alive; stories provide an opportunity for a renewed sense of organizational community. (Dawson, P. 2003:p128, quoted from Boje and Dennehy 1993:18)

Storytelling in organizations is a hot topic nowadays. As an ancient form of art, the glittering of storytelling has been re-discovered from the last decade. Quite a number of studies and researches have been conducted in this field and many advantages derived from the practice of organizational storytelling have been recognized. Based on the literature pertinent to this area, the article has revealed some of the significant impacts which storytelling embodies on the modern organizations. Such as, the advantages of storytelling over the abstract thinking; the reasons why modern organizations have the necessities to use storytelling; the efficiency and effectiveness which storytelling shows in organizational communications; how powerful storytelling is as a mechanism for sharing knowledge and experiences; and lastly, the dynamic relationships and triangulation between organizational change activities, the stories implied from those change programs and their contributions to the verification of organizational change theory has been probed briefly.

Human beings are born storytellers and listeners. According to some expertise study, at the age of two, human beings begin to listen to stories and tell stories. Storytelling as an ancient form of sharing information has a long history. For the ancient cavemen, the world was a strange and unexpected place to live. Storytelling around campfires enabled the village to pool information about baffling problems that faced the village, such as why the wild wolves were attacking and why the crops failed or why the weather was so harsh, so dry or so wet, so on and so forth. As human beings began to master these things over the last couple of thousands of years, they started to feel as though they understood what was going on. Now, the world is becoming turbulent and uncertain, and things are looking unexpected. Once again, human beings feel the urge to sit around a "conceptual campfire" and swap stories. Therefore, this very old art of storytelling resonates with us and come back again.)

Storytelling is pervasive in modern organizations. Human beings live in a story void. Everyday, they are surrounded by big or small stories to make life work. The big stories make sense of the groups or systems within which they are part of; while small stories deal with precise roles of each individual in a great context. When human beings were born, they utilize a very simplistic and straightforward way of learning---storytelling, but when they grew up, coming into the gate of schools, they were taught abstract theories, concepts and ideologies whereas stories are regarded as something only for children— stories are seen as a nickname for simplicity and being naive. Actually, human beings have been losing something, which is precious and effective for learning knowledge and exchanging information. As a "precious jade", stories have been buried deep into the earth for many years. Not hopelessly, the charms and attractions of storytelling as an art to exchange experience and transfer knowledge have been re-recognized in the last decade. This "lost–but-found treasure" has been re-glittering in many ways today, though there is a huge cultural, social, intellectual, political and financial superstructure that has a vested interest in favoring abstract thinking and communication which is hostile to narrative thinking and narrative modes of communication.

As organizations start their knowledge journey, they inevitably find great difficulties in communicating complicated ideas through abstract forms of communication. This is even more true where this knowledge journey also implies large-scale changes in behavior and understanding of the mission of the organization. Telling stories that build on real knowledge sharing situations enables individuals to gather in some of the understanding of the storyteller as well as recast the story into their own contextual work environment; hence adding their own understanding to the process, as Dawson P. (2003-2004) proposes the three key roles as a processual researcher: a storyteller, a chronicler and an analyst. Organizations are finding that the marriage of narrative and abstract communications provides a more powerful tool for sharing knowledge than merely abstract communications.

In many ways, abstract thinking has served the world well. But it is an approach with diminishing returns in a period of massive turbulence. As the organizations enter the 21st Century, there has been a growing recognition that abstract thinking alone doesn't help much in coping with a rapidly changing world, where innovation is the key to success. Innovation, what Dyson calls as "the creative chaos" (Denning, S. 2002) and Joseph S. called it "destructive creativity" (the Economist, June 1996). It breeds on the connections between things. As participants, firms can grasp the inter-relatedness of things in the world and so are able to connect them in new ways --- much more readily than when it has been seen as an external observer through the window of rigid analytic propositions.

5.3 STORYTELLING AND ORGANIZATIONAL COMMUNICATION

It has been unanimously agreed that when used effectively, storytelling offers numerous advantages in organizational communications, comparing with the more traditional organizational communication techniques. Stephen Denning (2002) has concluded the advantages of storytelling in organizational communication over some conventional communication tools:

- Stories communicate ideas holistically, conveying a rich yet clear message, and so they are an excellent way of communicating complicated ideas and concepts in an easy-to-understand form.
- Stories therefore allow people to convey tacit knowledge that might otherwise be difficult to articulate. In addition, because stories are told with feelings, they can allow people to communicate more than they realize they know. Thus "organizational storytelling generates creativity and safely allows suppressed emotions to surface" (Allan, J. 2000).
- Storytelling provides the context in which knowledge arises as well as the knowledge itself, and hence can increase the likelihood of accurate and meaningful knowledge transfer (Jones, R. et.al. 2003).
- Stories are an excellent vehicle for learning, as true learning requires interest which abstract principles and impersonal procedures rarely provide.
- Stories are memorable - their messages have the feature of being 'sticky' and the audience can be easily indulged in it.
- Stories can provide a 'living, breathing' example of how to do something and why it works rather than telling people what to do, hence people are more open to their lessons.

- Stories therefore often lead to direct action - they can help to close the 'knowing-doing gap' (the difference between knowing how to do something and actually doing it).
- Storytelling can help to make organizational communication more 'human' – not only do they use natural day-to-day language, but they also elicit an emotional response as well as thoughts and actions.
- Stories can nurture a sense of community and help to build relationships. This point has its unique significance in today's organizations. Just as Owen Hargies (Hargies, O. et al 2004) stated there is no such a great hero who could save everyone from the catastrophe. "Today's Captain Kirk relies on the network of teams, which are well organized, highly promoted, trained and committed to the goal of organizations". Stories and storytelling helps establish team identification, group norms and cohesion and facilitate organizational performance.
- People enjoys sharing stories – stories enliven and entertain. With the organizational downsizing and de-layering, workplace stress and pressure has been increasing. Employees are desperate and struggling in their workplaces. Organizational stories can become a powerful vehicle for employees' entertainment, job enrichment and satisfaction. Hence employee morale can be increased, organizational vision and mission strengthened and productivity increased. (Hargies, O. et al 2004)

5.4 STORYTELLING VS LEADERSHIP

How stories could help leaders define their personality for their followers, boosting their confidence in the leader's integrity and providing some ideas of how they might act in a given situation.

The ability to tell the right story at the right time is emerging as an essential leadership skill.

The age-old practice of storytelling is one of the most effective tools leaders can use. But they need to pick their stories carefully and match them to the situation. Though good business arguments are developed through use of numbers, they are typically approved on the basis of a story. Storytelling can translate those dry and abstract numbers into compelling pictures of a leader's goals. (Stephen Denning HBR May 2004)

Stories fulfill a profound human need to grasp the patterns of living---not merely as an intellectual exercise, but within a very personal and emotional experience. One of the principles of good storytelling is the understanding that we are all living in dread. Fear is when you do not know what's going to happen. Dread is what's going to happen and there is nothing you can do to stop it. Organizations do the same thing: they deny the existence of the negative while inflicting their dread on other institutions or their employees. "We follow people in whom we believe"---Storytelling that moves people's fear and increase the organizational productivity (Robert Mckee, HBR June 2003)

Is it alright that CEOs have to sit at the head of the table or in front of the microphone and navigate their companies through the storms of bad economies and tough competition? No, a great CEO is somebody who has come to terms with his own mortality and as a result, has compassion for others. This compassion is expressed in stories. Self-knowledge is the root of all great storytelling,. The more you understand your own humanity, the more you can appreciate the humanity of others in all their good-versus-evil struggles. Humans have self-insight and self-respect balanced by skepticism. … Great storytellers, great leaders are skeptics who understand their own mask as well as the masks of life, and this understanding makes them humble.

Persuasion is the central-piece of business activity. Executives can engage listeners on a whole new level if they toss their PowerPoint slides and learn to tell good stories. There are two ways to persuade people: the first is by using conventional rhetoric, which is what most executives are trained in---it's an intellectual process. The other way to persuade people and ultimately a much more powerful way is by uniting an idea with an emotion---the best way to do so is by telling a compelling story. If you can harness imagination and the principles of a well-told story, then you get people rising to their feet amid thunderous applause instead of yawning and ignoring you. (Robert Mckee, June HBR)

Boyce (1996) suggested 6 reasons why shared storytelling is important across all organizational levels: 1) Allow organizational members and clients to express their experience; 2) Confirm shared experiences and meaning of individuals and groups within an organization; 3) Stories are also devices for orienting and socializing organizational members, and for altering or amending organizational reality; 4) Telling stories allow organizational purposes to be developed, shared and reviewed; 5) Storytelling prepares groups for planning and decision-making in line with shared purposes; 6) It can play a major role in co-creating vision and strategy.

Carolyn *et.al.* in Storytelling: a Tool for Leadership to shape culture has pointed out that storytelling can be a powerful tool to influence others. Storytelling empowers trust, build relationship, shape culture, assist both leaders and staff in reaching strategic goals of an institution. Leadership is about creating vision, inspiring those you lead to take on that vision, and providing the knowledge tools, and inspirations and through the efforts of those you lead.

Effective leaders are often recognized for how they perform in 5 areas: ideas, values, energy, edge and storytelling. Leadership in general lies in the ability of leaders to get one or more individuals to perform in a certain way, to move in a certain direction, to meet certain performance metrics, perhaps even to accomplish what might first appear to be impossible goals. Ideas form the basis for action plans to achieve future state; values are about those things that are important to an individual, a group and an organization; energy is the investment the leaders regularly make in creating and sustaining a well-run organization, streamlining processes, work-flows, improving communications, recognizing excellent performance and creating a sense of urgency about what is needed to be successful all define the energy it takes to propel an organization forward; edge is about making tough decisions and sticking to that; storytelling is perhaps the most important area. It has to do with the ability of leaders tell stories that touch people's emotions as well as their intellects. (Tichy 2002)

Effective stories should 1) Spark action that allows listeners to imagine a "what if" scenario; 2) Communicate "who am I" story which in turn would lead to 3) "Who we are" in organizational stories. That will transmit values and incorporate collaboration into stories that build rapport and prompt discussions. Staff in organization knows storytelling is part of the culture. They are encouraged to submit their stories for different events; stories submitted by staff prior to their performance review describe their practice (Sue Ellen Pinkerton 2006)

Leadership can be as simple as stamp collecting and can be as difficult as getting a PhD in history. Scott W. Spreier et.al has identified 6 leadership styles as directive, visionary, affiliative, participative, pace setting and coaching. For directive, which entails strong even coercive behavior; for visionary, which focuses on clarity and communication; affiliative, which emphasizes harmony and relationship; participative, which is collaborative and democratic; pace-setting which is personalized by personal heroics an coaching which focuses on long-term development and mentoring. (Scott w. Spreier, et.al. Leadership Run—Amok June HBR)

In "Simple Heuristics that make us smart" by Murrary Gell-Mann (Oxford University Press 2000) is clearly expounded that the most valued personal trait in the 21 century would be a facility for synthesizing information. The ability to decide what information to heed, what to ignore and how to organize and communicate that which we judge to be important is becoming a core competence for those living in the developed world. This means that leaders have to find an effective and efficient way to transmit information within an organization at least and the best way to do so is through storytelling.

Many researches and studies have been accomplished for the last decade in the field of storytelling and organizational management. Those studies and research findings have strongly revealed that storytelling in organizations play a very unique role in exchanging information, sharing knowledge and experiences, facilitating organizational communication, building trust, cultivating social and group norms, transferring tacit knowledge, facilitating unlearning and generating emotional connections... The curiosity about the relationship between the organizational change activities, the stories generated from those change activities and the verification of the stories to the organizational change theory. Though stories are powerful tools in many aspects to accommodate organizational management, attention should be paid at the same time that storytelling is not a panacea - it doesn't always work. Understanding how and why storytelling works and learning what kinds of stories work in different situations, and what kinds of effects different kinds of stories have can enable managers and leaders to be more adept storytellers in organizational contexts. Only through appropriate use of storytelling, can its significance and strengths excel at the most powerful degree.

5.5 CASE STUDY ON THE LEADERSHIP OF THE DIRECTOR OF CCCL FROM THE ORGANIZATIONAL STORYTELLING PERSPECTIVE

Due to the significant merits of organizational storytelling, in this chapter, the author is trying to reveal the leadership styles of the CEO of a very renowned firm in the circle of cultural products in China. Permission has been obtained from the legal representative of the firm to guarantee the legitimacy of this case study. However, to avoid the unnecessary trouble and show respect to the persons involved in this research, the names of the persons being interviewed and the company name will keep anonymity. but in the major causes of the sudden disappearance of a Chinese firm --- Xi'an CCCL Coin Culture Co., Ltd. The mentioned firm was once enjoying a legendary and iconic status in cultural gifts sector in Chinese market. Its "fall from grace" has been spectacular and dramatic and the company is now surviving for its life like a dying man at the last spur of the moment. Based on the extensive interview with concerning personnel from various departments and utilizing a case-study approach, this paper provides an exploratory study into its sudden failure in the context of internal and external factors.

5.5.1 Methodologies in This Case Study

1. In Depth Interviews with Employees

In-depth interviews have been conducted for several times with carefully selected persons who have witnessed the raise and fall of the company and can represent the overall picture of the development of the company. These interviewees are working in different departments of the company and have the opportunity to observe the first hand information of the company. Mainly, each interviewee represents a key department. To be specific, they are from marketing department, sales department, R & D department, the secretarial sector of the board of directors, financial department, consultancy team, which consists of numismatic experts who are in charge of the collecting and authenticating the coins and related ancient cultural relics; the expertise who are specialized in Chinese culture and civilization; the advertising department and public relations department, as well as the head who is in charge of the coin museums. Due to the considerate selection of interviewees, more objective and realistic picture can be induced. The interview questions have been granted skillfully upon different interview participants by making slight twists of the expressions to cross-check the reliability of the replies from different sources. The interview questions have been constructed according to rigid research methodology and arranged in structural and semi-structural paradigm free from leading questions to secure the quality of the interview. To protect the privacy of the interviewees and to guarantee that the interviewed questions being replied realistically and objectively, the real names of the interviewees have been shaded by suing pseudo names. Possible gifts have been provided for the interviewees to motivate them to have a deeper involvement in this research. Due to the time constraints and variances of every interviewee, the beforehand intercourse has been made with them to guarantee that interview will not bring about any inconvenience to them. To meet the purpose of the interview and to provide a relaxed and pleasant place for interviewees to utter their mind freely and expressively, the interview venues have been carefully selected with the priorities to coffee shops, tea-houses, veranda of the high buildings free from crowds or offices after work. In secure a panoramic picture of the views upon the leadership styles of their director, interviewees have been also carefully selected to cover almost all the key units of the company. The interviewed persons and their affiliations, together with the duration during which they are working in CCCL firm can be seen from the following table (see more details from Table 1). With the permission of the interviewees, the interview questions from the interviewer

Table 1. Information about the interview

Interview Time	Name	Units	Position	Tenure
Oct. 18, 2007	LZJ	Marketing & Client Support Dept.	Sales manager	3 years
2007.10.18	TW	R & D Dept.	Designer	6 years
2007.10.19	LXM	R & D, Marketing Dept.	CMO	7 years
2007.10.19	ZY	HR Dept.	Recruiter	5 years
2007.10.21	YJ	Fiscal Dept. (Beijing/ Shanghai)	Accountant	5 years
2007.10.23	ZSW	Administrative Office	Dean	3 years
2007.10.23	ZL	Production Dept.	Quality inspector	4 years
2007.10.24	WP	Advertising Dept.	Dean	3 years
2007.10.25	YB	Sales Dept.	Dept. manager	6 years
2007.10.26	CJH	Marketing & Sales Dept.	Vice CMO	4 years
2007.10.30	ZYF	GM's Office	Secretary	4 years
2007.10.30	ZTG	Secretary of the Board	Vice CIO	8 years

and the answers from the interviewees have been recorded in MP3 format for later codification. During the process of interviews, blurred information has been clarified with the interviewees through repeating, reviewing and reconfirming of the messages and key points have been noted down to avoid short memory.

2. On-Site Observation

Being neutral, the author once worked there for about a year to be a part time translator and interpreter. At the moment, the most attractive thing to accept such a position was not because of its humble salary, but because of the unique company culture and very characteristic company image--- the element of culture. The deepest impression still lies in the author's memory: on the 3rd floor of Xi'an CCCL Mansion, there is a very delicate and cozy room, in the center of which, where there is a rectangular stone container, which was once used to fill the straws and other food for horses in the ancient times, but now served as a unique ash tray, which is the most huge ash tray I have ever seen in the world! Whenever employees need a relaxation or share ideas with peers, they would like to come into this room. While chatting with peers, they never forget to enjoy the world' most lovely smoking sector here. The smokers flip their cigarettes ash and butts into the "ash tray" in a casual and steady manner. Several round or square stone stools are surrounding the stone container for people to sit on. The walls of this small room are specially designed without any artificial whitewashing, so that they serve as a good platform to release the pressure or stress from work or life. Here, on the wall, you can write down your complaints about your boss, curse persons that you do not like, etc. In a word, you can do whatever you like (sure should be within the permission of law) to throw away your unhappiness, worries, anxieties and relax yourself.

3. Second-Hand Information From the Company and Other Sources

After amiable negotiation through telephone calls and face to face discussion with the president of the company, he agreed to provide the company sources to help finish this study. The relevant information has been provided timely. Though it is in narrative form, it does not affect the usefulness and value for this research. From the narration, lots of things can be induced, such as the annual sales volume, the increasing number of employment and development of coin museums in various cities in China and the huge social significance of the profit-free museums, especially from those narrations, it is of great value to imply and interpret the leadership styles of the director under different contexts. To verify the validity and reliability of the first hand information, the author of this study has also connected with other sources which once have close relationship with the leaders of the company, which include the Advertising Dept. of Shaanxi TV Station, of Xi'an TV Station, the journalists who once interviewed and business connections with the leaders of CCCL company.

4. An Interview with the Director Himself

The author is so delighted to find a piece of invaluable text with recorded message from the second hand materials provided by the CCCL firm. It is the dialogue between VMM (hereinafter as V.), a famous CCTV journalist and WG, the director of CCCL company (hereinafter as W). the dialogue mention above best represents the company's vision, mission, long term and short term strategy as well as the corporate culture, and of course, it is a precious material for the author to do her research in this case study. For the purpose of this leadership research, no one can frankly and crisply ask the questions as "what is your leadership style?". Such straight forward questions would plunge the interview into an embarrassed and awkward situation and interviews can not keep going. Therefore, the author has carefully schemed series of questions before the dialogue has been actually conducted. These questions are aiming at inducing some valuable information for interpret and imply his leadership styles. The following dialogue works as a transition in this study and from it, concluding remarks relevant to leadership style will be drawn out.

V.: CCCL mainly deals in ancient coins, why you establish museums as well?

W.: "If a company wants to develop sustainable, it must have its own brand. There are many approaches to establish brand and the best way has to be chosen based on the features of the products. Our products are tiny and we have to choose a unique way to set up our brand. Therefore, we thought of exhibition might be a better way to set up brand and create greater social significance. With the increased value of the intangible asset, the value of our tangible products will also be increased. Based on this consideration, we choose museum as the best approach to establish our brand quickly and efficiently." *This is a very clear minded and visionary leader. He knows very well where the company should go and how to establish the company's sustainable advantages.*

V.: What has impelled you to set up museums?

W.: As early as 1996, during the period of Xi'an Ancient Culture Art Festival, there was the need for cultural products as highlight. At that time, the provincial government summoned some numismatic experts to hold a coin exhibition, which caused a great whirl and gave us a clear indication that coin museums can be a profound opportunity. But how to manage this idea into practice is not yet so transparent at that moment. As we all know, even many national museums could not make ends meet, if we merely take the form of museums, the only thing waiting for us is death as well. As a single company could not make ends meet by selling museum tickets. Therefore, while we are holding museums, we must also have some tangible products to support the operations and keep the museums going on. Then we thought of making coin products to let the museum going alive. We began to consider expanding the external market by setting up museums. Museums can upgrade the value of our intangible assets and thus promote the enterprise for further development and once more, with the selling of the tangible products, the museums will keep going on, which will form a benign cycle. *This is a pretty wise and smart leader who knows the advantages and disadvantages of his firm and who is expertise with industry knowledge. Therefore, he*

*visualizes the merits and demerits of his business and realizes the core
competence of is firm.*

V.: As far as I know, you have already set up 4 museums nationwide, how
did they develop so far?

W.: The first museum was set up in Xi'an, which is rather small actually, but
we have millions of visitors. From 1997 to 1999, we rent the Shaanxi
History Museum to hold grand coin exhibitions for one or two months
annually. These exhibitions have arrested the interests of numismatic
experts, connoisseurs and antique funds from home and abroad, even
inclusive of government leaders like Qian Wei'chang, the vice chairman
of China. The first formal museum has been set up in Beijing in 1998,
which has laid a solid foundation for the Beijing market. The second
museum has been set up in Shanghai just before the "Shanghai Fortune
Forum" started. The museum was located in Duo'lun Celebrities' street
and formerly the location was the residential building of "Tang'en'bo",
a senior official of Kuomintang. This museum has become the window
on the world of our company in the financial center of China. As a firm
from western part of China, it was really a great whirlwind in Shanghai and many government leaders came to visit our museum which
automatically promoted the sale of our products. The third museum
was set up in Xia'men, which focuses on Taiwan and Fu'jian market.
It lies in Gu'lang Islet, the former British Consul in Fu'jian Province.
This year, we have bought a modern building and Xi'an Coin Museum
will be set up here. *This is a pretty wise and smart leader who knows
the advantages and disadvantages of his firm and who is expertise with
industry knowledge. Therefore, he visualizes the merits and demerits
of his business and realizes the core competence of is firm. He is well
known about the firm's future.*

V.: You have already achieved a great scale in setting up museums; will you
extend such an action all over the country?

W.: There are still 6 museums we are intending to open. Our initial plan is
to set up 10 museums in China. Shen'zhen and Tian'jin museums are
just under construction. The establishment of museums will become a
bright attraction to the modern cities. As an indicator of public facility,
the amount of museums that an individual occupies symbolizes the
degree of modernization of the city. In China, millions of citizens own
one museum, but in advanced countries, several hundreds of citizens
have a museum. Museums can not be developed merely by government.
With the entrance of WTO, we have to catch up with the international
standard in every aspects and as a usual practice, enterprises should

take out part of their profit to deal in public facilities. In the long run, this will still be a good and efficient way to establish company image and brands.

V.: Is it true that atmospheres like museums also nurtured unique and specialized consumers?

W.: It is true but even more I should say. Many visitors have little or no knowledge about coin, numismatics and let alone to know the evolution of currencies. Money is the most familiar and the oddest thing in people's life. Every piece of coin has its own story. Our coin museum is not only a statement about coins---the evolution of currencies, but we regard each piece of coin as a carrier, which connote profound aspects of culture. Money is a miniature of human life which represents economy, politics, culture and art. That is why we can use money as carrier to transmit such rich connotations.

V.: What makes you deal in coin business?

W.: I was born in the ancient city Xi'an. When I was young, I have been immersed into a very simple and rich cultural atmosphere: the colored roofs and carved pillars of my house, the plain but delicate displays and some antiques in my family. From then on, I begin to take a stout interest in collection of ancient things. When I gathered enough experience in doing business, I thought of shifting into the line of antique collections. In the past, many connoisseurs hide their collections and appreciate it themselves, fear of being exposed to others. However, modern connoisseurs should expose what they have collected and share with others. Through exposure and exhibition, we are intending to show the value of our collections and create more value. At that time, the price for a piece of genuine coin was even cheaper than making a fake one. As a business man, I invest in collecting genuine coins, because it pays! In this way, we have collected large number of invaluable coins exhibited in our coin museums, at the same time; we also collected large varieties of coins which were lying in the waste collection stations. To be honest, we did not know what we should do with those so-called wastes, but there is one thing in our mind: the preciousness and value of the coins should not only be judged by the quantities stored. Maybe they are not rare; at least they are fresh and vivid which provide people with vivid history and culture. Based on such mindset, we categorized these coins into different groups and bestow them with profound meaning in our products. No wonder these coin products enjoy vey good sale and bring us with very generous profit. Through this way, we not only enjoy good business, but also protected many rare and precious coins.

V.: Obviously you choose such a micro-product as your investment, why was that?

W.: As a business man, the sector I choose should have large room of profit. The reason why we choose this field is that we have realized the substantial potentiality in adding value. At that time, it was almost blank in domestic market and people like these kinds of collections. Although in the field of collection, ancient coins are in great quantity, but when it has been put in the whole country, even the whole world, and the quantities will be comparatively less. Many people only draw their conclusion from the limited field of collection but they ignored the even greater area outside of collection sector. And this is where we are aiming to develop.

V.: I have found that you are always addressing yourself as a businessman, but at the same time, many people think you are a cultural preacher. How did you integrate these two titles together?

W.: Businessman is businessman first, as he must make his firm going on the right track, but at the same time he should sometimes jump out of being a businessman. If a firm wants to maintain sustainable development beyond survival, it must have something to support its survival and sustainability, this something is culture. If a person has no brain, he could not take any action; if a firm has no culture, it surely can not sustain long.

V.: How could you forge such an ancient culture into the modern concept of enterprises?

W.: while we are managing our firm, we have not let the ancient tradition hinder our actions. In China, many firms try to follow the suit of how the ancestors once did. During the course of investigating the western firms, we have found that not all the things that our ancestors left us are completely right. What's more, contemporary people are different from ancient people. This also explains why our products could not get worldwide recognition though we have thousands of years' history and culture. Culture itself is also transforming and modern firms must realize this transformation and adjust its policy. Based on the market survey, we must position our products, manage our firms in a scientific way.

V.: What is your criterion to R & D your products?

W.: First of all, we must make market research and make ourselves clear about what the consumers want and need. According to the wants, needs and demands of the market, we R & D our products. For example, we have developed a coin product called <Chinese Coins of Successive Dynasties>, some people like it very much, while others think it is too expertise and not easy to be understood. Later, we combined together the coins, calligraphy on the coins and anecdotal stories related to the coins to meet more people's needs, we have achieved great success.

V.: I also found very plain and ordinary products like cards, how was it developed?

W.: China has been renowned as a country with enormous rites and etiquette. And on special occasions like Spring Festival, people like to give gifts one another. Then, we have developed a card product called "May you be wealthy and prosperous generation by generation", such product has enjoyed warm welcome. In the following year, we have developed another series of card products with traditional designs and good connotations. This year and later on, we will develop more products favorable to people.

V.: How did you price your products?

W.: Our products have been priced in the shape of a pyramid. At the very top lies the most precious and expensive product, such as <The Grand History of China>, which has involved our scores of years' unyielding efforts and we only made a collection of 2000 copies at the cost price of 20,000RMB; while at the bottom of the pyramid, we also have products worthy of 40 to 50 RMB. That our products have been priced in such a escalating-shape which enables us to develop large varieties of goods at differentiated strata in order to meet the needs of different consumers at different social stratum. Though we could not satisfy the needs of all the customers at the beginning, our products have already expanded to varied consumer groups within two years. Today, many people think CCCL company has made a great leap forward, but I should say it just begins. Since we label ourselves as the cultural preacher, I hope all the staff in CCCL, from the production work floor to the management level, when they go out, they will also be regarded as the cultural preachers.

V.: What do you mean by saying the term "the black hole of the enterprise"?

W.: When I say "the black hole of the enterprise", we mean the infusion process of the 5000 years of Chinese culture, which is the real and true attraction to anyone working in CCCL Company.

V.: How did you nurture the citizenship and belongingness of your employees?

W.: To answer this question, we should start from an ancient Chinese saying "you can not work together if you do not have the common goal". I sincerely hope that everyone who comes to CCCL Company to work should share the common goal with the firm. We are a firm taking transmitting ancient culture as our objective, but not merely making money. All the tangible resources are limited, only cultural resources are boundless. We regard it as our mission to disseminate our national culture. Not only I, but also our dealers, distributors, consumers and our staff are all the cultural preachers.

V.: While wandering around your company, I have such an impression that even the drinking cups of your staff have been placed very neatly on their tables, how will you think of such minor details?

W.: In the course of the firm integration, detail management is very important. Only when everyone takes the same pace, the whole firm can move forward quickly and efficiently. If a firm wants to develop and expand, there might meet with lots of hurdles. Due to the differences in cultural background, and worldview, different people may have different mind towards the same thing, we should not satisfy everyone's mind by modifying our overall strategy. In a firm, there are various rules and regulations, someone may like it, someone may not like it, but once the rules and regulations are released formally to the staff, everyone must obey it. I think this is the most important point to guarantee the implementation of the firm policy. *This is a pretty wise and smart leader who knows the advantages and disadvantages of his firm and who is expertise with industry knowledge. Therefore, he visualizes the merits and demerits of his business and realizes the core competence of is firm. He is also a leader with very great reinforcement in implementation.*

V.: Will you introduce the "Stress Release Room" in your company?

W.: Actually that is our smoking room. While you are smoking, you can release your anxieties and dissatisfaction there. We are advocating a liberal culture in the firm. We do not wish our employees to squeeze their anxieties dissatisfaction in their heart. Therefore, we created such a release room to let the staff work in a light-hearted atmosphere. This is also a place to collect the mindsets of the staff in order for our senior managers to modify our management style accordingly. *This is a pretty wise and smart leader who knows the advantages and disadvantages of his firm and who is expertise with industry knowledge. Therefore, he visualizes the merits and demerits of his business and realizes the core competence of is firm. He is a leader with open mind and democratic freedom.*

V.: While managing your firm, did you apply any of the advanced western management theories into practice?

W.: We do not merely copy the western management experiences in our management practice. Management should be conducted according to the specific situation of our own firm. We should on the one hand copy the traditional experiences or on the other hand just duplicate the western management experiences; we must learn to manage our firm with great innovation and flexibility. We also challenge the traditional culture. In China, when you are starting a new business, some people may ask you "who has taught you so?" But if the same case in the west, no one asks you such questions and you might create a new field by exerting your innovation and enthusiasm. Therefore, it is even harder to start a brand-new business in China as against that in the west. Every staff is required to try all means to protect the company brand. How a firm goes and how far the firm goes depends on the efforts of each staff and therefore you should ask yourself what you have brought to the staff. This is of key importance.

V.: Will you please introduce your new marketing mechanism?

W.: In the past years, we have been developing very fast, and museums have been set up one after another. The branches and subsidiaries have also been arranged well. Our next strategy for further development will be withdrawing from the sales channels. A firm can not on the one hand be a coach and on the other hand be the athletes. Our core competence is culture and we have very powerful R & D personnel. Thus we should focus on R & D and outsource the marketing and sales to specialized firms. This is based on the analysis on our competitive advantage.

V.: How do you choose your cooperation partners?

W.: First of all, we will consider its position in the field. It takes lots of time and efforts to get to know more details about the potential partners, but we still think it worthwhile to do so.

V.: At the beginning while you are inviting your business partners, what kind of chain stores do you prefer to choose?

W.: We will initially choose 100 provincial cities in China and in each city, we will choose one distributor for pure chain operation. These chain distributors will have the same logo, same CI (company image) and the same VI. Our museums will help promote the products for our distributors and the comprehensive full set of marketing scheme, advertising etc. will be provided for these 100 distributors. We also hope that these 100 distributors will display our products in the 100 most famous department stores and shopping malls. Once again, I should emphasize that our partners should fully understand our core value and share the common goal with us. Secondly, we will work as a bridge for these business partner and provide as many support as we can for them; thirdly, we have the very famous and strong brand recognition, anyone who deals in our products will be proud of our brand and in turn, that will do good for them to upgrade their own firm's reputation; lastly, the profit. Our products have much margin of profit as against other products in this line.

V.: After the permission of entering of WTO, foreign cultural products would come to Chinese market, as you are dealing in the traditional cultural products, won't that be a challenge for you? What will you react?

W.: We have wide and substantial connections with lots of foreign firms dealing in cultural products. As early as 1999, our products have been regarded as the national gift by Shanghai Municipal Government at "the Global Fortune Forum" held in Shanghai. Our products have been bestowed as gifts upon the Fortune 500. At that forum, our firm has been seen as the most promising multinational firm in the next 50 years in China and Fortune magazine has reported it. At that time, it was really beyond our expectation to have got such a special title. Many CEO and directors of the Fortune 500firms have unanimously praised our products and agreed that "in the 21st century, we are not afraid of the industrial development in China; we are not afraid of the hi-tech in China, but the only thing we are afraid is the emergence and development of Chinese cultural products". China has over 5000years of culture and civilization. Before the founding of new China, just like the material wealth being taken away from China by the West, the same is true of Chinese Culture. In the 21st century, will China suffer the same fate? I hope all the Chinese should have a clear mind. Actually, such worries have already been testified as true: the well-known <Hua'mulan---Story of a Girl in Man's Clothes > is a good example. From such a severe situation, we also feel great pressure. Today, we are selling coins only, but the cultural sparkles and glitters are far from being developed due to our insufficient capability in excavation, development and transmission, which might also caused by the so deep and profound cultural burden. Therefore, after 1999 "Fortune Global Forum", we have conducted great variety kinds of connections and communications with western firms dealing in cultural products with the hope that we can learn from them and cooperate with them. In this way, we can make full use of the advanced transmission mode of the west combined with our research results to achieve the best effects. Our cultural products will not only be understood by us Chinese, but also by foreigners. Only and only through this way, can Chinese culture go outward to the whole world. Today, we use ancient coins as the carrier to disseminate Chinese culture, and tomorrow we hope we will develop more cultural products rather than coins to disseminate our culture.

V.: Will WTO be a kind of challenge to you?

W.: WTO to us is not merely a challenge; we see it more as an opportunity. 21st century will provide substantial opportunities for the development of cultural industry.

5.5.2 Glorious and Splendid Times

CCCL was established in 1998 with only ten persons and located in a very small corner of Xi'an city. But within very short time, it has become very successful and set a model for the firms dealing in cultural gifts. This grandeur seems a legend suddenly appeared in China and shines so brightly that people even could not have the time to retrospect how it has been successful! Such a legend has arrested the attention from all sources both at home and abroad. In the 1999 Fortune Global forum held in Shanghai, CCCL has been predicted by Fortune Magazine as one of the Fortune 500 in the future with its great potentiality and market. In 2001, its annual production value has roared up to 70 million Yen with fixed assets reaching several hundred millions. It has made itself into the No. one largest Coin Company in Asia---a rising transnational company is just over there.

Due to the unique positioning of the company and its products, during the process of the initial development, there were almost no competitors, even though there was one or two rivalries, the rivals could never match in every aspect of the business operations. CCCL has the largest inventory of ancient coins for over 500 metric tons; it has hired high talents for its staff with over 90 percent of the staff was undergraduates. During the interview, we have been informed that quite a number of talents were attracted by the strong odor of culture dispersed in the company, they did not want to care anything else and just wanted to work for the company. The information obtained from triangulation approaches have revealed that almost all of the employees in CCCL were admiring the personal charm of the director very much and regarded him as their idol. With the combination of rare resources, appropriate positioning of the company and the products, as well as the right leadership of the director, CCCL Company made a great leap forward in no more than three years. The company has been seen as the benchmark for other companies in the same or similar business sector. With the magnificent success of the initial development, the director of CCCL Company began to think about the further development of his kingdom. Many splendid ideas and proposal came into his mind: real estate, which has been seen as the most profitable business in China; subsidiaries nationwide and even had the mind to set up branches in the UK and the USA. It seemed that everything was going on very well on the right track.

5.5.3 Organizational Crisis and Failure--- Is It Due to Wrong Leadership Style?

With the expansion of the company in business scope and scale, the reputation of the firm also reached its peak. The business scope not only includes the arts and crafts products relevant to ancient coins in the forms of frames for hanging and displaying, booklets, swords and cards to meet the tastes of people from all works of life, but also extended to real estate business, interior decoration, museums, as well as film-making industry. Everything has been going on smoothly and it has revealed to everyone internal and external that CCCL will become the new star of tomorrow, but suddenly in the end of 2003, the company clasped with no signs of failure at all. Is it because the board of director made a wrong strategy? Or is it because that the competitors were so ferocious as to defeat CCCL company or Is it because the director of CCCL company did not conduct his duties and responsibilities in proper leadership styles? The following analysis may piece the veil from one extent to another:

First of all, in order to analyze the failure of CCCL firm, we have to be very clear about whether the company has sustainable competitive advantages and whether the leaders of the company have formulated BHAG (big hairy attainable goal) based on the hedgehog concept. Because resources and capabilities cannot be evaluated in isolation, the VRIO framework presents four interconnected and increasingly difficult hurdles for them to become a source of sustainable competitive advantage, we adopt VRIO model to analyze the factors of CCCL firm. According to the VRIO model, if a company wants to obtain sustainable competitive advantages, the leaders of the firm must ask themselves such questions as VRIO, here, "V" stands for valuable, "R" stands for rarity, "I" stands for inimitable and "O" stands for organization. This model is most frequently used for firms to identify their resources for business development and expansion. As a transparent and efficient tool for firms to analyze the reality and potentiality of business operations, VRIO model is an essential and quick approach to:

- Build the firm's resources and capabilities strengths before beginning the search for the most attractive industry or segment.
- Imitation is not a successful strategy—creating new ways of adding value forces competitors to play the best performing firm's game.
- Competitive advantage does not last forever—strategic foresight is necessary to anticipate needs and move early to build resources and capabilities for future competition.

Table 2. The VRIO framework: features of a resource or capability

Valuable?	Rare	Inimitable	Exploited by Organization?	Competitive Implication	Firm performance
1. No*** 2. Yes*** 3. No 4. Yes	1. Yes*** 2. No 3. Yes 4. No	1. No 2. Yes*** 3. No 4. Yes	1. Yes*** 2. No 3. Yes 4. No	1.Competitive Disadvantage 2.Competitive Parity 3.Temporary Competitive Advantage*** 4.Sustained Competitive Advantage***	1.Below Average 2. Average 3.Above Average*** 4.Persistently Above Average***

Note: *** in the above VRIO model stands for the states in which the CCCL company falls into after analyzing its resources.

This Model can be illustrated as shown in Table 2.

From the checking list, it is obvious that the company has obtained over 500 metric tons of ancient coins, which can be valuable or can not be of great value depending on how the company has developed them. This non-producible resource is in reality very scarce and even rare. Since they are genuine ancient coins, which work as miniatures to represent the history, economy, culture, appreciation on beauty, etc. of specific dynasties, it is of course inimitable and it is not worthwhile to forge the fake coins in the perspective of cost. Such large quantities of genuine ancient coins can be temporary competitive advantage or sustained competitive advantage again depending on how to explore and exploit them into cultural products and according to the company records, as well as the publicly released documents, CCCL company's performance was above the average of the industry sector but will it be persistently above the average is a question mark.

It is for sure that a company's success story or failure story can not be a single factor. It is without any exception that the failure or success of a firm has been induced by multiple factors with great complexity. Taking into consideration of this research, attention will mainly be laid on the leadership style of the director of CCCL firm as it is common knowledge that leader plays a key role in the business operations of firms.

The dialogue between the CCTV correspondents, the in-depth interviews on the carefully selected employees and the information obtained from other sources provide sufficient bundle of information to identify the director's leadership style. The universally adopted leadership traits chart has been used for the interviewees to identify the leadership style of their director. The replies to the questions raised in the dialogue have worked as a rich repository to analyze the leadership style of the director from the perspective of himself. The assessment results of the leadership traits of the director can be summarized in the following table as can be seen from Table 3.

5.6 POST- EFFECT FROM CCCL COMPANY

Though such a giant has got lost overnight, it leaves people lots of room to think about it. In China, there are millions of private-owned enterprises, which jointly play a very important role in the economic development and the overall GDP growth. It would be partial and prejudicial for any one to study the Chinese phenomena without consideration of these large numbers

Table 3. Positive leader attributes: Self-assessment from the dialogue

Leadership Traits	Corresponding Leadership Scale	Self-Assessment	Assessed by Others
Trustworthy	Integrity	yes	yes
Just	Integrity	yes	yes
Honest	Integrity	yes	yes
Foresight	Charisma 1: visionary	yes	yes
Plans ahead	Charisma 1: visionary	yes	yes
Encouraging	Charisma 2: inspirational	yes	yes
Positive	Charisma 2: inspirational	yes	yes
Dynamic	Charisma 2: inspirational	yes	yes
Motive arouser	Charisma 2: inspirational	yes	yes
Confidence builder	Charisma 2: inspirational	yes	yes
Motivational	Charisma 2: inspirational	yes	yes
Dependable	Malevolent (reverse score)	yes	yes
Intelligent	Malevolent	yes	yes
Decisive	Decisiveness	yes	yes
Effective bargainer	Diplomatic	yes	yes
Win-win problem solver	Diplomatic	yes	yes
Administratively skilled	Administratively competent	yes	yes
Communicative	team integrator	yes	yes
Informed	team integrator	yes	yes
Coordinator	team integrator	yes	yes
Team builder	team integrator	yes	yes
Excellence oriented	Performance oriented	yes	yes

of private-owned enterprises. Therefore, CCCL's rise and fall is not a single case, it represents the fate and fortune of all the private-owned enterprises in China. One of the positive effects of its fall is that it has created a brand-new field in the arts and crafts market, or rather, to put numerous connotations to every piece of coins, which has broadened people's views on how to develop such a unique numismatic antique into high-quality gifts with rich cultural glitters. No boasting that CCCL has fostered a new industry in China and meanwhile has nurtured a large number of people to get to know this new industry, have keen interest in this new industry, love this new industry and take this new industry as a life-long career.

After the fall of CCCL, most employees have to find a new job or start their own career. Surprisingly, during my interview and consultation, I have got to know that still many people who once were working in CCCL Coin Culture Co., Ltd. are in this line for their life long career. Some of them are working for other employers in this line; and still others have started their businesses in this line; still some others are doing a wonderful job in this line. For example, in 2005, when the president of Tai'wan Kuomintang Lian'zhan and his wife visited China, they have been given an invaluable gift which was made of ancient Chinese coins designed and produced by one of the employees of CCCL. Among all the interviewees I have conducted, no matter what they have said during the interview, they all unanimously agree that Wang'gang, the president and general manager of CCCL Coin Culture Co., Ltd. was the principal of Huang'pu School. From their appearance, I could sense that the title "the principal of Huang'pu Military School" was not at all an irony or satire, but a great honor and cordial admiration of W.C. from the bottom of their heart.

In order to testify the positive post-ECCL effect, one of the interviewees has provide a name list on which are some of the employees who once worked in CCCL company but now started their own businesses in the field of Chinese coins and coin related cultural products. These firms are playing a key role in the gift sector of domestic market and some of them have already explored the international market due to attraction design of the cultural products and excellent quality. Retrospect to the success of their firms, they unanimously attribute their success to CCCL and the director of CCCL company. No matter what kind of leadership styles they once experienced while working in CCCL, one thing fore sure is that they all regard CCCL Company as the incubator for their business success and the director, also the main actor in this case study has been seen as the icon in their mind. As they admit that he is a powerful leader with great potentiality in being a different leader under different circumstances.

Summary of the Case

In summary, there is no right or wrong leadership style. It is always the case that a leader performs his leadership style according to the contexts under which he is leading. It is the interaction between leader, follower and situation. To be specific, the formulation and formation of the leadership style of a person result in very complex factors; a person's leadership style can be influenced by multiple factors internal and external and cultures, as well as values system is one the most complicated one against all other factors; even for a single person, his or her leadership style can not remain unchanged, however it changes all the time according to the situation, as well as his or her followers. This case has testified the validity of the questionnaires we have adopted in this research, since in the case, the leadership style of the interviewed leader not only assessed his leadership style himself but also been assessed through 360 degree dimensions. This case once again has enhanced the conclusion that we have got from the empirical samples of 778 business leaders in China. Apart from the leader we have interviewed in this case, we have also extended the same interviews with other peoples from other industries to secure the reliability and validity of the research results. To make this case condense and crisp, we have maintained the leadership stories of other leaders from all works of life for further research purposes (for more details, please see the attached name list of other interviewees---Table 4).

Table 4. Interviews conducted with other leaders

Interviewee	Position & Name of the Company	Nature of the Ownership	Interview Time	Interview Venue
James LIU	Director of a Commercial Bank	State Owned Enterprise (SOE)	Nov. 12, 2006	Zhengzhou
Aaron LEE	Manager of a Bookstore	Private Firm	Nov. 23, 2006	Zhengzhou
Teresa CHEN	Director of an Auction Company	Private Firm	Dec. 8, 2006	Beijing
Vilene SHI	Vice GM of a Clothing Firm	Sino-Japan Joint Venture (JV)	Feb. 14, 2007	Suzhou
Lily WANG	GM of a Machinery Plant	State Owned Enterprise (SOE)	April 3, 2007	Yinchuan
Marc WU	Director of a Consulting Firm	Sino-USA Joint Venture (JV)	June 2, 2007	Shanghai
William HE	Vice Director of US Subsidiary in China	Whole Owned Subsidiary (WOS)	July 6, 2007	Xi'an
Jack ZANG	GM of a Food Chain Store	Private Firm	Sept. 6, 2007	Shenzhen
John BAI	GM of a Film Studio	SOE	Sept. 22, 2007	Beijing

REFERENCES

Allman, J. L., Ohair, D., & Stewart, R. (1994). Communication and Aging: A study of the Effects of Cohort-Centrism and Perceived Decoding Ability on Communication Competence and Communication Satisfaction. *Communication Quarterly*, *42*(4), 363–376. doi:10.1080/01463379409369943

Anderson, J. C., & Gerbing, D. W. (1988). Structural Equation Modeling in Practice: A review and Recommended Two-Step Approach. *Psychological Bulletin*, 103.

Antal, A. B., Lenhardt, U., & Rosenbrock, R. (2001). Barriers to Organizational Learning. In M. Dierkes, A. B. Antal, J. Child, & I. Nonaka (Eds.), *Handbook of Organizational Learning and Knowledge* (pp. 865–885). Oxford University Press.

Arogyaswarny, B., & Byles, C. M. (1987). Organizational Culture: Internal & External Fits. *Journal of Management*, *13*(4), 647–659. doi:10.1177/014920638701300406

Ashforth, B. E., & Mael, F. (1989). Social Identity Theory and the Organization. *Academy of Management Review*, (14), 20–39.

Badaracco, J. (1992). *Knowledge Link: How Firms Compete Through Strategic Alliance*. Boston: Harvard Business School.

Barney, J. (1991). Firm Resources and Sustained Competitive Advantage. *Journal of Management*, *17*(1), 99–120. doi:10.1177/014920639101700108

Barney, J., & Jay, B. (1986). Strategic Factor Markets: Expectation, Luck and Business Strategy. *Management Science*, *32*(10), 1231–1241. doi:10.1287/mnsc.32.10.1231

Bass, B. M., & Avlio, B. J. (1994). Transformational Leadership and Organizational Culture. *Public Administration Quarterly*, (17), 112–118.

Bhatt, G. (2001). Knowledge Management in Organizations: Examining the Interaction between Technologies, Techniques and People. *Journal of Knowledge Management*, *5*(1), 68–75. doi:10.1108/13673270110384419

Brislin, R. W., Lonner, W. J., & Thorndike, R. M. (1973). *Cross-cultural Research Methods*. New York: John Wiley.

Carless, S. A. (1998). Gender Difference in Transformational Leadership: An Examination of Superior, Leader, and Subordinate Perspectives. Sex Role, (39), 887-902.

Chinese Culture Connection. (1987). Chinese Values and the Search for Culture-Free Dimensions of Culture. *Journal of Cross-Cultural Psychology*, (18), 143–164.

Collison & Parcell. (2001). *Learning to fly: practical lessons from one of the world are leading knowledge companies*. Oxford, UK: Capstone.

David, A. (2006). Stability and Change in Managerial Work Values: A Longitudinal Study of China, Hong Kong, and the U. S. A. *Management and Organization Review*, 2(1), 67–94. doi:10.1111/j.1740-8784.2006.00031.x

David, W., & Hutchings, K. (2005). Cultural Embeddedness and Contextual Constraints: Knowledge Sharing in Chinese and Arab Cultures. *Knowledge and Process Management*, 12(2), 89–98. doi:10.1002/kpm.222

Davies, R. (1998). An Evolutionary Approach to Facilitating Organizational Learning: An Experiment by the Christian Commission for Development in Bangladesh. *Impact Assessment and Project Appraisal*, 16(3), 243–250. do i:10.1080/14615517.1998.10590213

Downton, J. V. (1973). *Rebel Leadership*. New York: Free Press.

Dutton, J. E., Dukerich, J. M., & Harquail, C. V. (1994). Organizational Images and Member Identification. *Administrative Science Quarterly*, 39(34), 239–263. doi:10.2307/2393235

Finkelstein, S., & Hambrick, D. C. (1996). *Strategic leadership: Top executives and their effects on organizations*. St. Paul, MN: West Publishing Company.

Ford, D. P., & Chan, Y. E. (2003). Knowledge Sharing in Multicultural Setting: A Case Study. *Knowledge Management Research and Practice*, 1(1), 11–27. doi:10.1057/palgrave.kmrp.8499999

Ginnette, R. C. (1993). *Crews as Groups: Their Formation and Their Leadership*. Academic Press Inc.

Glisby, M., & Holden, N. (2003). Contextual Constraints in Knowledge Management Theory: Cultural Embeddedness of Nonakas Knowledge Creating Company. *Knowledge and Process Management*, 10(1), 29–36. doi:10.1002/kpm.158

Hambrick, D. C. (1989). Guest editors introduction: Putting top managers back in the strategy picture. *Strategic Management Journal, 10*(10), 5–15. doi:10.1002/smj.4250100703

Hambrick, D. C., & Mason, P. (1984). Upper echelons: The organization as a reflection of its top managers. *Academy of Management Review,* (9), 193–206.

Harzing, A. W. (2006). Response styles in cross-national survey research: A 26-country study. *International Journal of Cross Cultural Management, 6*(2), 243–261. doi:10.1177/1470595806066332

Hooijberg, R., & Quinn, R. E. (1992). Behavioral complexity and the development of effective leaders. In R. L. Phillips & J. G. Hunt (Eds.), *Strategic management: A multi organizational level perspective* (pp. 161–176). New York: Quorum.

Hunt, J. G., Dachler, H. P., & Schriesheim, C. A. (Eds.). (1988). Emerging leadership vistas. Lexington.

Hwang, K. K. (1997). Guanxi and Mientze: Conflict resolution in Chinese society. *Intercultural Communication Studies, 7*(1), 17–37.

John, K. B. Jr, & Randall, J. F. (1999). Transformational Leadership Behaviors, Upward Trust and Satisfaction in Self-Managed Work Teams. *Organization Development Journal,* (1), 17–33.

Kaye, M. (1996). *Myth-makers and storytellers.* Sydney, Australia: Business & Professional Publishing Pty Ltd.

Koh, W. L., Steers, R. M., & Terborg, J. R. (1995). The Effect of Transformational Leadership on Teacher Attitudes and Student Performance in Singapore. *Journal of Organizational Behavior, 16*(4), 319–333. doi:10.1002/job.4030160404

Lambert. (Eds.). (n.d.). *Handbook of Cross-Cultural Psychology Perspectives* (Vol. 1). Boston: Allyn & Bacon.

Latham, G. P., & Saari, L. M. (1979). The Application of Social Learning Theory to Training Supervisors throughout Behavior Modeling. *The Journal of Applied Psychology, 64*(72), 239–246. doi:10.1037/0021-9010.64.3.239

Logan, E. (2001). *A pipeline for collaboration: Leveraging knowledge through storytelling at SIEP* (Vol. 20). Knowledge Management.

Lombardo, M. M. (1983). I felt it as soon as I walked in. *Issues and Observations*, *3*(4), 7–8.

Marin, G., Triandis, H. C., Betancourt, H., & Kashima, Y. (1983). Ethnic affirmation versus social desirability: Explaining discrepancies in bilinguals responses to a questionnaire. *Journal of Cross-Cultural Psychology*, *14*(2), 173–186. doi:10.1177/0022002183014002003

McClelland, D. C., Atkinson, J. W., Clark, R. A., & Lowell, E. L. (Eds.). (1953). *The achievement motive*. New York: Appleton-Century-Crofts. doi:10.1037/11144-000

McFarland, L. J., Senen, S., & Childress, J. R. (1993). *Twenty-first-century leadership*. New York: Leadership Press.

Miller, D., & Droge, C. (1986). Psychological and traditional determinants of structure. *Administrative Science Quarterly, 31*(4), 539-560.

Misumi, J. (1985). *The behavioral science of leadership: An interdisciplinary Japanese research program*. Ann Arbor, MI: University of Michigan Press.

Moore, R. H., & Blakely, G. L. (1995). Individualism-Collectivism as an Individual Difference Predictor of Organizational Citizenship Behavior. *Journal of Organizational Behavior*, *16*(2), 127–142. doi:10.1002/job.4030160204

Morris, C. W. (1956). *Varieties of Human Value*. Chicago: University of Chicago Press. doi:10.1037/10819-000

Nutt, P. C., & Backoff, R. W. (1997). Crafting vision. *Journal of Management Inquiry*, *6*(6), 308–328. doi:10.1177/105649269764007

O'Connell, M. S., Lord, R. G., & O'Connell, M. K. (1990, August). *Differences in Japanese and American leadership prototypes: Implications for cross-cultural training*. Paper presented at the meeting of the Academy of Management, San Francisco, CA.

Putnam, R. D. (1993). *Making democracy work*. Princeton, NJ: Princeton University Press.

Schein, E. H. (1992). *Organizational culture and leadership: A dynamic view* (2nd ed.). San Francisco: Jossey-Bass.

Schneider, B. (1987). The people make the place. *Personnel Psychology*, *40*(3), 437–454. doi:10.1111/j.1744-6570.1987.tb00609.x

Schneider, B., Goldstein, H. W., & Smith, D. B. (1995). The ASA Framework: An update. *Personnel Psychology*, *48*(4), 747–783. doi:10.1111/j.1744-6570.1995. tb01780.x

Schriesheim, C. A., & Hinkin, T. R. (1986). *Influence Tactics Used by Subordinates: A Theoretical and Empirical Analysis and Refinement of the Kipnis, Schmidt, and Wilkinson Sub-scales*. Paper presented at the annual Academy of Management meetings, San Diego, CA.

Simonton, D. K. (1994). *Greatness: Who makes history and why*. New York: Guilford Press.

Sipe, W. P., & Hanges, P. J. (1997). Reframing the glass ceiling: A catastrophe model of changes in the perception of women as leaders. In R. G. Lord (Chair), *Dynamic systems, leadership perceptions, and gender effects*. Symposium presented at the Twelfth Annual Conference of the Society of Industrial and Organizational Psychology.

Smith, P. B., Misumi, J., Tayeb, M. H., Paterson, M., & Bond, M. H. (1989). On the generality of leadership style across cultures. *Journal of Occupational Psychology*, (30): 526–537.

Staw, B. M., Sandelands, L. E., & Dutton, J. E. (1981). Threat-rigidity effects in organizational behavior: A multilevel analysis. *Administrative Science Quarterly*, *26*(4), 501–524. doi:10.2307/2392337

Thompson, K. R., & Luthans, F. (1990). Organizational culture: A behavioral perspective. In B. Schneider (Ed.), *Organizational Climate and Culture* (pp. 319–344). San Francisco: Jossey-Bass.

Triandis, H. C. (1995). *Individualism and Collectivism*. Boulder, CO: Westview Press.

Walumbwa, F. O., Wang, P., Lawler, J. J., & Shi, K. (2004). The Role of Collective Efficacy in the Relations between Transformational Leadership and Work Outcomes.. *Journal of Occupational and Organizational Psychology*, *77*(4), 515–530. doi:10.1348/0963179042596441

Wiener, Y. (1982). Commitment in Organizations: A Normative View. *Academy of Management Review*, *7*(3), 421–429.

Zaccaro, S. J., Gilbert, J. A., Thor, K. K., & Mumford, M. D. (1991). Leadership and social intelligence: Linking social perceptiveness to behavioral flexibility. *The Leadership Quarterly*, (2): 317–347. doi:10.1016/1048-9843(91)90018-W

Chapter 6
Conclusions, Implications, and Future Research

Through over two years of survey on the same batch of Guinea pigs on their cultures and values system as well as leadership styles, 778 pieces of valid questionnaires have been collected and processed by appropriate statistical software. Based on the statistical results, the following possible results have been drawn from:

Culture and values systems have been ingrained and embedded into people's blood which leaves footprints all the way through his life. Therefore, person's behavior and conducts are the miniatures of the cultures and values systems in which the person is soaked, especially things that they have obtained before 13 years old. Thus, when people come to the post being a leader, their leadership styles will also be significantly influenced by their culture and values system.

There is no one-for-all leadership style in the world. Even though the same person's leadership style may alter according to different occasions, when the contexts within which he leads change. It is wrong and at least not exact to say that a person has a specific leadership style all through the periods when he is acting as a leader. It is more reasonable and acceptable to say that a person has a higher tendency in one leadership style over the other leadership styles

DOI: 10.4018/978-1-5225-2277-5.ch006

due to the nature of the industry, the tenure of his career in the firms, as well as the characteristics of the subordinates under which he leads.

Additionally, one's leadership styles have been largely affected by numerous other factors which are relevant to the leader. Such as the nature of the industry, the ownership specificity of the enterprise, the education level, gender, age, the competitive environment in which the enterprises belong to, as well as the geographic locations of the enterprises and the tenure. To be specific, in traditional industries such as manufacturing sectors, leaders are more likely to follow autocratic leadership styles; whereas in the high-tech industries, leaders are more likely to adopt democratic and free reign leadership styles; male leaders are more likely to adopt autocratic leadership styles rather than female leaders; leaders with higher education levels are more probably to adopt democratic leadership style and free reign leadership style than those who are at lower education levels.

Statistics results have revealed that among the demographic factors, age and education level of the guinea pigs have much greater influence on their leadership styles as against all other demographic factors. This has verified that leader's leadership styles have been deeply affected by his experiences in life and work. With the increase of age, people are intending to have more rational and mature views on lots of things in their life and work and as a result, their leadership styles are more likely to demonstrate in multidimensional scale. They may express different leadership styles according to the specific situation in which they are handling. Education is also a key factor to influence people's leadership style. The higher the education level, the more like the Guinea pigs are intending to conduct in a democratic style or free reign leadership style, as higher education levels have armed themselves on how to empower the subordinates and be delegated by the followers.

The geographic location of the enterprise and tenure of the surveyed population will definitely influence the leadership styles. Research results have indicated that business leaders whose enterprises are located along the east-southern coastal lines are more likely to adopt democratic leadership style and free reign leadership style. Moreover, those who have longer tenure in the firms are more probably to adopt democratic and free reign leadership styles. This might be explained as follows: companies which are located in the east-southern coastal lines have been experiencing more open policy and the location has enabled them to know, understand, and learn more western management styles due to the more and quicker information flow especially during the first half of the period when China has implemented open door policy. The longer the tenure of the leader in the enterprise, the more likely he is to adopt democratic and free reign leadership styles, which is because the long the time he stays in the enterprises, the more trust and friendliness he has established with his subordinates.

In values survey testing, we have obvious demonstrations that the value sets of tradition and universalism only have significant correlations with company location and company scale respectively; while educational level of the respondents and work ages of the respondents have very strong and significant correlations with almost all the ten sets of value orientations (eight sets out of the total ten sets of values orientations). Additionally, permanent residential areas, position in the companies and the nature of company ownership, as well as the nature of industries have medium degree on the influence of participants' value orientations and the remaining four factors (company location, company scale, age brackets and gender) have the least influence on participants' value orientations.

However, in testing the leadership style survey, we have found in this research the following significant outcomes: company scale has not at all a bit correlation with leadership style 1 (autocratic leadership style) and the nature of company ownership, as well as the company location have played no role in the influence on leadership style 2 (democratic leadership style); whereas, education level, position in the company, work age and the nature of company ownership have very strong and significant correlation with leadership style 3 (free reign leadership style). Moreover, it is transparent outcome that these three factors (educational level, position in the company and work age of the respondents) have significant correlations with all the three kinds of leadership styles.

To enhance and strengthen this research, in the last chapter of this dissertation, a case study has been provided as a supplementary support for the conclusions we have obtained from the empirical study of 778 sampled populations. The findings from the case study have again reinforced the conclusions we have got: that is, there is no right or wrong leadership style. In real business world, any one who takes the leadership position will behave flexibly and differently according to the different scenarios in which he or she encounters. Therefore, leadership research follows the rule of idiosyncratic approach as there is no one-for-all leadership style in the world. Every leader takes a mixed and complex leadership style among autocratic, democratic and free reign style in a multidimensional space. Future research has to lay more emphases on the triangulation approaches rather than merely quantitative or qualitative method.

Future studies of the similar type should lay more emphases on the issues raised from this research as why company scale has no correlation with leadership style 1 (the autocratic leadership style)? Why the nature of company ownership and company location have no correlations with leadership style 2 (the democratic leadership style)? And why educational level, positions in the company and the nature of company ownership and work age have significant correlations with leadership style 3 (namely, the free reign leadership style)? Lastly, for future research, more attention should be paid on the obvious results from this empirical study, that is, why educational level, positions in the company and work age have very strong and significant correlations with all the three types of leadership styles? For the obvious reasons and downsides of empirical studies with questionnaires survey, future research should call for much larger samples and rigid procedures in conducting questionnaires survey should be followed to the letter in order to guarantee the quality of collected questionnaires and thus to secure the quality of testing results. Meanwhile, comparative studies should have been made under different cultural contexts to verify the generalizability and universal application of the research findings. In addition, horizontal comparative studies of the similar type should have been implementing on younger generations of future Chinese business leaders and investigate the values shift in Chinese culture, as well as the changing trends of leadership styles with young leaders as against that of the older generation business leaders.

More profound thinking and consideration for future research and practice pertaining to this topic have to take into account with new situations in which we are all inserted without exception and avoidance. To be specific, Due to the rapid development of science and technology, especially with the ubiquity of internet, virtual reality and artificial intelligence, information, data and knowledge has become so easy to obtain, share and disseminate; people's working environment has also been experiencing great changes; more and more people are working in small office, home office and even freelance; project-based virtual organizations are every where; It is obvious that Chinese younger generations have been undergoing a substantial value shifts, in particular those who were born after 1985 as against the older generations like those who were born before 1980s, jobs once seen as an "iron-bowl", "golden-bowl" or even "platinum-bowl" are no longer the pursuit for younger generations in China; new industries and work positions are emerging now and then... All these changes have been blurring the demarcation between leader and follower; the authority-ship of leaders has been diminishing; new challenges in work place for leaders and subordinates have to be encountered. Therefore, business management and academic scholars are to face the music and be prepared for these changes.

REFERENCES

Abram, D., Ando, K., & Hinkle, S. (1998). Psychological Attachment to the Group: Cross-Cultural Differences in Organizational Identification and Subjective Norms as Predictor of Workers Turnover Intentions. *Personality and Social Psychology Bulletin*, *24*(10), 1027–1039. doi:10.1177/01461672982410001

Allman, J. L., Ohair, D., & Stewart, R. (1994). Communication and Aging: A study of the Effects of Cohort-Centrism and Perceived Decoding Ability on Communication Competence and Communication Satisfaction. *Communication Quarterly*, *42*(4), 363–376. doi:10.1080/01463379409369943

Amado, G. (1999). Bilateral Transformational Leadership: An Approach for Fostering Ethical Conduct in Public Service Organizations. *Administration & Society*, *31*(2), 247–260. doi:10.1177/00953999922019111

Anderson, J. C., & Gerbing, D. W. (1988). Structural Equation Modeling in Practice: A review and Recommended Two-Step Approach. *Psychological Bulletin*, 103.

Antal, A. B., Lenhardt, U., & Rosenbrock, R. (2001). Barriers to Organizational Learning. In M. Dierkes, A. B. Antal, J. Child, & I. Nonaka (Eds.), *Handbook of Organizational Learning and Knowledge* (pp. 865–885). Oxford University Press.

Bandura, A. (1977). Self-Efficacy: Toward a Unifying Theory of Behavioral Change. *Psychological Review*, *84*(2), 191–215. doi:10.1037/0033-295X.84.2.191 PMID:847061

Baransons, J. (1966). Transfer of Technical Knowledge by International Corporations to Developing Economics. *The American Economic Review*, (56), 259–260.

Barnard, C. (1968). *The Functions of the Executive*. Harvard University Press.

Boomsma, A. (1982). Non-convergence, Improper Solutions and Starting Values in LISREL Maximum Likelihood Estimation. *Psychometrika*, 50.

Busse. (2014). Corporate culture, organizational change and meaning at work-linking human resources with business ethics. *Human Systems Management, 33*, 47-50.

Busse, R. (2014). Is culture driving innovation? A multinational quantitative analysis. *Human Systems Management, 33*, 91–98. doi:10.3233/HSM-140813

Busse, R. (2014). Comprehensive leadership review-literature, theories and research. *Advances in Management, 7*(5), 52–66.

Busse, R., & Zhu, V. (2014). Demographic and business related effects on leadership styles of Chinese and German managers. *Advances in Management, 7*(2), 29–38.

Busse, R., & Zhu, V. C. Y. (2014). Comparing value orientations of German and Chinese managers: impacts of demographic and business-related factors. *Asia Pacific Business Review*. Retrieved from http://www.tandfonline.com/loi/fapb20

Chatman, J. A., & Jehn, K. A. (1994, June). Assessing the Relationship between Industry Characteristics and Organizational Culture: How Different Can You Be? [J]. Academy of Management Journal. *Briarcliff Manor, 37*(3), 522–532.

Chinese Culture Connection. (1987). Chinese Values and the Search for Culture-Free Dimensions of Culture. *Journal of Cross-Cultural Psychology,* (18), 143–164.

Hanges, P. J., Lord, R. G., Day, D. V., Sipe, W. P., Smith, W. C., & Brown, D. J. (1997). Leadership and gender bias: Dynamic measures and nonlinear modeling. In R. G. Lord (Chair), *Dynamic systems, leadership perceptions, and gender effects.* Symposium presented at the Twelfth Annual Conference of the Society of Industrial and Organizational Psychology.

Hickman, G. R. (1998). Leadership and the social imperative of organizations in the 21st century. In Leading organizations: Perspectives for a new era. Sage.

Ireland, R. D., & Hitt, M. A. (1999). Achieving and maintaining strategic competitiveness in the 21st century: The role of strategic leadership. *The Academy of Management Executive, 13,* 43–57.

Johnson, R. E., Lanaj, K., & Barnes, C. M. (2014). The good and bad of being fair: Effects of procedural and interpersonal justice behaviors on regulatory resources. *The Journal of Applied Psychology, 99*(4), 635–650. doi:10.1037/a0035647 PMID:24446913

Kimberly, B. B., & Hooijberg, R. (2000). Strategic Leadership research Moving on. *The Leadership Quarterly, 11*(4), 515–549. doi:10.1016/S1048-9843(00)00057-6

Kotter, J. (1996). *Leading Change.* Harvard Business School Press.

Kotter, J. (1997). *Realizing Change*. Harvard Business School Press.

Lanaj. (2015). Benefits of transformational behaviors for leaders: a daily investigation of leader behaviors and need fulfillment. *Journal of Applied Psychology*. 10.1037/apl0000052

Lin. (2016). When ethical leader behavior breaks bad: how ethical leader behavior can turn abusive via ego depletion and moral licensing. *Journal of Applied Psychology*..10.1037/apl0000098

McFarland, L. J., Senen, S., & Childress, J. R. (1993). *Twenty-first-century leadership*. New York: Leadership Press.

Miller, D., & Droge, C. (1986). Psychological and traditional determinants of structure. *Administrative Science Quarterly, 31*(4), 539-560.

O'Connell, M. S., Lord, R. G., & O'Connell, M. K. (1990, August). *Differences in Japanese and American leadership prototypes: Implications for cross-cultural training*. Paper presented at the meeting of the Academy of Management, San Francisco, CA.

Putnam, R. D. (1993). *Making democracy work*. Princeton, NJ: Princeton University Press.

Ralston, D. A., Carolyn, P. E., Stewart, S., Robert, H. T., & Kaicheng, Y. (1999). Doing Business in the 21st Century with the New Generation of Chinese Managers: A Study of Generational Shifts in Work Value in China. *Journal of International Business Studies, 30*(2), 415–427. doi:10.1057/palgrave.jibs.8490077

Rokeach, M. (1973). *The nature of human values*. New York: Free Press.

Schneider, B. (1987). The people make the place. *Personnel Psychology, 40*(3), 437–454. doi:10.1111/j.1744-6570.1987.tb00609.x

Schneider, B., Goldstein, H. W., & Smith, D. B. (1995). The ASA Framework: An update. *Personnel Psychology, 48*(4), 747–783. doi:10.1111/j.1744-6570.1995.tb01780.x

Schriesheim, C. A., & Neider, L. L. (1989). Leadership Theory and Development: The Coming New Phase. *Leadership and Organization Development Journal, 10*(6), 17–26. doi:10.1108/EUM0000000001145

Segall, M. H., Dasen, P. R., Berry, J. W., & Poortinga, Y. H. (1990). *Human Behavior in Global Perspective: An Introduction to Cross-Cultural Psychology*. New York: Pergamon.

Shaw, J. B. (1990). A cognitive categorization model for the study of intercultural management. *Academy of Management Review, 15*(4), 626–645.

Simonton, D. K. (1994). *Greatness: Who makes history and why*. New York: Guilford Press.

Sipe, W. P., & Hanges, P. J. (1997). Re-framing the glass ceiling: A catastrophe model of changes in the perception of women as leaders. In R. G. Lord (Chair), *Dynamic systems, leadership perceptions, and gender effects*. Symposium presented at the Twelfth Annual Conference of the Society of Industrial and Organizational Psychology.

Smith, P. B., & Bond, M. H. (1993). *Social psychology across cultures: Analysis and perspectives*. London: Harvester Wheatsheaf.

Smith, P. B., Misumi, J., Tayeb, M. H., Paterson, M., & Bond, M. H. (1989). On the generality of leadership style across cultures. *Journal of Occupational Psychology*, (30), 526–537.

Staw, B. M., Sandelands, L. E., & Dutton, J. E. (1981). Threat-rigidity effects in organizational behavior: A multilevel analysis. *Administrative Science Quarterly, 26*(4), 501–524. doi:10.2307/2392337

Thompson, K. R., & Luthans, F. (1990). Organizational culture: A behavioral perspective. In B. Schneider (Ed.), *Organizational Climate and Culture* (pp. 319–344). San Francisco: Jossey-Bass.

Triandis, H. C. (1993). The contingency model in cross-cultural perspective. In M. M. Chemers & R. Ayman (Eds.), *Leadership theory and research: Perspectives and directions* (pp. 167–188). San Diego, CA: Academic Press.

Triandis, H. C. (1995). *Individualism and Collectivism*. Boulder, CO: Westview Press.

Tushman, M. L., Newman, W. H., & Nadler, D. A. (1988). Executive leadership and organizational evolution: Managing incremental and discontinuous change. In R. H. Kilman & T. J. Covin (Eds.), *Corporate transformation: Revitalizing organizations for a competitive world* (pp. 102–130). San Francisco: Jossey-Bass.

Appendix 1

DEFINITION OF KEY TERMS

1.Culture:
    1.1 "Culture is the way of life of a group of people" (Foster, 1962).

    1.2 "Culture is that complete whole which includes knowledge, beliefs, art, law, morals, customs and any capabilities and habits acquired as a member of a society" (Tylor, 1977).

    1.3 "Culture is the collective programming of the mind which distinguishes the members of one human group from another .... The interactive aggregate of common characteristics that influences a groups response to its environment" (Hofstede, 1980).

    1.4 "Culture is a set of learned core values, beliefs, standards, knowledge, morals, laws, and behaviors shared by individuals and societies that determines how an individual acts, feels, and views oneself and others. (From Mitchell, C. (2000) The Short course in International Trade Series: International Business Culture, Shanghai: Shanghai Foreign Language Education press).

2.   **Value:** The value concept, more than any other, should occupy a central position...able to unify the apparently diverse interests of all the sciences concerned with human behavior. (Psychologist Rokeach, 1973:3, Sociologist Williams, 1968; Anthropologist Kluckhohn, 1951). Values are viewed as the criteria people use to select and justify actions and to evaluate people and events.

3.   **Convergence:** The concept which holds that industrialization and technology are the primary driving forces for the global merging of work values (Dunphy, 1987; Yip, 1992; Keefer and Knack, 1997; Suarez-Villa, 2000).

4.   **Divergence:** It advocates that values system of a society is deeply embedded in its cultural roots and values system has been seen as the product of social-cultural influences (Inkeles, 1997), national culture differences reflect enduring cultural heritages that are deeply embedded in individuals (Ricks, Toyne, and Martinez, 1990). The values and

beliefs learned during childhood socialization endure throughout one's lifetime irrespective of business ideology changes in the society, and that these values are passed from generation to generation (Inglehart and Baker, 2000, Egri, Stewart, Terpstra, and Yu, 1999).

5. **Crossvergence:** It is defined as the synergistic interaction of social cultural and economic ideology influences within a society that result in q unique value system (Ralston et.al., 1997)economic ideology reflects the economic system that individuals within a society experience, with technology being an implicit part of it.

6. **Relationship Among Convergence, Divergence and Crossvergence:** Business ideology forces leading to convergence and the social-cultural forces leading to divergence will synergistically interact with one another.

7. **Terminal Values:** Terminal values are those social-culturally ingrained values deeply rooted in the core of social fabric of the society which are not susceptible to change.

8. **Instrumental Values:** These are the values that more peripheral and susceptible to change when there are economic, political or technological changes.

9. **Emic (Which Derived from the Term Phonemic):** As Pike defines it, the emic perspective focuses on the intrinsic cultural distinctions that are meaningful to the members of a given society (e.g., whether the natural world is distinguished from the supernatural realm in the worldview of the culture) in the same way that phonemic analysis focuses on the intrinsic phonological distinctions that are meaningful to speakers of a given language. The native members of a culture are the sole judges of the validity of an emic description, just as the native speakers of a language are the sole judges of the accuracy of a phonemic identification.

10. **Etic (Which Derived from the Term Phonetic):** The etic perspective, again according to Pike, relies upon the extrinsic concepts and categories that have meaning for scientific observers (e.g., per capita energy consumption) in the same way that phonetic analysis relies upon the extrinsic concepts and categories that are meaningful to linguistic analysts (e.g., dental fricatives). Scientists are the sole judges of the validity of an etic account, just as linguists are the sole judges of the accuracy of a phonetic transcription.

Besides Pike, the scholar most closely associated with the concepts of "emics" and "etics" is the cultural anthropologist Marvin Harris, who has made the distinction between the emic and etic perspectives an integral part of his paradigm of cultural materialism. Pike and Harris continue to disagree about the precise definition and application of emics and etics (Headland et al. 1990). The most significant area of their disagreement concerns the goal of the etic approach. For Pike, etics are a way of getting at emics; for Harris, etics are an end in themselves. From Pike's point of view, the etic approach is useful for penetrating, discovering, and elucidating emic systems, but etic claims to knowledge have no necessary priority over competing emic claims. From Harris's perspective, the etic approach is useful in making objective determinations of fact, and etic claims to knowledge are necessarily superior to competing emic claims. Pike believes that objective knowledge is an illusion, and that all claims to knowledge are ultimately subjective; Harris believes that objective knowledge is at least potentially obtainable, and that the pursuit of such knowledge is essential for a discipline that aspires to be a science.

The terms "emic" and "etic" are current in a growing number of fields--including education, folklore, management, medicine, philology, psychiatry, psychology, public health, semiotics, and urban studies--but they are generally used in ways that have little or nothing to do with their original anthropological context.

Emic constructs are accounts, descriptions, and analyses expressed in terms of the conceptual schemes and categories that are regarded as meaningful and appropriate by the members of the culture under study. Am emic construct is correctly termed "emic" if and only if it is in accord with the perceptions and understandings deemed appropriate by the insider's culture.

Etic constructs are accounts, descriptions, and analyses expressed in terms of the conceptual schemes and categories that are regarded as meaningful and appropriate by the community of scientific observers. An etic construct is correctly termed "etic" if and only if it is in accord with the epistemological principles deemed appropriate by science.

Finally, most cultural anthropologists agree that the goal of anthropological research must be the acquisition of both emic and etic knowledge. Emic knowledge is essential for an intuitive and empathic understanding of a culture, and it is essential for conducting effective ethnographic fieldwork. Furthermore, emic knowledge is often a valuable source of inspiration for etic hypotheses. Etic knowledge, on the other hand, is essential for cross-cultural comparison, the sine qua non of ethnology, because such comparison necessarily demands standard units and categories.

11. **Leader:** A leader is a person who is able to partner with followers in the creation and implementations of a common goal or vision.

12. **Leadership:** It is the ability of an individual to influence, motivate, and enable others to contribute towards the effectiveness and success of organizations of which they are members (House et.al., 1997P548).
13. **Followers:** These are those individuals who voluntarily engage in the leadership process by partnering with leaders and other followers for the purpose of achieving a common goal or vision.
14. **Nomothetic Approach:** It is an approach in leadership research field which insists that leadership phenomenon and leadership content should be applied globally. It is possible to obtain a one-for-all global leadership style (House, Wright and Aditya, 1997).
15. **Idiographic Approach:** This approach admits that leadership phenomenon is a universal issue, but leadership content is embedded into cultures. With the variances of cultures, leadership content is also varying. One leadership style is effective in one culture may not be effective in another culture (Chemes, 993; Hofstede, 1980).
16. **Hermeneutic Approach:** It is a process begun with F. Schleiermacher (1768-1834) which is adopted as a research methodology especially in social science research. The researchers and scholars are attempting to understand the mind of the authors when they are reading some ancient literature. Hermeneutics is both science and art. This approach is always going along with narrative approach (organizational storytelling method).
17. **Halo Effect:** Due to the unique characteristics of the subordinate (followers), superiors (leaders) are intending to overestimate the performance of the follower. (Performance Evaluation Trap).
18. **Horn Effect:** It is such phenomenon that the assessor (leader) is intending to underestimate the performance of the assessed (the follower) due to an event or a piecemeal of view (Performance Evaluation Trap).
19. **Pygmalion Effect:** It is such the case that Followers (Subordinates) are working at their utmost efforts while Leaders (Superiors) admit the high performance and give timely encouragement and reward, which will result in a benign cycling of the follower performance.
20. **Dyadic Theory:** It is a theory which reflects such a case that the same leader behaves differently in dealing with different followers.
21. **Upper Echelon Theory:** It is the theory which proposes that the succession in organization may or may not affect the organization performance. An overall consideration should be taken into this issue as the general characteristics of the whole team of the top management. This theory differs from other two theories as the "Common Sense Theory" and "Vicious Circle Theory".

22. **Level 5 Leadership:** It is proposed by Jim Collins, which is the latest concept about leadership style. The key ingredient of Level 5 Leadership is Humility. The concept can be simplified in such a simple equation: Humility + Will = Level 5. it is a study in duality---- modest and willful, shy and fearless.

23. **Transformational Leadership:** Bennis & Nanus (1985) have summarized transformational leadership style into these 4 dimensions initiated in 4I's. That is, Idealized influence or charisma, leaders being a role model; Inspirational Motivation, leaders advocate team spirit, motivate followers and intend to confront challenges; Intellectual Stimulation, leaders are keen on creativity and innovation; Individualized Consideration, leaders know the importance of empowerment and they like to work as mentors or coaches.

24. **Transactional Leadership:** This theory is derived from the Leader-Member-Exchange Theory and Path-Goal Theory. It is based on a series of transactional relations between the leader and the follower. If the degree of leadership perception by the follower is high, the follower will be rewarded as he is expected, vice versa. The transactional objects can be tangible as raise of the pay or intangible as loyalty, belongingness and trust. Transactional theory has two sub-dimensions: Contingent Reward and management by exception.

Appendix 2

SCHWARTZ VALUE SURVEY (ENGLISH VERSION)

Part One: Objectives and Statement of This Survey

Thank you for participating in this value survey. We are aiming at finding out how the values system affect Chinese business leaders. Meanwhile, we have added some personal information in order to find out the most important demographic factors that influence the behaviors of the participated business leaders in order to investigate the configuration of their leadership styles.

Part Two: Personal Background

1. Age: __ years old
2. Gender: (1) Male (2) Female
3. Birth Place (Area where you were born):
4. The area where you have lived longest (Five or more years):
5. Education conducted (Please choose the one which suits you)
   (1) Four or less years _____
   (2) Five to eight years _____
   (3) Nine to 12 years _____
   (4) 13 to 16 years ____
   (5) Master's degree _____
   (6) PhD. degree _____
6. Current position:
   (1) non-managerial post_____
   (2) Preliminary managerial post(e.g.Team leader)_____
   (3) Middle management(e.g.Dept. head)
   (4) Senior management(e.g. Company CEO or Director)_____
7. Accumulated work duration: years
8. Company scale:
   (1) Less than 100 employees
   (2) 100 to 1,000 employees
   (3) More than 1,000employees

9. The Ownership of my organization (can choose more than one items):
    (1) SOE
    (2) Collective business firm
    (3) Share holding organization
    (4) Joint business firm_____
    (5) Company limited_____
    (6) Share holding Co. Ltd._____
    (7) Private firm_____
    (8) Sino - foreign JV._____
    (9) JV with HK, Maucao & Taiwan_____
    (10) Foreign WOS_____
    (11) HK,Maucao & Taiwan WOS_____
    (12) Others (if not applicable to the above)_____

10. Business section of my organization:
    (1) Agriculture, mining, fishery, forestry _____
    (2) Construction _____
    (3) Manufacturing _____
    (4) Transport, communication and energy _____
    (5) Wholesale, retailing
    (6) Financing, insurance and real estate
    (7) tertiary industry (e.g. Hotels, restaurants)
    (8) Publish administration
    (9) Health-care
    (10) Others (if the above is not applicable) _____(and state specifically)

11. Company location(s) if not located in one place:
    (1) Eastern China
    (2) Northern China
    (3) Middle of China
    (4) Southern China
    (5) Northwestern China
    (6) Southwestern China
    (7) Northeastern China

Part Three: Value Orientation Survey

1. **Schwartz Value Survey on Chinese Business Leaders**

INSTRUCTIONS: This part consists of 2 sections comprised of *Values List 1* and *Values List 2*.

When responding to each of these sections, please ask yourself: "What values are important to ME as guiding principles in MY life, and what values are less important to me?" There are two lists of values on the following pages. These values come from different cultures. In the parentheses following each value item is an explanation that may help you to understand its meaning.

You are asked to rate how important each value is for **YOU** as *a guiding principle in your life*. Use the rating scales below:

0 means the value is not at all important, it is not relevant as a guiding principle for you.
3 means the value is important.
6 means the value is very important.

The higher the number (0,1,2,3,4,5,6), the more important the value is as a guiding principle in YOUR life.

-1 is for rating any values opposed to the principles that guide you.
7 is for rating a value of supreme importance as a guiding principle in your life; For these two extremes of value rating -1 and 7, you can only choose twice at most.

In the space before each value, write the number (-1,0,1,2,3,4,5,6,7) that indicates the degree of importance of that value for you personally. Try to distinguish as much as possible between the values by using all the numbers. You will, of course, need to use numbers more than once.

Please begin by reading values 1 to 30 on *Values List 1*, choose the one value that is most important to you and rate its importance. Next, choose the value that is most opposed to your values and rate it -1. If there is no such value, choose the value least important to you and rate it 0 or 1 according to the degree of its importance. Then, rate the rest of the values.

Values List 1

AS A GUIDING PRINCIPLE IN MY LIFE, this value is:

-1 opposed of   0 not important   1   2   3 important   4   5
6 very important   7 supreme importance

1. _____ EQUALITY (equal opportunity for all)
2. _____ INNER HARMONY (at peace with myself)

3. _____ SOCIAL POWER (control over others, dominance)
4. _____ PLEASURE (gratification of desires)
5. _____ FREEDOM (freedom of action and thought)
6. _____ A SPIRITUAL LIFE (emphasis on spiritual, not material matters)
7. _____ SENSE OF BELONGING (feeling that others care about me)
8. _____ SOCIAL ORDER (stability of society)
9. _____ AN EXCITING LIFE (stimulating experiences)
10. _____ MEANING IN LIFE (a purpose in life)
11. _____ POLITENESS (courtesy, good manners)
12. _____ WEALTH (material possessions, money)
13. _____ NATIONAL SECURITY (protection of my nation from my enemies)
14. _____ SELF RESPECT (belief in one's own worth)
15. _____ RECIPROCATION OF FAVORS (avoidance of indebtedness)
16. _____ CREATIVITY (uniqueness, imagination)
17. _____ A WORLD AT PEACE (free of war and conflict)
18. _____ RESPECT FOR TRADITION (preservation of time-honored customs)
19. _____ MATURE LOVE (deep emotional and spiritual intimacy)
20. _____ SELF-DISCIPLINE (self-restraint, resistance to temptation)
21. _____ DETACHMENT (detachment from worldly concerns)
22. _____ FAMILY SECURITY (safety for loved ones)
23. _____ SOCIAL RECOGNITION (respect, approval by others)
24. _____ UNITY WITH NATURE (fitting into nature)
25. _____ A VARIED LIFE (life filled with challenge, novelty and change)
26. _____ WISDOM (a mature understanding of life)
27. _____ AUTHORITY (the right to lead or command)
28. _____ TRUE FRIENDSHIP (close, supportive friends)
29. _____ A WORLD OF BEAUTY (beauty of nature and the arts)
30. _____ SOCIAL JUSTICE (correcting injustice, care for the weak)

Now rate how important each of the following values is for you as *a guiding principle in YOUR life*. These values are phrased as ways of acting that may be more or less important for you. Once again, try to distinguish as much as possible between the values by using all the numbers.

Before you begin, read values 31 to 56 on *Values List 2,* choose the one that is most important to you and rate its importance. Next, choose the value that is most opposed to your values, or--if there is no such value, choose the value least important to you, and rate it -1, 0, or 1 according to the degree of its importance. Then, rate the rest of the values.

Values List 2

AS A GUIDING PRINCIPLE IN MY LIFE, this value is:

-1 opposed of   0 not important   1   2   3 important   4   5
6 very important   7 supreme importance

31. _____ INDEPENDENT (self-reliant, self-sufficient)
32. _____ MODERATE (avoiding extremes of feeling and action)
33. _____ LOYAL (faithful to my friends, group)
34. _____ AMBITIOUS (hard working, aspiring)
35. _____ BROAD-MINDED (tolerant of different ideas and beliefs)
36. _____ HUMBLE (modest, self-effacing)
37. _____ DARING (seeking adventure, risk)
38. _____ PROTECTING THE ENVIRONMENT (preserving nature)
39. _____ INFLUENTIAL (having an impact on people and events)
40. _____ HONORING OF PARENTS AND ELDERS (showing respect)
41. _____ CHOOSING OWN GOALS (selecting own purposes)
42. _____ HEALTHY (not being sick physically or mentally)
43. _____ CAPABLE (competent, effective, efficient)
44. _____ ACCEPTING MY PORTION IN LIFE (submitting to life's circumstances)
45. _____ HONEST (genuine, sincere)
46. _____ PRESERVING MY PUBLIC IMAGE (preserving my "face")
47. _____ OBEDIENCE (dutiful, meeting obligations)
48. _____ INTELLIGENT (logical, thinking)
49. _____ HELPFUL (working for the welfare of others)
50. _____ ENJOYING LIFE (enjoying food, sex, leisure, etc.)
51. _____ DEVOUT (holding to religious faith and belief)
52. _____ RESPONSIBLE (dependable, reliable)
53. _____ CURIOUS (interested in everything, exploring)
54. _____ FORGIVING (willing to pardon others)
55. _____ SUCCESSFUL (achieving goals)
56. _____ CLEAN (neat, tidy)

Table 1. Schwartz Value Survey Values Dimensions

Value	Items
Power	3, 12, 27, 46
Achievement	34, 39, 43, 55
Hedonism	4, 50
Stimulation	9, 25, 37
Self-direction	5, 16, 31, 41, 53
Universalism	1, 17, 24, 26, 29, 30, 35, 38
Benevolence	33, 45, 49, 52, 54
Tradition	18, 32, 36, 44, 51
Conformity	11, 20, 40, 47
Security	8, 13, 15, 22, 56

Values Dimensions

Openness-to-Change: Self-direction + Stimulation
Conservation: Tradition + Conformity + Security
Self-Enhancement: Power + Achievement + Hedonism
Self-Transcendence: Benevolence + Universalism

Value items 1-30 are terminal (or end) values, while value items 31-56 are instrumental values.

These 56 value items can be shaped into ten sub- dimensions of

- Power
- Achievement
- Hedonism
- Stimulation
- Self-direction
- Universalism
- Benevolence
- Tradition
- Conformity
- Security

Part Four: M.H. Bond Value Survey

The aim of this study is to find out what matters are important or unimportant to people. You will find that there are 40 items in all in this survey list. Please indicate how important to you is each of these 40 items.

To express your opinion, imagine an importance scale which varies from 1 to 7 as the maximum. 1 stands for "no importance for me at all" and 7 stand for "supreme importance for me", in other words, the larger the number, the greater the degree of importance to you. Give one number (either 1, 2, 3, 4, 5, 6 or 7) to each item in the brackets to express how important is that item to you personally.

You can concentrate better by asking yourself the following question while rating each item: "how important is this item to me personally?" Repeat the same question when you are rating the next item, until you finish all the 40 items.

Thank you!

1 Not at all Important   2 Unimportant   3 Not so Important   4 Neutral
5 Somewhat Important   6 Important   7 Very Important

( ) 1. Filial piety (obedience to parent,respect for parents, honoring of ancestors,financial support of parents)
( ) 2. Industry (Working hard)
( ) 3. Tolerance of others
( ) 4. Harmony with others
( ) 5. Humbleness
( ) 6. Loyalty to Superiors
( ) 7. Observation of rites and social rituals
( ) 8. Reciprocation of greetings, favors and gifts
( ) 9. Kindness (Forgiveness and compassion)
( ) 10. Knowledge (Education)
( ) 11. Solidarity with others
( ) 12. Moderation, following the middle way
( ) 13. Self-cultivation
( ) 14. Ordering relationships by status and observing this order
( ) 15. Sense of righteousness
( ) 16. Benevolent authority
( ) 17. Non-competitiveness
( ) 18. Personal-steadiness and stability
( ) 19. Resistance to corruption

( ) 20. Patriotism
( ) 21. Sincerity
( ) 22. Keeping oneself disinterested and pure
( ) 23. Thrifty
( ) 24. Persistence (Perseverance)
( ) 25. Patience
( ) 26. Repayment of both the good or the evil that another person has caused
   you
( ) 27. A sense of cultural superiority
( ) 28. Adaptability
( ) 29. Prudence (Carefulness)
( ) 30. Trustworthiness
( ) 31. Having a sense of shame
( ) 32. Courtesy
( ) 33. Contentedness with one's position in life
( ) 34. Being conservative
( ) 35. Protecting your "Face" (Being face-saving)
( ) 36. A close, intimate friend
( ) 37. Chastity in women
( ) 38. Having few desire
( ) 39. Respect for tradition
( ) 40. Wealth

Part Five: Acknowledgment and Sharing of Research Results

Our sincere thanks to you for supporting this survey. If you have interest in the research results, please leave your contact information here and we will send the research results to you in due course.

E-mail address: _____

Other channels of communication: _____

Survey conducted on the date of: _____

   In: _____

   Coached by _____

Thanks again and with best regards!

Appendix 3

LEADERSHIP STYLES SURVEY (ENGLISH VERSION)

Part One: Objectives and Statement of This Survey

This questionnaire is to help you assess what leadership style you normally operate out of. The lowest score possible for any stage is 10 (Almost never) while the highest score possible for any stage is 50 (Almost always).

The highest of the three scores indicates what style of leadership you normally use. If your highest score is 40 or more, it is a strong indicator of your normal style.

The lowest of the three scores is an indicator of the style you least use. If your lowest score is 20 or less, it is a strong indicator that you normally do not operate out of this mode.

If two of the scores are close to the same, you might be going through a transition phase, either personally or at work, except if you score high in both the participative and the delegative then you are probably a delegative leader.

If there is only a small difference between the three scores, then this indicates that you have no clear perception of the mode you operate out of, or you are a new leader and are trying to feel out the correct style for yourself.

Part Two: Personal Background

1. **Age:** years old
2. **Gender:** (1) Male (2) Female
3. **Birth Place (Area where you were born):**
4. **The area where you have lived longest (Five or more years):**
5. **Education conducted (Please choose the one which suits you)**
    (1)   Four or less years _____
    (2)   Five to eight years_____
    (3)   Nine to 12 years _____
    (4)   13 to 16 years _____
    (5)   Master's degree _____
    (6)   PhD. degree _____

6. **Current position:**
   (1) non-managerial post_____
   (2) Preliminary managerial post(e.g.Team leader)_____
   (3) Middle management(e.g.Dept. head)
   (4) Senior management(e.g. Company CEO or Director)_____
7. **Accumulated work duration:** years
8. **Company scale:**
   (1) Less than 100 employees
   (2) 100 to 1,000 employees
   (3) More than 1,000employees
9. **The Ownership of my organization (can choose more than one items):**
   (1) SOE
   (2) Collective business firm
   (3) Share holding organization
   (4) Joint business firm_____
   (5) Company limited_____
   (6) Share holding Co. Ltd._____
   (7) Private firm_____
   (8) Sino - foreign JV._____
   (9) JV with HK, Maucao & Taiwan_____
   (10) Foreign WOS_____
   (11) HK, Maucao & Taiwan WOS_____
   (12) Others (if not applicable to the above)_____
10. **Business section of my organization:**
    (1) Agriculture, mining, fishery, forestry _____
    (2) Construction _____
    (3) Manufacturing _____
    (4) Transport, communication and energy _____
    (5) Wholesale, retailing
    (6) Financing, insurance and real estate
    (7) tertiary industry (e.g. Hotels, restaurants)
    (8) Publish administration
    (9) Health-care
    (10) Others (if the above is not applicable) _____ (and state specifically)

11. **Company location(s) if not located in one place:**
    (1) Eastern China
    (2) Northern China
    (3) Middle of China
    (4) Southern China
    (5) Northwestern China
    (6) Southwestern China
    (7) Northeastern China

Part Three: Leadership Survey Items

Please read the following each statement in this survey and choose the NUMBER from 1, 2, 3, 4, or 5 which best suits you in conducting your leadership in your workplace and fill in the Leadership Survey Grading Table.

The connotations of the FIVE NUMBERS are indicated as below:

5 Always like this   4 Often like this   3 Sometimes like this
2 Seldom like this   1 Never like this

Table 1. The Statement of Leadership Survey Items(30 Statements in all)

1	I always have the final decision making power in my department or my team.	5	4	3	2	1
2	Though I have the final decision making power, I always let one or more subordinates to discuss issues with me.	5	4	3	2	1
3	For every important decisions, my subordinates and I make the final decision by voting.	5	4	3	2	1
4	I do not consider the suggestions of my subordinates, because I have no time to listen to them.	5	4	3	2	1
5	I consult and apply the advice of my subordinates in our future plan and project.	5	4	3	2	1
6	A key decision must be consented by individual or majority of people in my group before it is made.	5	4	3	2	1
7	I tell my subordinates what to do and how to do it.	5	4	3	2	1
8	Once things go wrong and I need to make strategic decisions, I always seek advice from my subordinates to make things going right.	5	4	3	2	1
9	I use email, memo and voice mail for communication but not face-to-face meetings. The only thing my subordinates do is to follow my orders.	5	4	3	2	1
10	Once my subordinates make mistake, I tell them not to make the same mistake again and draw lessons from it.	5	4	3	2	1
11	I create such an air for my subordinates: they have the ownership of the project and I allow them to participate in the decision-making process.	5	4	3	2	1
12	I allow my subordinates to decide what they do and how to do it.	5	4	3	2	1

continued on following page

Table 1. Continued

13	Unless with my consent, new subordinates are not allowed to make any decision.	5	4	3	2	1
14	I consult my subordinates their views on how things will go. Once I agree with them, I would accept their opinions.	5	4	3	2	1
15	My subordinates know more clearly about their work, so I allow them to make decisions automatically in order to accomplish their work.	5	4	3	2	1
16	Once things go wrong, I tell my subordinates what have been wrong with the work and establish a new procedure.	5	4	3	2	1
17	I allow my subordinates to arrange their work as per the priority according to my instructions.	5	4	3	2	1
18	To enact a new procedure, I always follow it myself.	5	4	3	2	1
19	To guarantee outcome of a certain assignment, I conduct rigid supervisory control of my subordinates.	5	4	3	2	1
20	Once role expectation diverse discrepancy, I ask them to find out the variance and solve the problem.	5	4	3	2	1
21	Every subordinate has the responsibility to define his /her work assignments.	5	4	3	2	1
22	I like the power bestowed by my position to supervise my subordinates.	5	4	3	2	1
23	I like excel my power and help my subordinates grow.	5	4	3	2	1
24	I like to share my power with my subordinates.	5	4	3	2	1
25	To accomplish organizational goal, subordinates must be supervised, punished and even intimidated.	5	4	3	2	1
26	If subordinates have responsibility in their work, they can mind and constrain their behaviors.	5	4	3	2	1
27	Subordinates have the right to decision their organizational goal.	5	4	3	2	1
28	Subordinates are mainly seeking for safety.	5	4	3	2	1
29	Subordinates know how to solve the organizational problems through their wisdom and creativity.	5	4	3	2	1
30	My subordinates are able to guide their behavior just like I do.	5	4	3	2	1

Table 2. Leadership Survey Grading Table

Item	Score	Item	Score	Item	Score
1	_____	2	_____	3	_____
4	_____	5	_____	6	_____
7	_____	8	_____	9	_____
10	_____	11	_____	12	_____
13	_____	14	_____	15	_____
16	_____	17	_____	18	_____
19	_____	20	_____	21	_____
22	_____	23	_____	24	_____
25	_____	26	_____	27	_____
28	_____	29	_____	30	_____
TOTAL	_____	TOTAL	_____	TOTAL	_____
	Authoritarian Style		Participative Style		Delegative Style
	(autocratic)		(democratic)		(free reign)

Part Four: Acknowledgment and Sharing of Research Results

Our sincere thanks to you for supporting this survey. If you have interest in the research results, please leave your contact information here and we will send the research results to you in due course.

E-mail address: _____

Other channels of communication: _____

Survey conducted on the date of: _____

     In: _____

     Coached by _____

Thanks again and with best regards!

Appendix 4

INTERVIEW FRAMEWORK: RESEARCH ON LEADERSHIP STYLES UNDER DIFFERENT CULTURAL CONTEXTS

Stories of Chinese Leadership

Historical Stories of Chinese Leadership (the Past)

Purpose: To identify the historical 'grand stories' of Chinese leadership from the trilogy of Confucianism, Taoism, and Buddhism. To discern similarities and variations in the interpretation of these historical texts from the perspective of traditional Chinese philosophers as well as the discourse on Eastern philosophies in the modern leadership literature.

Procedures: An expert panel of Chinese philosophers will be asked to identify stories that in their view, are most influential and relevant for leadership textual analysis of leadership qualities and practices following hermeneutic principles and procedures -- from the Eastern perspective and from the Western perspective. May want to also include other persons to verify coding. These are then reviewed and commented on by the expert panel of Chinese philosophers

Textual analysis of modern interpretations of these Eastern philosophies as presented in the Chinese and Western leadership literature. This will involve a literature search in electronic databases for articles as well as books (e.g., Heider's book entitled "Tao of Leadership").

Modern Stories of Chinese Leadership (the Present)

Purpose: To learn the modern stories of Chinese leadership and to discern the extent to which these reflect traditional Chinese philosophies and modern Western leadership theories. Empirical test of theories of cultural convergence, divergence, and cross-vergence in Chinese leadership theories in practice.

Procedures: Research Participants: Chinese executives in the XJTU EMBA program (targeted number of participants = 50 to 60). Involvement in the research will include the completion of a survey questionnaire and participation in a qualitative interview.

Step 1: Quantitative Survey Questionnaires to include validated measures of Chinese leadership style (check previous research conducted in China, Hong Kong, and Taiwan); Confucian values measures (e.g., Bond's Chinese Values Survey), cross-culturally validated personal values measure (e.g., Schwartz Value Survey), Western leadership styles (e.g., Goleman's emotional intelligence, visionary leadership, transformational leadership, Level 5 leadership)

Questionnaires will be sent to participating executives prior to their interviews and will be collected at the time of the interview.

Participating executives will be subsequently provided with a "Personal Leadership Profile" report as well as a summary report of study findings

Quantitative analysis of questionnaires will focus determining relationships among personal values and leadership styles, demographic differences in values/leadership (e.g., gender, age/generation)

Step 2: Qualitative interviews with Chinese executives who will be asked for three stories of leadership, each in a different context.
1. Their personal story of leadership.
2. A story about a leader in their work experience who has significantly impacted their leadership philosophy/practice
3. A story about a leader in their personal/community experience who has significantly impacted their leadership philosophy/practice

Sample probing questions: Why is this an important story for you? What is this an interesting story for you? How has this leader impacted your leadership philosophy and/or practice?

To develop interview protocols, will review organizational storytelling literature (e.g., David Boje)

- Content analysis of leadership stories will focus on identifying:
- Common and unique themes within and across contexts
- Themes consistent with historical Chinese philosophies
- Themes consistent with Western leadership theories

Step 3: Comparative analysis of qualitative and quantitative leadership data for a holistic understanding of antecedents and practice of organizational leadership in the modern Chinese society.

A Thorny Question: I am still considering whether the analysis of leadership philosophy and principles reflective of Chinese communist ideology should be included or not, as it has evolved over time since the founding of P.R. China in 1949.

Research Report: Based on this research proposal, I have done about 300 questionnaires as against the proposed 50 or 60 in order to secure more degree of reliability and generality. The next step will have to input all the raw data into relevant software as SPSS, or LISREL to process the data and present interpretations based on the findings. These findings will be compared with literature review as most of the leadership literature has been developed in the western world. Personal interviews will be conducted with the participants carefully singled out from the questionnaires list to cover different industries, different geographic areas, different genders and age groups, etc. in order to secure the broad coverage of the research.

Appendix 5

Stories of Other Business Leaders Interviewed

Table 1. Interviews conducted with other business leaders

Interviewee	Position and Name of the Company	Nature of the Ownership	Interview Time	Interview Venue
James LIU	Director of a Commercial Bank	State Owned Enterprise (SOE)	Nov. 12, 2006	Zhengzhou
Aaron LEE	Manager of a Bookstore	Private Firm	Nov. 23, 2006	Zhengzhou
Teresa CHEN	Director of an Auction Company	Private Firm	Dec. 8, 2006	Beijing
Vilene SHI	Vice GM of a Clothing Firm	Sino-Japan Joint Venture (JV)	Feb. 14, 2007	Suzhou
Lily WANG	GM of a Machinery Plant	State Owned Enterprise (SOE)	April 3, 2007	Yinchuan
Marc WU	Director of a Consulting Firm	Sino-USA Joint Venture (JV)	June 2, 2007	Shanghai
William HE	Vice Director of US Subsidiary in China	Whole Owned Subsidiary (WOS)	July 6, 2007	Xi'an
Jack ZANG	GM of a Food Chain Store	Private Firm	Sept. 6, 2007	Shenzhen
John BAI	GM of a Film Studio	SOE	Sept. 22, 2007	Beijing

Related Readings

To continue IGI Global's long-standing tradition of advancing innovation through emerging research, please find below a compiled list of recommended IGI Global book chapters and journal articles in the areas of leadership development, business culture, and strategic leadership. These related readings will provide additional information and guidance to further enrich your knowledge and assist you with your own research.

Aguirre, S. J. (2017). The Lived Experiences of Authentic Leaders: A Phenomenological Study Exploring the Defining Experiences that Informed Their Development. In F. Topor (Ed.), *Handbook of Research on Individualism and Identity in the Globalized Digital Age* (pp. 287–309). Hershey, PA: IGI Global. doi:10.4018/978-1-5225-0522-8.ch013

Altındağ, E. (2016). Current Approaches in Change Management. In A. Goksoy (Ed.), *Organizational Change Management Strategies in Modern Business* (pp. 24–51). Hershey, PA: IGI Global. doi:10.4018/978-1-4666-9533-7.ch002

Atiku, S. O., & Fields, Z. (2017). Multicultural Orientations for 21st Century Global Leadership. In N. Baporikar (Ed.), *Management Education for Global Leadership* (pp. 28–51). Hershey, PA: IGI Global. doi:10.4018/978-1-5225-1013-0.ch002

Balogh, A. (2017). Knowledge Management and Its Approaches: Basics of Developing Company Knowledge Management Systems. In A. Bencsik (Ed.), *Knowledge Management Initiatives and Strategies in Small and Medium Enterprises* (pp. 1–24). Hershey, PA: IGI Global. doi:10.4018/978-1-5225-1642-2.ch001

Baporikar, N. (2016). Talent Management Integrated Approach for Organizational Development. In A. Casademunt (Ed.), *Strategic Labor Relations Management in Modern Organizations* (pp. 22–48). Hershey, PA: IGI Global. doi:10.4018/978-1-5225-0356-9.ch002

Baporikar, N. (2017). Corporate Leadership and Sustainability. In Z. Fields (Ed.), *Collective Creativity for Responsible and Sustainable Business Practice* (pp. 160–179). Hershey, PA: IGI Global. doi:10.4018/978-1-5225-1823-5. ch009

Barron, I., & Novak, D. A. (2017). i-Leadership: Leadership Learning in the Millennial Generation. In P. Ordoñez de Pablos, & R. Tennyson (Eds.), Handbook of Research on Human Resources Strategies for the New Millennial Workforce (pp. 231-257). Hershey, PA: IGI Global. doi:10.4018/978-1-5225-0948-6.ch011

Begum, R., & Mujtaba, B. G. (2016). Business Ethics for Employee Development in Pakistan. In U. Aung & P. Ordoñez de Pablos (Eds.), *Managerial Strategies and Practice in the Asian Business Sector* (pp. 11–29). Hershey, PA: IGI Global. doi:10.4018/978-1-4666-9758-4.ch002

Bencsik, A. (2017). Appropriate Leadership Style in Knowledge Management System (KMS) Building. In A. Bencsik (Ed.), *Knowledge Management Initiatives and Strategies in Small and Medium Enterprises* (pp. 91–112). Hershey, PA: IGI Global. doi:10.4018/978-1-5225-1642-2.ch005

Bencsik, A., & Filep, B. (2017). Relationship between Knowledge Management and Innovation. In A. Bencsik (Ed.), *Knowledge Management Initiatives and Strategies in Small and Medium Enterprises* (pp. 67–90). Hershey, PA: IGI Global. doi:10.4018/978-1-5225-1642-2.ch004

Bisschoff, T. C., & Nieto, M. L. (2017). Leadership and Followership in Post-1992 University Business Schools in England. In S. Mukerji & P. Tripathi (Eds.), *Handbook of Research on Administration, Policy, and Leadership in Higher Education* (pp. 461–495). Hershey, PA: IGI Global. doi:10.4018/978-1-5225-0672-0.ch018

Bissessar, C. (2017). Leadership Challenges Confronting Middle Managers at a Secondary School in Trinidad. In C. Bissessar (Ed.), *Assessing the Current State of Education in the Caribbean* (pp. 1–23). Hershey, PA: IGI Global. doi:10.4018/978-1-5225-1700-9.ch001

Blomme, R. J., & Morsch, J. (2016). Organizations as Social Networks: The Role of the Compliance Officer as Agent of Change in Implementing Rules and Codes of Conduct. In A. Goksoy (Ed.), *Organizational Change Management Strategies in Modern Business* (pp. 110–121). Hershey, PA: IGI Global. doi:10.4018/978-1-4666-9533-7.ch006

Bognár, T., & Rácz, I. (2017). From Giftedness to Compliance: The Best Practices in Utilizing Human Capital. In A. Bencsik (Ed.), *Knowledge Management Initiatives and Strategies in Small and Medium Enterprises* (pp. 204–225). Hershey, PA: IGI Global. doi:10.4018/978-1-5225-1642-2.ch010

Boice, G. S. (2017). Balancing the Leadership Equation: Know Yourself and Know Your Follower – A Modern Case Study of Metacognition and Servant Leadership. In V. Wang (Ed.), *Encyclopedia of Strategic Leadership and Management* (pp. 16–28). Hershey, PA: IGI Global. doi:10.4018/978-1-5225-1049-9.ch002

Boice, W. L. (2017). Non-Profit Leadership Success: A Study of a Small, Non-Profit Organization's Leadership and Culture through the Lens of Its Volunteers. In V. Wang (Ed.), *Encyclopedia of Strategic Leadership and Management* (pp. 485–506). Hershey, PA: IGI Global. doi:10.4018/978-1-5225-1049-9.ch035

Boice, W. L. (2017). Raising Strategic Leaders: A Call for Action – An Army Perspective and Conceptual Framework for Organizations and Institutions Worldwide. In V. Wang (Ed.), *Encyclopedia of Strategic Leadership and Management* (pp. 538–552). Hershey, PA: IGI Global. doi:10.4018/978-1-5225-1049-9.ch038

Bowman, S. G., & Mulvenon, S. W. (2017). Effective Management of Generational Dynamics in the Workplace. In V. Wang (Ed.), *Encyclopedia of Strategic Leadership and Management* (pp. 833–844). Hershey, PA: IGI Global. doi:10.4018/978-1-5225-1049-9.ch058

Breithaupt, J., & Durante, R. (2017). Multiple Intelligences for Global Leadership Development. In V. Wang (Ed.), *Encyclopedia of Strategic Leadership and Management* (pp. 470–484). Hershey, PA: IGI Global. doi:10.4018/978-1-5225-1049-9.ch034

Brown, S. L. (2017). A Case Study of Strategic Leadership and Research in Practice: Principal Preparation Programs that Work – An Educational Administration Perspective of Best Practices for Master's Degree Programs for Principal Preparation. In V. Wang (Ed.), *Encyclopedia of Strategic Leadership and Management* (pp. 1226–1244). Hershey, PA: IGI Global. doi:10.4018/978-1-5225-1049-9.ch086

Brown, S. L., & Hartman, A. (2017). Feminist Creative Leadership Approaches. In V. Wang (Ed.), *Encyclopedia of Strategic Leadership and Management* (pp. 233–243). Hershey, PA: IGI Global. doi:10.4018/978-1-5225-1049-9.ch017

Bruno, G. (2017). Product Knowledge Management in Small Manufacturing Enterprises. In A. Bencsik (Ed.), *Knowledge Management Initiatives and Strategies in Small and Medium Enterprises* (pp. 157–179). Hershey, PA: IGI Global. doi:10.4018/978-1-5225-1642-2.ch008

Brzozowski, M., & Ferster, I. (2017). Educational Management Leadership: High School Principal's Management Style and Parental Involvement in School Management in Israel. In V. Potocan, M. Üngan, & Z. Nedelko (Eds.), *Handbook of Research on Managerial Solutions in Non-Profit Organizations* (pp. 55–74). Hershey, PA: IGI Global. doi:10.4018/978-1-5225-0731-4.ch003

Burton, S. L. (2017). Leadership Shifts: Perceptions and Consequences, In-Person, or Cyber. In V. Wang (Ed.), *Encyclopedia of Strategic Leadership and Management* (pp. 371–397). Hershey, PA: IGI Global. doi:10.4018/978-1-5225-1049-9.ch028

Buzady, Z. (2017). Resolving the Magic Cube of Effective Case Teaching: Benchmarking Case Teaching Practices in Emerging Markets – Insights from the Central European University Business School, Hungary. In D. Latusek (Ed.), *Case Studies as a Teaching Tool in Management Education* (pp. 79–103). Hershey, PA: IGI Global. doi:10.4018/978-1-5225-0770-3.ch005

Byrd-Poller, L., Farmer, J. L., & Ford, V. (2017). The Role of Leaders in Facilitating Healing After Organizational Trauma. In S. Háša & R. Brunet-Thornton (Eds.), *Impact of Organizational Trauma on Workplace Behavior and Performance* (pp. 318–340). Hershey, PA: IGI Global. doi:10.4018/978-1-5225-2021-4.ch014

Campbell, A. (2016). Leadership Education within Transitional Justice Instruments. In K. Pandey & P. Upadhyay (Eds.), *Promoting Global Peace and Civic Engagement through Education* (pp. 190–211). Hershey, PA: IGI Global. doi:10.4018/978-1-5225-0078-0.ch011

Campbell, L. O., Truitt, J. H., Herlihy, C. P., & Plante, J. D. (2017). A Thematic Analysis of Leadership Qualities of Women Leaders in Technology: Viewed through Social Media. In V. Wang (Ed.), *Encyclopedia of Strategic Leadership and Management* (pp. 1–15). Hershey, PA: IGI Global. doi:10.4018/978-1-5225-1049-9.ch001

Carvalho, A. B., & Nogueira, F. (2016). The Key of Franchising Chains and Human Resource Management: A Question of Commitment. In A. Casademunt (Ed.), *Strategic Labor Relations Management in Modern Organizations* (pp. 209–222). Hershey, PA: IGI Global. doi:10.4018/978-1-5225-0356-9.ch013

Chedid, M., & Teixeira, L. (2017). Knowledge Management and Software Development Organization: What Is the Challenge? In A. Bencsik (Ed.), *Knowledge Management Initiatives and Strategies in Small and Medium Enterprises* (pp. 226–246). Hershey, PA: IGI Global. doi:10.4018/978-1-5225-1642-2.ch011

Conrero, S. (2016). External Consulting in Change Processes: Change Management Consulting and Human Resource Management. In A. Casademunt (Ed.), *Strategic Labor Relations Management in Modern Organizations* (pp. 76–88). Hershey, PA: IGI Global. doi:10.4018/978-1-5225-0356-9.ch004

De León, A., Ozuem, W., & Okoya, J. (2016). Reframing Diversity in Management: Diversity and Human Resource Management. In A. Casademunt (Ed.), *Strategic Labor Relations Management in Modern Organizations* (pp. 105–120). Hershey, PA: IGI Global. doi:10.4018/978-1-5225-0356-9.ch006

Delmas, P. M. (2017). Research-Based Leadership for Next-Generation Leaders. In R. Styron Jr & J. Styron (Eds.), *Comprehensive Problem-Solving and Skill Development for Next-Generation Leaders* (pp. 1–39). Hershey, PA: IGI Global. doi:10.4018/978-1-5225-1968-3.ch001

Deshpande, M. (2017). Best Practices in Management Institutions for Global Leadership: Policy Aspects. In N. Baporikar (Ed.), *Management Education for Global Leadership* (pp. 1–27). Hershey, PA: IGI Global. doi:10.4018/978-1-5225-1013-0.ch001

Dickenson, P., & Montgomery, J. L. (2016). The Role of Teacher Leadership for Promoting Professional Development Practices. In K. Dikilitaş (Ed.), *Innovative Professional Development Methods and Strategies for STEM Education* (pp. 91–114). Hershey, PA: IGI Global. doi:10.4018/978-1-4666-9471-2.ch006

Domínguez, M. B. (2016). International Human Capital as a Source of Competitive Advantage for Organizations: International Human Resource Management. In A. Casademunt (Ed.), *Strategic Labor Relations Management in Modern Organizations* (pp. 1–21). Hershey, PA: IGI Global. doi:10.4018/978-1-5225-0356-9.ch001

Drago-Severson, E., Maslin-Ostrowski, P., & Hoffman, A. M. (2017). In One Voice: Aspiring and Practicing School Leaders Embrace the Need for a More Integrated Approach to Leadership Preparation and Development. In V. Wang (Ed.), *Adult Education and Vocational Training in the Digital Age* (pp. 147–168). Hershey, PA: IGI Global. doi:10.4018/978-1-5225-0929-5.ch009

Durante, R. (2017). Value-Based Leadership and Personality Type: The Influence on Organizational Change. In V. Wang (Ed.), *Encyclopedia of Strategic Leadership and Management* (pp. 662–685). Hershey, PA: IGI Global. doi:10.4018/978-1-5225-1049-9.ch046

Ellington, L. (2017). A Strategy: A 21st Century Strategic Leader Profile. In V. Wang (Ed.), *Encyclopedia of Strategic Leadership and Management* (pp. 1299–1313). Hershey, PA: IGI Global. doi:10.4018/978-1-5225-1049-9.ch090

Ellington, L. (2017). Strategic Leadership: An Organic Intellect. In V. Wang (Ed.), *Encyclopedia of Strategic Leadership and Management* (pp. 1623–1636). Hershey, PA: IGI Global. doi:10.4018/978-1-5225-1049-9.ch113

Ellis, A. (2016). Cultural Intelligence and Experiential Learning Powering Faculty Intercultural Leadership Development. In V. Wang (Ed.), *Handbook of Research on Learning Outcomes and Opportunities in the Digital Age* (pp. 354–375). Hershey, PA: IGI Global. doi:10.4018/978-1-4666-9577-1.ch016

Ellis, M., & Kisling, E. (2017). Collaborative Approach to Successful Virtual Team Leadership. In V. Wang (Ed.), *Encyclopedia of Strategic Leadership and Management* (pp. 55–70). Hershey, PA: IGI Global. doi:10.4018/978-1-5225-1049-9.ch005

Elufiede, O. J., & Flynn, B. B. (2017). Mentor the Leader: A Transformational Approach. In R. Styron Jr & J. Styron (Eds.), *Comprehensive Problem-Solving and Skill Development for Next-Generation Leaders* (pp. 188–209). Hershey, PA: IGI Global. doi:10.4018/978-1-5225-1968-3.ch009

Erne, R. (2016). Change Management Revised. In A. Goksoy (Ed.), *Organizational Change Management Strategies in Modern Business* (pp. 1–23). Hershey, PA: IGI Global. doi:10.4018/978-1-4666-9533-7.ch001

Esquivel, M. I., Tjernstad, C. D., Mac Quarrie, A., & Tamariz, M. I. (2017). Personal Growth and Leadership: Interpersonal Communication with Mindfulness into Action. In V. Wang (Ed.), *Encyclopedia of Strategic Leadership and Management* (pp. 507–525). Hershey, PA: IGI Global. doi:10.4018/978-1-5225-1049-9.ch036

Esquivel, M. I., Wallace, B., Du, X., Chang, Y., Brito, A., Ong, F. L., & Morales-Abbud, J. A. et al. (2017). Leadership Skills Development: Co-Creating Sustainability through Indigenous Knowledge. In V. Wang (Ed.), *Encyclopedia of Strategic Leadership and Management* (pp. 398–416). Hershey, PA: IGI Global. doi:10.4018/978-1-5225-1049-9.ch029

Esquivel, M. I., Wallace, B., Du, X., Parks, C., Chang, Y., Brito, A., & Dennis, Y. et al. (2017). Readdressing Situational Leadership in the New World Order through Technology. In V. Wang (Ed.), *Encyclopedia of Strategic Leadership and Management* (pp. 553–566). Hershey, PA: IGI Global. doi:10.4018/978-1-5225-1049-9.ch039

Esquivel, M. I., Wallace, B., Mewani, A., Reyes, A., Marsick, V., Yorks, L., & Green, J. et al. (2017). Conflict Resolution and Leadership Mindfulness into Action (MIA) for Cultural Humility and Awareness (MIA-CHA): Toward Ending Microaggressions and Fostering Harmony. In V. Wang (Ed.), *Encyclopedia of Strategic Leadership and Management* (pp. 71–82). Hershey, PA: IGI Global. doi:10.4018/978-1-5225-1049-9.ch006

Evans, C. M. (2017). Interpersonal Communication Application to Leadership. In V. Wang (Ed.), *Encyclopedia of Strategic Leadership and Management* (pp. 296–316). Hershey, PA: IGI Global. doi:10.4018/978-1-5225-1049-9.ch022

Fenyvesi, É., & Vágány, J. B. (2017). Knowledge-Sharing Is One of the Guarantees of Success in Family Businesses. In A. Bencsik (Ed.), *Knowledge Management Initiatives and Strategies in Small and Medium Enterprises* (pp. 291–315). Hershey, PA: IGI Global. doi:10.4018/978-1-5225-1642-2.ch014

Ferreira-Cotón, X., & Carballo-Penela, A. (2016). Why Manage Human Resources from a Social Responsibility Perspective?: An Analysis of the Job Seekers' and Employees' Perceptions. In A. Casademunt (Ed.), *Strategic Labor Relations Management in Modern Organizations* (pp. 149–171). Hershey, PA: IGI Global. doi:10.4018/978-1-5225-0356-9.ch009

Figueiredo, P., & Sousa, M. J. (2016). Leaders and Followers: The Leadership Style Perceived in Modern Organizations. In G. Jamil, J. Poças Rascão, F. Ribeiro, & A. Malheiro da Silva (Eds.), *Handbook of Research on Information Architecture and Management in Modern Organizations* (pp. 195–218). Hershey, PA: IGI Global. doi:10.4018/978-1-4666-8637-3.ch009

Gao, J. H. (2016). Examining Corporate Social Responsibility and Employee Engagement in Macao: The Mediating Role of Perceived Organizational Support and Chinese Values. In U. Aung & P. Ordoñez de Pablos (Eds.), *Managerial Strategies and Practice in the Asian Business Sector* (pp. 59–81). Hershey, PA: IGI Global. doi:10.4018/978-1-4666-9758-4.ch005

Gao, Z., Li, J., Hu, H., & Wang, Y. (2016). Internationalization of Chinese Pharmaceutical Firms-Strategies and Drivers. In U. Aung & P. Ordoñez de Pablos (Eds.), *Managerial Strategies and Practice in the Asian Business Sector* (pp. 150–168). Hershey, PA: IGI Global. doi:10.4018/978-1-4666-9758-4.ch009

Garcia, A. G., & Villarino, R. F. (2016). The Social Role of Human Resources Teachers: Human Resource Management. In A. Casademunt (Ed.), *Strategic Labor Relations Management in Modern Organizations* (pp. 172–182). Hershey, PA: IGI Global. doi:10.4018/978-1-5225-0356-9.ch010

García-Cabrera, A. M., Suárez-Ortega, S. M., & Hernández, F. G. (2016). Managerial Practices as Antecedents of Employees' Resistance to Change: Organizational Change and Human Resource Management. In A. Casademunt (Ed.), *Strategic Labor Relations Management in Modern Organizations* (pp. 89–104). Hershey, PA: IGI Global. doi:10.4018/978-1-5225-0356-9.ch005

Gordon, K. (2017). The Impact of Improved Organizational Citizenship on Employee Retention. In V. Wang (Ed.), *Encyclopedia of Strategic Leadership and Management* (pp. 1128–1139). Hershey, PA: IGI Global. doi:10.4018/978-1-5225-1049-9.ch079

Guo, J., Zhang, H., & Zong, Y. (2017). Leadership Development and Career Planning. In L. Ruan, Q. Zhu, & Y. Ye (Eds.), *Academic Library Development and Administration in China* (pp. 264–279). Hershey, PA: IGI Global. doi:10.4018/978-1-5225-0550-1.ch016

Hendel, R. J. (2017). Leadership for Improving Student Success through Higher Cognitive Instruction. In R. Styron Jr & J. Styron (Eds.), *Comprehensive Problem-Solving and Skill Development for Next-Generation Leaders* (pp. 230–254). Hershey, PA: IGI Global. doi:10.4018/978-1-5225-1968-3.ch011

Henry-Campbell, S., & Hadeed, S. (2017). Managing a Diverse Workforce. In V. Wang (Ed.), *Encyclopedia of Strategic Leadership and Management* (pp. 953–964). Hershey, PA: IGI Global. doi:10.4018/978-1-5225-1049-9.ch066

Hitch, L. P. (2017). Leadership as a Wicked Problem. In V. Wang (Ed.), *Encyclopedia of Strategic Leadership and Management* (pp. 340–349). Hershey, PA: IGI Global. doi:10.4018/978-1-5225-1049-9.ch025

Hubball, H. T., Clarke, A., & Pearson, M. L. (2017). Strategic Leadership Development in Research-Intensive Higher Education Contexts: The Scholarship of Educational Leadership. In S. Mukerji & P. Tripathi (Eds.), *Handbook of Research on Administration, Policy, and Leadership in Higher Education* (pp. 1–19). Hershey, PA: IGI Global. doi:10.4018/978-1-5225-0672-0.ch001

Hunt, L., & Chalmers, D. (2017). Change Leadership, Management and Strategies to Promote Quality University Teaching and Learning. In S. Mukerji & P. Tripathi (Eds.), *Handbook of Research on Administration, Policy, and Leadership in Higher Education* (pp. 377–403). Hershey, PA: IGI Global. doi:10.4018/978-1-5225-0672-0.ch015

James, S., & Hauli, E. (2017). Holistic Management Education at Tanzanian Rural Development Planning Institute. In N. Baporikar (Ed.), *Management Education for Global Leadership* (pp. 112–136). Hershey, PA: IGI Global. doi:10.4018/978-1-5225-1013-0.ch006

Jeong, S., Lim, D. H., & Park, S. (2017). Leadership Convergence and Divergence in the Era of Globalization. In P. Ordóñez de Pablos & R. Tennyson (Eds.), *Handbook of Research on Human Resources Strategies for the New Millennial Workforce* (pp. 286–309). Hershey, PA: IGI Global. doi:10.4018/978-1-5225-0948-6.ch014

Joseph, L. M., Rutigliano, N. K., & Frost, A. (2017). Navigating the Turbulent Waters of Career Transitions: What Every Leader and Manager Should Know. In V. Wang (Ed.), *Encyclopedia of Strategic Leadership and Management* (pp. 1022–1035). Hershey, PA: IGI Global. doi:10.4018/978-1-5225-1049-9.ch071

Juhasz, T., & Gabriella, H. (2017). The Practice of Mentoring: Based on Empirical Research Carried Out at Hungarian Companies. In A. Bencsik (Ed.), *Knowledge Management Initiatives and Strategies in Small and Medium Enterprises* (pp. 342–360). Hershey, PA: IGI Global. doi:10.4018/978-1-5225-1642-2.ch016

Kasemsap, K. (2016). Analyzing the Roles of Human Capital and Competency in Global Business. In S. Sen, A. Bhattacharya, & R. Sen (Eds.), *International Perspectives on Socio-Economic Development in the Era of Globalization* (pp. 1–29). Hershey, PA: IGI Global. doi:10.4018/978-1-4666-9908-3.ch001

Kasemsap, K. (2016). Promoting Leadership Development and Talent Management in Modern Organizations. In U. Aung & P. Ordoñez de Pablos (Eds.), *Managerial Strategies and Practice in the Asian Business Sector* (pp. 238–266). Hershey, PA: IGI Global. doi:10.4018/978-1-4666-9758-4.ch013

Kasemsap, K. (2017). Investigating the Roles of Neuroscience and Knowledge Management in Higher Education. In S. Mukerji & P. Tripathi (Eds.), *Handbook of Research on Administration, Policy, and Leadership in Higher Education* (pp. 112–140). Hershey, PA: IGI Global. doi:10.4018/978-1-5225-0672-0.ch006

Kasemsap, K. (2017). Management Education and Leadership Styles: Current Issues and Approaches. In N. Baporikar (Ed.), *Innovation and Shifting Perspectives in Management Education* (pp. 166–193). Hershey, PA: IGI Global. doi:10.4018/978-1-5225-1019-2.ch008

Kasemsap, K. (2017). Mastering Business Process Management and Business Intelligence in Global Business. In M. Tavana, K. Szabat, & K. Puranam (Eds.), *Organizational Productivity and Performance Measurements Using Predictive Modeling and Analytics* (pp. 192–212). Hershey, PA: IGI Global. doi:10.4018/978-1-5225-0654-6.ch010

Kasemsap, K. (2017). Organizational Learning: Advanced Issues and Trends. In A. Bencsik (Ed.), *Knowledge Management Initiatives and Strategies in Small and Medium Enterprises* (pp. 42–66). Hershey, PA: IGI Global. doi:10.4018/978-1-5225-1642-2.ch003

Kasemsap, K. (2017). Professional and Business Applications of Social Media Platforms. In V. Benson, R. Tuninga, & G. Saridakis (Eds.), *Analyzing the Strategic Role of Social Networking in Firm Growth and Productivity* (pp. 427–450). Hershey, PA: IGI Global. doi:10.4018/978-1-5225-0559-4.ch021

Keene, B., & Stelson, U. M. (2017). Managing People as a Leader. In V. Wang (Ed.), *Encyclopedia of Strategic Leadership and Management* (pp. 965–976). Hershey, PA: IGI Global. doi:10.4018/978-1-5225-1049-9.ch067

King, D. R. (2016). Management as a Limit to Organizational Change: Implications for Acquisitions. In A. Goksoy (Ed.), *Organizational Change Management Strategies in Modern Business* (pp. 52–73). Hershey, PA: IGI Global. doi:10.4018/978-1-4666-9533-7.ch003

Kishna, T., Blomme, R. J., & van der Veen, J. A. (2016). Organizational Routines: Developing a Duality Model to Explain the Effects of Strategic Change Initiatives. In A. Goksoy (Ed.), *Organizational Change Management Strategies in Modern Business* (pp. 363–385). Hershey, PA: IGI Global. doi:10.4018/978-1-4666-9533-7.ch018

Larkin, B. (2017). When Management Policies Collide: An Examination of How the Autonomous Intent of Charter School Laws Work with the Rigid Accountability of Idea. In V. Wang (Ed.), *Encyclopedia of Strategic Leadership and Management* (pp. 1179–1191). Hershey, PA: IGI Global. doi:10.4018/978-1-5225-1049-9.ch082

Lauzon, A. (2017). Meeting the Cognitive Demands of Leading in Times of Uncertainty. In V. Wang (Ed.), *Encyclopedia of Strategic Leadership and Management* (pp. 434–443). Hershey, PA: IGI Global. doi:10.4018/978-1-5225-1049-9.ch031

Liu, Z., Kim, H. M., & Zhang, K. (2016). Manufacturing and Logistics Networks of Korean Firms in China: A Case Study of Suzhou Industrial Park. In U. Aung & P. Ordoñez de Pablos (Eds.), *Managerial Strategies and Practice in the Asian Business Sector* (pp. 193–219). Hershey, PA: IGI Global. doi:10.4018/978-1-4666-9758-4.ch011

Lorber, M., Treven, S., & Mumel, D. (2017). Leaders' Behavior in Association with Job Satisfaction and Organizational Commitment. In V. Potocan, M. Üngan, & Z. Nedelko (Eds.), *Handbook of Research on Managerial Solutions in Non-Profit Organizations* (pp. 111–133). Hershey, PA: IGI Global. doi:10.4018/978-1-5225-0731-4.ch006

Lucia-Casademunt, A. M., Ariza-Montes, A., & Montero-Romero, T. (2016). Strategic Antecedents of Emotional Involvement in Europe: Emotions at Work Context and Human Resource Management. In A. Casademunt (Ed.), *Strategic Labor Relations Management in Modern Organizations* (pp. 195–208). Hershey, PA: IGI Global. doi:10.4018/978-1-5225-0356-9.ch012

Manuel, N. N. (2016). Angolan Higher Education, Policy, and Leadership: Towards Transformative Leadership for Social Justice. In N. Ololube (Ed.), *Handbook of Research on Organizational Justice and Culture in Higher Education Institutions* (pp. 165–189). Hershey, PA: IGI Global. doi:10.4018/978-1-4666-9850-5.ch007

Marinakou, E., & Giousmpasoglou, C. (2017). Gendered Leadership as a Key to Business Success: Evidence from the Middle East. In P. Ordoñez de Pablos & R. Tennyson (Eds.), *Handbook of Research on Human Resources Strategies for the New Millennial Workforce* (pp. 200–230). Hershey, PA: IGI Global. doi:10.4018/978-1-5225-0948-6.ch010

McNeil, S., Trimbath, S., Atique, F., & Burke, R. (2017). Predictive Analytics for Infrastructure Performance. In M. Tavana, K. Szabat, & K. Puranam (Eds.), *Organizational Productivity and Performance Measurements Using Predictive Modeling and Analytics* (pp. 1–16). Hershey, PA: IGI Global. doi:10.4018/978-1-5225-0654-6.ch001

Moore, B. (2017). Authentic Leadership: Applications in Academic Decision-Making. In R. Styron Jr & J. Styron (Eds.), *Comprehensive Problem-Solving and Skill Development for Next-Generation Leaders* (pp. 76–94). Hershey, PA: IGI Global. doi:10.4018/978-1-5225-1968-3.ch004

Moyano, M. (2016). Cultural Intelligence in Organizational Contexts and Human Resource Management. In A. Casademunt (Ed.), *Strategic Labor Relations Management in Modern Organizations* (pp. 121–134). Hershey, PA: IGI Global. doi:10.4018/978-1-5225-0356-9.ch007

Mupepi, S., Mupepi, M., & Modak, A. (2017). Highly Productive 21st Century Workforce: Tech-Savvy Women in-Charge. In M. Mupepi (Ed.), *Effective Talent Management Strategies for Organizational Success* (pp. 218–234). Hershey, PA: IGI Global. doi:10.4018/978-1-5225-1961-4.ch015

Naidoo, V. (2017). E-Learning and Management Education at African Universities. In N. Baporikar (Ed.), *Management Education for Global Leadership* (pp. 181–201). Hershey, PA: IGI Global. doi:10.4018/978-1-5225-1013-0.ch009

Naik, K. R., & Srinivasan, S. R. (2017). Distinctive Leadership: Moral Identity as Self Identity. In P. Ordoñez de Pablos & R. Tennyson (Eds.), *Handbook of Research on Human Resources Strategies for the New Millennial Workforce* (pp. 90–110). Hershey, PA: IGI Global. doi:10.4018/978-1-5225-0948-6.ch005

Nedelko, Z., & Potocan, V. (2017). Priority of Management Tools Utilization among Managers: International Comparison. In V. Wang (Ed.), *Encyclopedia of Strategic Leadership and Management* (pp. 1083–1094). Hershey, PA: IGI Global. doi:10.4018/978-1-5225-1049-9.ch075

Neimann, T. D. (2017). Retention of Rural Latina College Students, Engaging Strategic Leadership: A Chicana Feminist Theory Perspective on Retention. In V. Wang (Ed.), *Encyclopedia of Strategic Leadership and Management* (pp. 580–603). Hershey, PA: IGI Global. doi:10.4018/978-1-5225-1049-9.ch041

Norris, S. E. (2017). What Motivates an Individual to Lead and Engage in Leadership Development? In V. Wang (Ed.), *Encyclopedia of Strategic Leadership and Management* (pp. 696–706). Hershey, PA: IGI Global. doi:10.4018/978-1-5225-1049-9.ch048

Norris, S. E. (2017). What Motivates an Individual to Lead and Engage in Leadership Development? In V. Wang (Ed.), *Encyclopedia of Strategic Leadership and Management* (pp. 696–706). Hershey, PA: IGI Global. doi:10.4018/978-1-5225-1049-9.ch048

Noszkay, E. (2017). Best Practice Model Tools and Methods for Developing KM Systems. In A. Bencsik (Ed.), *Knowledge Management Initiatives and Strategies in Small and Medium Enterprises* (pp. 137–156). Hershey, PA: IGI Global. doi:10.4018/978-1-5225-1642-2.ch007

Noszkay, E. (2017). Correlations of Company Strategy and KM. In A. Bencsik (Ed.), *Knowledge Management Initiatives and Strategies in Small and Medium Enterprises* (pp. 113–135). Hershey, PA: IGI Global. doi:10.4018/978-1-5225-1642-2.ch006

O'Connor, J. R. Jr. (2017). A Strategic Approach to Decision Making. In V. Wang (Ed.), *Encyclopedia of Strategic Leadership and Management* (pp. 1265–1275). Hershey, PA: IGI Global. doi:10.4018/978-1-5225-1049-9.ch088

Obermayer, N., Csepregi, A., & Kővári, E. (2017). Knowledge Sharing Relation to Competence, Emotional Intelligence, and Social Media Regarding Generations. In A. Bencsik (Ed.), *Knowledge Management Initiatives and Strategies in Small and Medium Enterprises* (pp. 269–290). Hershey, PA: IGI Global. doi:10.4018/978-1-5225-1642-2.ch013

Ololube, N. P., Agbor, C. N., & Agabi, C. O. (2017). Effective Leadership and Management in Universities through Quality Management Models. In N. Baporikar (Ed.), *Innovation and Shifting Perspectives in Management Education* (pp. 224–245). Hershey, PA: IGI Global. doi:10.4018/978-1-5225-1019-2.ch010

Orazbayeva, B., & Baaken, T. (2017). Intercultural Knowledge Transfer in Teams. In A. Bencsik (Ed.), *Knowledge Management Initiatives and Strategies in Small and Medium Enterprises* (pp. 248–268). Hershey, PA: IGI Global. doi:10.4018/978-1-5225-1642-2.ch012

Ozuem, W., Lancaster, G., & Sharma, H. (2016). In Search of Balance between Talent Management and Employee Engagement in Human Resource Management. In A. Casademunt (Ed.), *Strategic Labor Relations Management in Modern Organizations* (pp. 49–75). Hershey, PA: IGI Global. doi:10.4018/978-1-5225-0356-9.ch003

Park, C. K., Lim, D. H., & Ju, B. (2016). Transformational Leadership and Teacher Engagement in an International Context. In J. Keengwe, J. Mbae, & G. Onchwari (Eds.), *Handbook of Research on Global Issues in Next-Generation Teacher Education* (pp. 22–42). Hershey, PA: IGI Global. doi:10.4018/978-1-4666-9948-9.ch002

Pasamar, S., & López-Fernández, M. (2016). Work-Life Balance: The Importance of Human Resource Managers' Role. In A. Casademunt (Ed.), *Strategic Labor Relations Management in Modern Organizations* (pp. 223–238). Hershey, PA: IGI Global. doi:10.4018/978-1-5225-0356-9.ch014

Patro, C. S. (2016). Influence of Retention Policies on Employee Efficiency and Organization Productivity. In U. Aung & P. Ordoñez de Pablos (Eds.), *Managerial Strategies and Practice in the Asian Business Sector* (pp. 124–149). Hershey, PA: IGI Global. doi:10.4018/978-1-4666-9758-4.ch008

Pawliczek, A., & Rössler, M. (2017). Knowledge of Management Tools and Systems in SMEs: Knowledge Transfer in Management. In A. Bencsik (Ed.), *Knowledge Management Initiatives and Strategies in Small and Medium Enterprises* (pp. 180–203). Hershey, PA: IGI Global. doi:10.4018/978-1-5225-1642-2.ch009

Petrelli, H. M. (2017). Millennial Leadership Model. In V. Wang (Ed.), *Encyclopedia of Strategic Leadership and Management* (pp. 444–459). Hershey, PA: IGI Global. doi:10.4018/978-1-5225-1049-9.ch032

Pinto, H. (2017). The Transfer of Knowledge and University-Firm Tensions: Contributions from S&T Studies to the Understanding of a New Institutional Paradigm. In A. Bencsik (Ed.), *Knowledge Management Initiatives and Strategies in Small and Medium Enterprises* (pp. 361–381). Hershey, PA: IGI Global. doi:10.4018/978-1-5225-1642-2.ch017

Putman, P. G. (2017). Strategic Leadership Competency Development. In V. Wang (Ed.), *Encyclopedia of Strategic Leadership and Management* (pp. 1495–1520). Hershey, PA: IGI Global. doi:10.4018/978-1-5225-1049-9.ch104

Qin, L., & Neimann, T. D. (2017). Fostering English Learners' Intercultural Competence and Multicultural Awareness in a Foreign Language University in Northeastern China. In V. Wang (Ed.), *Encyclopedia of Strategic Leadership and Management* (pp. 890–913). Hershey, PA: IGI Global. doi:10.4018/978-1-5225-1049-9.ch062

Roberts, C. (2017). Advancing Women Leaders in Academe: Creating a Culture of Inclusion. In S. Mukerji & P. Tripathi (Eds.), *Handbook of Research on Administration, Policy, and Leadership in Higher Education* (pp. 256–273). Hershey, PA: IGI Global. doi:10.4018/978-1-5225-0672-0.ch012

Rouzbehani, K. (2016). A Revolutionary Look at Knowledge Management: Considering Intellectual Assets as Facilitating Infrastructure. In U. Aung & P. Ordoñez de Pablos (Eds.), *Managerial Strategies and Practice in the Asian Business Sector* (pp. 169–192). Hershey, PA: IGI Global. doi:10.4018/978-1-4666-9758-4.ch010

Ruffin, T. R., & Boice, W. L. (2017). Leader Development in an Unpredictable World: Transferable Skills and Organizational Development. In V. Wang (Ed.), *Encyclopedia of Strategic Leadership and Management* (pp. 328–339). Hershey, PA: IGI Global. doi:10.4018/978-1-5225-1049-9.ch024

Rugutt, J. K., Chemosit, C. C., Ngeno, V., & Soi, D. (2016). The Impact of School Leadership and Professional Development on Professional Commitment: A Hierarchical Linear Modeling Approach. In J. Keengwe, J. Mbae, & G. Onchwari (Eds.), *Handbook of Research on Global Issues in Next-Generation Teacher Education* (pp. 260–275). Hershey, PA: IGI Global. doi:10.4018/978-1-4666-9948-9.ch015

Ruiz-Lozano, M., & Nieto, R. R. (2016). Ethics and Corporate Social Responsibility in Human Resource Management. In A. Casademunt (Ed.), *Strategic Labor Relations Management in Modern Organizations* (pp. 135–148). Hershey, PA: IGI Global. doi:10.4018/978-1-5225-0356-9.ch008

Ruizalba, J., & Soares, A. (2016). Internal Market Orientation and Strategy Implementation. In A. Casademunt (Ed.), *Strategic Labor Relations Management in Modern Organizations* (pp. 183–194). Hershey, PA: IGI Global. doi:10.4018/978-1-5225-0356-9.ch011

Rutigliano, N. K., & Frost, A. (2017). Leading with Intention: The Power of Must, Will, and Now. In V. Wang (Ed.), *Encyclopedia of Strategic Leadership and Management* (pp. 417–433). Hershey, PA: IGI Global. doi:10.4018/978-1-5225-1049-9.ch030

Rutigliano, N. K., Samson, R. M., & Frye, A. S. (2017). Mindfulness: Spiriting Effective Strategic Leadership and Management. In V. Wang (Ed.), *Encyclopedia of Strategic Leadership and Management* (pp. 460–469). Hershey, PA: IGI Global. doi:10.4018/978-1-5225-1049-9.ch033

Rutigliano, N. K., Wedderburn, N. V., & Beckem, J. M. II. (2017). Navigating Organizational Change: From Resistance to Acceptance, Learning, and Growth. In V. Wang (Ed.), *Encyclopedia of Strategic Leadership and Management* (pp. 1005–1021). Hershey, PA: IGI Global. doi:10.4018/978-1-5225-1049-9.ch070

Saini, D. (2017). Relevance of Teaching Values and Ethics in Management Education. In N. Baporikar (Ed.), *Management Education for Global Leadership* (pp. 90–111). Hershey, PA: IGI Global. doi:10.4018/978-1-5225-1013-0.ch005

Satpathy, B., & Muniapan, B. (2016). Ancient Wisdom for Transformational Leadership and Its Insights from the Bhagavad-Gita. In U. Aung & P. Ordoñez de Pablos (Eds.), *Managerial Strategies and Practice in the Asian Business Sector* (pp. 1–10). Hershey, PA: IGI Global. doi:10.4018/978-1-4666-9758-4.ch001

Schenck, A. D. (2017). The Change Process in Korean Education: A Philosophical Tug-of-War between the Old and the New. In V. Wang (Ed.), *Encyclopedia of Strategic Leadership and Management* (pp. 1106–1117). Hershey, PA: IGI Global. doi:10.4018/978-1-5225-1049-9.ch077

Seo, G., & Huang, W. D. (2017). Social Perceptions, Gender Roles, and Female Leadership: A Theoretical Grounding for Understanding the Underrepresentation of Women in Top-Level Management. In V. Wang (Ed.), *Encyclopedia of Strategic Leadership and Management* (pp. 619–630). Hershey, PA: IGI Global. doi:10.4018/978-1-5225-1049-9.ch043

Sharma, A. J. (2017). Enhancing Sustainability through Experiential Learning in Management Education. In N. Baporikar (Ed.), *Management Education for Global Leadership* (pp. 256–274). Hershey, PA: IGI Global. doi:10.4018/978-1-5225-1013-0.ch013

Shetty, K. P. (2017). Responsible Global Leadership: Ethical Challenges in Management Education. In N. Baporikar (Ed.), *Innovation and Shifting Perspectives in Management Education* (pp. 194–223). Hershey, PA: IGI Global. doi:10.4018/978-1-5225-1019-2.ch009

Sihi, D. (2017). The Influence of Leadership and Strategic Emphasis on Social Media Use of Regional Nonprofit Organizations. *International Journal of Public Administration in the Digital Age, 4*(1), 1–18. doi:10.4018/IJPADA.2017010101

Siu, K. W., & Wong, Y. L. (2017). Leadership and Management in a Workshop-Based Educational Project: A Case Study of an Environmental Sustainability Project. In V. Wang (Ed.), *Encyclopedia of Strategic Leadership and Management* (pp. 929–940). Hershey, PA: IGI Global. doi:10.4018/978-1-5225-1049-9.ch064

Sorooshian, S. (2017). Structural Equation Modeling Algorithm and Its Application in Business Analytics. In M. Tavana, K. Szabat, & K. Puranam (Eds.), *Organizational Productivity and Performance Measurements Using Predictive Modeling and Analytics* (pp. 17–39). Hershey, PA: IGI Global. doi:10.4018/978-1-5225-0654-6.ch002

Starr-Glass, D. (2017). Psychological Contracts and Strategic Leadership. In V. Wang (Ed.), *Encyclopedia of Strategic Leadership and Management* (pp. 1450–1460). Hershey, PA: IGI Global. doi:10.4018/978-1-5225-1049-9.ch100

Storey, V. A., Anthony, A. K., & Wahid, P. (2017). Gender-Based Leadership Barriers: Advancement of Female Faculty to Leadership Positions in Higher Education. In V. Wang (Ed.), *Encyclopedia of Strategic Leadership and Management* (pp. 244–258). Hershey, PA: IGI Global. doi:10.4018/978-1-5225-1049-9.ch018

Storey, V. A., & Dambo, N. J. (2017). Educational Leadership Sustainability: Maintaining Wellness, Coping with Stress, and Preventing Burnout. In V. Wang (Ed.), *Encyclopedia of Strategic Leadership and Management* (pp. 182–193). Hershey, PA: IGI Global. doi:10.4018/978-1-5225-1049-9.ch014

Su-Keene, E. (2017). Women in Strategic Leadership and Management: Identifying Concerns and Implementing Strategic Gender-Specific Leadership Development. In V. Wang (Ed.), *Encyclopedia of Strategic Leadership and Management* (pp. 1192–1204). Hershey, PA: IGI Global. doi:10.4018/978-1-5225-1049-9.ch083

Swami, B. N., Gobona, T., & Tsimako, J. J. (2017). Academic Leadership: A Case Study of the University of Botswana. In N. Baporikar (Ed.), *Innovation and Shifting Perspectives in Management Education* (pp. 1–32). Hershey, PA: IGI Global. doi:10.4018/978-1-5225-1019-2.ch001

Torlak, N. G. (2016). Improving the Role of Organisational Culture in Change Management through a Systems Approach. In A. Goksoy (Ed.), *Organizational Change Management Strategies in Modern Business* (pp. 230–271). Hershey, PA: IGI Global. doi:10.4018/978-1-4666-9533-7.ch012

Torrisi-Steele, G. (2017). "But We've Got No Power": The Leadership Role of the Program Director. In V. Wang (Ed.), *Encyclopedia of Strategic Leadership and Management* (pp. 42–54). Hershey, PA: IGI Global. doi:10.4018/978-1-5225-1049-9.ch004

Torrisi-Steele, G. (2017). Design Leadership in the Context of Emerging Technologies. In V. Wang (Ed.), *Encyclopedia of Strategic Leadership and Management* (pp. 121–130). Hershey, PA: IGI Global. doi:10.4018/978-1-5225-1049-9.ch010

Torrisi-Steele, G. (2017). Leadership Learning through Virtual Play. In V. Wang (Ed.), *Encyclopedia of Strategic Leadership and Management* (pp. 361–370). Hershey, PA: IGI Global. doi:10.4018/978-1-5225-1049-9.ch027

Torrisi-Steele, G. (2017). Virtual Teams, Technology, and Leadership: A Primer. In V. Wang (Ed.), *Encyclopedia of Strategic Leadership and Management* (pp. 686–695). Hershey, PA: IGI Global. doi:10.4018/978-1-5225-1049-9.ch047

Toulassi, B. (2017). Educational Administration and Leadership in Francophone Africa: 5 Dynamics to Change Education. In S. Mukerji & P. Tripathi (Eds.), *Handbook of Research on Administration, Policy, and Leadership in Higher Education* (pp. 20–45). Hershey, PA: IGI Global. doi:10.4018/978-1-5225-0672-0.ch002

Van Wingerden, C., Goto, S., & Burstein, M. (2017). Creating Sustainable Communities: Adult and Leadership Theories and Principles in Practice. In V. Wang (Ed.), *Encyclopedia of Strategic Leadership and Management* (pp. 94–110). Hershey, PA: IGI Global. doi:10.4018/978-1-5225-1049-9.ch008

Varty, C. T., O'Neill, T. A., & Hambley, L. A. (2017). Leading Anywhere Workers: A Scientific and Practical Framework. In Y. Blount & M. Gloet (Eds.), *Anywhere Working and the New Era of Telecommuting* (pp. 47–88). Hershey, PA: IGI Global. doi:10.4018/978-1-5225-2328-4.ch003

Velencei, J., & Baracskai, Z. (2017). Decision Maker in the Global Village: Thinking Together. In A. Bencsik (Ed.), *Knowledge Management Initiatives and Strategies in Small and Medium Enterprises* (pp. 25–41). Hershey, PA: IGI Global. doi:10.4018/978-1-5225-1642-2.ch002

Verma, H. V., & Duggal, E. (2016). Grooming Market in India: Concept, Instrumentality, Outcomes, and Marketing. In U. Aung & P. Ordoñez de Pablos (Eds.), *Managerial Strategies and Practice in the Asian Business Sector* (pp. 82–106). Hershey, PA: IGI Global. doi:10.4018/978-1-4666-9758-4.ch006

Véry, Z. (2017). Managing Collective Knowledge at a Small Business Group (VID Group). In A. Bencsik (Ed.), *Knowledge Management Initiatives and Strategies in Small and Medium Enterprises* (pp. 316–341). Hershey, PA: IGI Global. doi:10.4018/978-1-5225-1642-2.ch015

Wang, C., Schofield, M., Li, X., & Ou, X. (2017). Do Chinese Students in Public and Private Higher Education Institutes Perform at Different Level in One of the Leadership Skills: Critical Thinking?: An Exploratory Comparison. In V. Wang (Ed.), *Encyclopedia of Strategic Leadership and Management* (pp. 160–181). Hershey, PA: IGI Global. doi:10.4018/978-1-5225-1049-9.ch013

Wang, V. C., & Torrisi-Steele, G. (2017). A Critical Review of Learning Organizations in the 21st Century. In V. Wang (Ed.), *Encyclopedia of Strategic Leadership and Management* (pp. 729–743). Hershey, PA: IGI Global. doi:10.4018/978-1-5225-1049-9.ch051

Wang, V. C., & Torrisi-Steele, G. (2017). Digital Leadership in the New Century. In V. Wang (Ed.), *Encyclopedia of Strategic Leadership and Management* (pp. 143–159). Hershey, PA: IGI Global. doi:10.4018/978-1-5225-1049-9.ch012

Related Readings

Witte, M. M., Teel, J. B., Cordie, L. A., & Witte, J. E. (2017). Building Capacity through Student Leadership Development and Practices. In V. Wang (Ed.), *Encyclopedia of Strategic Leadership and Management* (pp. 29–41). Hershey, PA: IGI Global. doi:10.4018/978-1-5225-1049-9.ch003

Yablonsky, S. (2016). Intermediaries in E-Commerce. In I. Lee (Ed.), *Encyclopedia of E-Commerce Development, Implementation, and Management* (pp. 48–73). Hershey, PA: IGI Global. doi:10.4018/978-1-4666-9787-4.ch005

Yüksel, A. H. (2017). Innoveadership: Marrying Strategic Leadership with Complexity. In V. Wang (Ed.), *Encyclopedia of Strategic Leadership and Management* (pp. 282–295). Hershey, PA: IGI Global. doi:10.4018/978-1-5225-1049-9.ch021

Zel, U. (2016). Leadership in Change Management. In A. Goksoy (Ed.), *Organizational Change Management Strategies in Modern Business* (pp. 272–288). Hershey, PA: IGI Global. doi:10.4018/978-1-4666-9533-7.ch013

Index

C

case study 52, 126, 133-134, 136, 149, 152, 158
CCCL 133-137, 141, 145-149
Chinese 9-10, 12-15, 34, 36-39, 41-44, 49-51, 53, 55, 59-61, 66-67, 75, 82, 85, 106, 109, 112, 122, 124, 133-134, 140-141, 144, 148-149, 152-153, 159, 161-162
Coin Culture Co., Ltd. 133, 149
communications 123, 127-129, 132, 144
correlations 1, 9-10, 36, 45-46, 59-61, 63, 72, 79, 89, 106, 108-109, 119-121, 158-159
cultural influences 89
cultures 1, 3, 7, 9-11, 30-32, 34-35, 37, 40, 42, 44-45, 51, 56-57, 59-61, 75, 82-83, 86-87, 106, 109, 150, 152, 155-156, 163

E

education 1, 4, 11, 32, 45, 49, 66-67, 78, 88, 91, 94, 98-99, 115, 119, 157-158
EMBA 13, 62, 66-68, 76

G

Guinea pigs 3-4, 8, 36, 61, 66-67, 75, 98, 156-157

L

leadership 1-32, 37-38, 45-61, 63, 66, 71, 75, 79, 81, 83-89, 91, 102, 106, 108-115, 117, 119-126, 130-134, 136-137, 145-163

Literature review 1, 8, 11, 14-15, 31, 45-46, 80

P

phenomena 126, 148
population 1, 4, 61, 63, 66-69, 94, 157

Q

questionnaires 1, 3, 10, 13-15, 45, 59-62, 75-76, 102, 106, 109-110, 150, 156, 159

R

raw data, 1, 109
research 1-19, 22-24, 26, 28-38, 45, 47, 50-57, 60-64, 66-67, 69, 72, 75-76, 79-83, 85-94, 106, 108-110, 113, 119, 123-126, 133-134, 136, 140, 144, 147, 150-154, 156-159, 161, 163
results 1, 3-4, 8-10, 12, 17, 44, 60-62, 66, 69, 72, 74-75, 80, 88-89, 91, 93-94, 106, 108-113, 119, 144, 148, 150, 156-157, 159

S

SEM (Structural Equation Modeling) 9, 60, 108
several rounds 13, 61, 75
specialized experts 61
Storytelling 8, 14, 30, 49, 80-84, 127-133, 153
survey 1, 3, 8-10, 13, 33-36, 44-46, 49, 59-62, 66-69, 71, 75-76, 78, 85, 91, 93, 106, 108, 110, 112, 140, 153, 156, 158-159

T

theories 1-3, 13-14, 17-19, 24, 26-27, 29-32,

46, 51-52, 58, 66, 126, 128, 142, 161

top tier journals 9, 60, 108

V

values 1, 3-4, 9-11, 13-14, 19-22, 31-37,

45-50, 53, 55-60, 63, 66, 69-70, 72,
74-76, 78-79, 81, 85-86, 88-89, 91,
93-96, 98-109, 112, 119-122, 124,

132, 150, 152, 156, 158-162

W

widely used 9, 60, 71, 75, 80, 108, 126

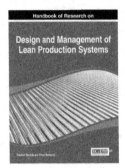
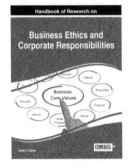

Printed in the United States
By Bookmasters